Representative American Speeches
2011–2012

Edited by
Brian Boucher

The Reference Shelf
Volume 84 • Number 6
H. W. Wilson
A Division of EBSCO Publishing, Inc.
Ipswich, Massachusetts
2013

The Reference Shelf

The books in this series contain reprints of articles, excerpts from books, addresses on current issues, and studies of social trends in the United States and other countries. There are six separately bound numbers in each volume, all of which are usually published in the same calendar year. Numbers one through five are each devoted to a single subject, providing background information and discussion from various points of view and concluding with an index and comprehensive bibliography that lists books, pamphlets, and articles on the subject. The final number of each volume is a collection of recent speeches. Books in the series may be purchased individually or on subscription.

Library of Congress Cataloging-in-Publication Data

Representative American speeches 2011–2012 / edited by Brian Boucher.
    p. cm. — (The reference shelf ; v. 84, no. 6)
  Includes index.
  ISBN 978-0-8242-1120-2 (issue 6, pbk.) — ISBN 978-0-8242-1249-0 (volume 84)
1. Speeches, addresses, etc., American. I. Boucher, Brian.
  PS668.2.R47 2013
  815.008—dc23

                 2012033121

Cover: U.S. Secretary of State Hillary Clinton, St. Petersburg, Russia on June 29, 2012. (Getty Images)

Visit: www.salempress.com/hwwilson

Printed in the United States of America

Contents

1

Remarks to the Graduating Class

In this speech, delivered at a commencement ceremony at Atlanta's Spelman College, America's oldest historically black college for women, First Lady Michelle Obama implores graduates to follow in the footsteps of Spelman's founders and give a chance to those who might otherwise have none.

Emmy- and Golden Globe–winning actress Jane Lynch addresses the 2012 graduating class of Smith College, advising graduates to forgo excessive planning and suggesting that plans often prevent us from taking the chances that truly shape our lives.

In an address at the 2012 Boston College commencement, television reporter Bob Woodruff shares four truths to live by that were reaffirmed in the wake of a near-fatal head injury he sustained while reporting from Iraq, insisting that it is life's challenges that recommit us to that which is truly important.

Writer and concentration-camp survivor Elie Wiesel addresses the new graduates of Washington University, telling them that they should work to prevent the political and racist fanaticism that plagued the twentieth century.

Share Our Strength founder Billy Shore speaks to the graduating class of Bronx Community College, urging them to do both well and good.

In a speech to the 2011 graduates of Sarah Lawrence College, Arianna Huffington affirms her faith in the next generation's ability to bring positive change to a chaotic world, espousing empathy over competition and wisdom over IQ.

3

A Decade after 9/11

New Hampshire Senator Jeanne Shaheen reflects on the legacy of the attacks, saying the story of 9/11 is not just about loss but about how America responded as a nation in the face of adversity.

4

Education Today

In a commencement speech to the graduating class of Fayetteville State University, US Deputy Secretary of Education Tony Miller emphasizes the importance of spreading and supporting the education of others and using one's education to better society. He also celebrates the success of historically black colleges and universities such as FSU and gives examples of graduates who have achieved great success in their professions.

Secretary of Defense Leon E. Panetta addresses the Military Child Education Co-alition on the importance of education for the children of military families. He asserts that children of parents in the military often follow in their parents' footsteps and enlist in the service, and argues that education for these children will ultimately strengthen and benefit the US military and the country.

Arne Duncan, the US secretary of education, addresses state higher education executives on the problems facing the education system in the United States. He expresses his concern over the United States' unsatisfactory ranking in the world's college attainment rate—sixteenth place—and disapproves of recent cuts to education in various states. He expresses optimism, however, about the Obama administration's efforts to decrease the burden of student loans and announces the goal to make the United States number one in college attainment by 2020.

Joanne Weiss, the chief of staff to Arne Duncan, the US secretary of education, speaks at the twenty-fifth anniversary celebration of the National Board for Professional Teaching Standards. Weiss celebrates the progress in professionalizing the teaching field. She emphasizes the importance of certifying teachers in order to increase the performance of schools in the United States.

bullying. Using the recent suicide of Tyler Clementi and other victims as examples of the devastating impact of cyberbullying, Duncan illustrates the far-reaching effect of bullying in children's lives, including academic performance.

Jane Clementi addresses the New Brunswick Superior Court of New Jersey after the suicide of her son, Tyler Clementi, whose roommate, Dharum Ravi, videotaped him having sexual relations with another man and used social media to exploit his sexuality. Mrs. Clementi speaks to the disastrous effects of cyberbullying and the high suicide rate among LGBTQ youth. She urges the court to sanction Ravi's crimes.

The Federal Trade Commission chair, Jon Leibowitz, compares the infringement upon consumer's privacy to the paparazzi and their abuse of celebrities' privacy. Leibowitz explains how this information can be misused and potentially harm the consumer.

In a speech at the House of Representatives, Edith Ramirez, a commissioner of the Federal Trade Commission, speaks of the importance of consumer privacy and security both on- and offline. She emphasizes the goal of protecting consumers' personal information in her attempt to convince Congress to pass legislation that would regulate corporate policies on data security, including notifying consumers when their personal information is being used.

Preface: Representative American Speeches

From heartwarming oratory delivered before cap-and-gown-clad college graduates to finger-pointing on the floor of the Senate, the addresses in this year's *Representative American Speeches* touch on some of the issues at the heart of the American experience today.

Commencement speeches are a perennial source of uplift. In a chapter devoted to commencement addresses at American colleges and universities, seven speakers dispense inspiration, encouragement, and humor. First Lady Michelle Obama instructs the alumnae of Spelman College to think big and to draw on the example set by the school's founders. Billy Shore refers to a classic theme of commencement addresses, the distinction between doing well and doing good, to remind graduating seniors at Bronx Community College that the two are no longer mutually exclusive. Concentration camp survivor Elie Wiesel asks the graduating class of Washington University to never "stand idly by," but to take action in the face of injustice.

Several commencement speakers take as their theme the extent to which unexpected events can shape our lives. David Evans tells of the winding path his professional life has cut, concluding that ambitious future plans, as worthy as they are, could never have plotted the course his career has taken. Arianna Huffington reveals that much of her career was made possible by a painful breakup with a man she loved, from which she gleaned the maxim, "In life, the things that go wrong are often the very things that lead to other things going right." Actress Jane Lynch asserts the applicability to life of the "yes and" principle that governs sketch comedy—to take what your partner (or the world) offers and run with it. And reporter Bob Woodruff outlines some principles he lives by after he underwent a most unexpected experience.

The two years covered in this volume saw debate in Congress over deeply divisive issues that touch upon core American principles. Remarks by ten senators and representatives are presented here to illustrate the scope and passion of those debates.

The most momentous and controversial legislation in years, the Patient Protection and Affordable Care Act, was signed into law on March 23, 2010, but remains the subject of ongoing debate. Senator Mike Enzi (R-WY) lambastes the Supreme Court's decision to uphold the constitutionality of the Act, while Harry Reid (D-NV) praises the law's salutary effect on health care for women, quipping that being a woman can no longer be considered a "preexisting condition."

Many of the talks by our elected officials focus on dollars and cents against the backdrop of a lagging economy. Senator Dianne Feinstein (D-CA) speaks in opposition to a budget authored by Paul Ryan (R-WI), a leader among House conservatives and Mitt Romney's vice presidential running mate. Congressman Mike Kelly (R-PA) articulates a conservative theme when he strikes out against excessive governmental regulation. For the Democrats, Senator Carl Levin (D-MI), by contrast, says the problem is tax cuts for the rich that do nothing to spur growth. Railing against inequality, Senator Bernie Sanders (D-VT) says that "the American people are angry" over a system that, he says, is rigged to benefit the wealthy at the expense of everyone else. Senator Debbie Stabenow (D-MI), speaking in support of the Paycheck Fairness Act, points out that when it comes to handing out pay, equal compensation for equal work should be the principle.

Money figures into not only economic recovery, but also the political process. Representative Raúl Grijalva (D-AZ) warns against the growing influence of money in political campaigns, abetted by so-called social welfare groups that are not obliged to reveal their donors' identities. In keeping with his long history fighting the influence of money in politics, Senator John McCain (R-AZ) speaks in opposition to the DISCLOSE Act, which he calls a slanted bill that would not require the same disclosure from all parties.

And finally, the process of politics comes under the microscope. In an era when it has become commonplace to observe that partisanship and gridlock paralyze Washington like never before, House Majority Whip Steny Hoyer (D-MD) takes his Republican counterparts to task for obstructionism in a debate over cutting taxes for the middle class.

The year 2011 marked a decade since the terrorist attacks of September 11, 2001, ten years during which American military and diplomatic efforts have focused on foiling similar assaults and systematically destroying al-Qaeda's power structure. On May 2, 2011, American forces killed Osama bin Laden, al-Qaeda's leader, in Abbottabad, Pakistan. In this chapter, terrorism expert Brian Michael Jenkins assesses the state of al-Qaeda after bin Laden's death, warning that deadly terrorist attacks may continue, even if they become smaller and less dramatic.

Several speakers in this chapter address the way the attacks brought out the best in Americans. Tragedy can inspire courage, Vice President Joe Biden tells those gathered at the Pentagon for the tenth anniversary of the attacks. Secretary of Defense Leon Panetta goes so far as to say that America is at its best when responding to crisis. Secretary of State Hillary Clinton, in the words of a man who lost his wife that day, sums up the effect of the tragedy: "A fog that makes you forget we are all connected and knitted together instantly got lifted." President Obama stresses that while much may be different since 9/11, the attacks have not changed key characteristics of the United States or the American people. The nature of America, says Senator Jeanne Shaheen, is to be found in the way its citizens responded to the tragedy by supporting one another.

Considering 9/11 from a distinct perspective is Maham Khan, an American Muslim. She delivers an address at her alma mater, where she was a student on September 11, 2001, in which she applies the theme of jihad, or struggle, to her own endeavors to protect Islam from its twisted representation by media outlets in the years following the attacks. She also applies the term to America's efforts on behalf of its people.

Five talks form a chapter on the state of American education. Secretary of Education Arne Duncan tells a conference of state college executives that America can reach its goal of being number one in the world in college attainment rates, and discusses what will be required of states and the federal government to attain that goal. Speeches from two members of Duncan's staff are also represented here. Duncan's deputy secretary, Tony Miller, touts the role of historically black colleges and universities, asserting that access to educational opportunity is the key civil rights issue of our time. Duncan's chief of staff, Joanne Weiss, calls on members of the National Board for Professional Teaching Standards to continue to elevate the field of teaching and professionalize its constituents. Secretary of Defense Leon Panetta links education and national defense, pointing out that an educated populace is essential to national security.

The fourth chapter in this volume is dedicated to a recent American social movement. On September 17, 2011, a ragtag group of protestors took up residence in Lower Manhattan's tiny Zuccotti Park in a movement they dubbed Occupy Wall Street. Their nominally leaderless movement, opposed to corporate greed, inequality, and the corrosive power of multinational corporations over the democratic process, quickly went global with the slogan "we are the 99 percent," a phrase that calls attention to the shift of the nation's wealth toward a tiny percentage of its citizens.

Three talks from movement supporters at demonstrations in New York and one address by a congressman form a chapter devoted to the Occupy movement. Professor and author Judith Butler makes an argument for the necessity, in an age when so much human interaction is virtual, for bodies to come together in physical space, as did those camping out in Zuccotti Park. Activist Virginia Rasmussen and professor and author Lawrence Lessig, speaking at the same demonstration, speak out against the Supreme Court's controversial 2010 ruling in the case *Citizens United v. Federal Election Commission*. In that case, the court ruled five to four that the government may not ban independent political spending by corporations, labor unions, or other organizations. The ruling has been widely and bitterly criticized for allowing shadowy groups to pour unlimited dollars into political advertising. Congressman Bobby Rush compares Occupy Wall Street to some of the most momentous movements for equality and civil rights in American history.

Finally, four speeches, ranging from the policy-oriented to the wrenchingly personal, are presented to explore and illustrate the ongoing efforts to find the balance of transparency and privacy on the Internet, and the awful consequences that can ensue when our privacy is violated.

Two representatives of the Federal Trade Commission (FTC) weigh in on their organization's efforts in this arena. In testimony in the House of Representatives, Edith Ramirez, an FTC commissioner, describes her organization's efforts to protect the privacy of America's citizenry in an age when so many of us put personal information in vulnerable places in order to take advantage of greater convenience. FTC chair Jon Leibowitz compares companies that gather and sell information about our Internet browsing habits to paparazzi, those photographers who take shots of celebrities in compromising situations without regard for the effect on their subjects. Secretary of Education Duncan speaks about the administration's efforts to combat bullying, touching on the times when bullying becomes fatal.

One tragic instance of cyberbullying occurred when Rutgers freshman Dharun Ravi mocked his roommate, Tyler Clementi, on Twitter after spying on him via webcam in an intimate embrace with a man. Clementi then committed suicide, and Ravi was subsequently charged with bias intimidation—a hate crime—along with other offenses. In a victim impact statement delivered at Ravi's sentencing, Tyler's mother, Jane Clementi, speaks movingly about her loss. She touches especially on how Ravi sought out information on her son through his Internet browsing habits. "Based on what he found out, he judged Tyler," she says. "The sad part is what he found out was only one part of who Tyler was. He would never really know Tyler." Explaining her appearance in court that day, Clementi says, simply, "What I want is justice."

Brian Boucher
October 2012

1

Remarks to the Graduating Class

(Bill Greenblatt/UPI /Landov)

Holocaust survivor and Nobel Peace Prize winner Elie Wiesel delivers his remarks as commencement speaker during commencement ceremonies at Washington University in St. Louis on May 20, 2011. Wiesel, who has received more than 100 honorary degrees, received a Doctor of Humane Letters from Washington University.

"Do Big Things"

First Lady Michelle Obama

In this speech, delivered at a commencement ceremony at Atlanta's Spelman College, America's oldest historically black college for women, Obama evokes the odds-defying history of the school, names some of its graduates and their achievements, and tells the students that graduating from Spelman confers on them an inheritance that brings with it a certain obligation. She describes that obligation as a duty to do for others what the founders of Spelman College, established in 1881 as the Atlanta Baptist Female Seminary, did for the eleven poor black women who were its first students: give a chance to those who might otherwise have none.

Well, goodness. Thank you. (Applause.) Let me tell you it is a pleasure and an honor—yes, Chicago—(laughter and applause)—to be with all of you today.

And I want to thank President Tatum for her leadership and for that very kind and generous introduction. She is such an inspiration to all of the women who are part of the Spelman family, so let's give her our thanks and round of applause. (Applause.)

I also want to acknowledge a few people who are here in the audience: Senator Isakson, Representative Johnson, and of course Mayor Reed. Thank you all so much for joining us today. Thank you all for your leadership. (Applause.)

And I want to give a special shoutout to one of my people, one of my staff members, Ms. Kristen Jarvis of Spelman class of 2003. (Applause.) Look, ladies, you want to know what Spelman does for you? Kristen is my right-hand woman. She travels with me all across the country and around the world. I don't know what I would do without her. She has been with me from the very beginning, looking after my girls, taking care of my mom. So I want to thank Spelman for giving me Kristen. (Applause.)

And again, let's take a moment to thank all of those beautiful people sitting behind you all today and standing behind you every day, the folks who brought you into this world (applause) the folks who showed you, with their love, that you belong here. They pushed you, they believed in you, and they answered calls those late nights, even when you were just calling for money. (Laughter.) So again, let's give a special round of applause for all the families here today. (Applause.)

And of course, most of all, to the Spelman class of 2011, congratulations! (Applause.) We are so, so proud of you. We're proud of the effort you've invested and the risks that you took. We're proud of the bonds that you forged, the growth that you've showed. We're proud of how, for the past four years, you've immersed yourselves in the life of this school and embraced all that it has to offer. In doing so, you didn't just

Delivered May 15, 2011, at the Spelman College commencement, Atlanta, Georgia, by First Lady Michelle Obama.

write a chapter in your own life story. You also became part of the Spelman story—a story that began 130 years ago about 10 miles down the road from where we are today.

And by now, all of you know the details: about how two white women from up North—Sophia Packard and Harriet Giles (laughter)—came here to Atlanta to establish the Atlanta Baptist Female Seminary. Now we want the world to know this story. They started out in a dank church basement loaned to them by a kindly preacher named Father Quarles. And their first class had just 11 students, many of whom were former slaves.

Back then, the thought of an African-American woman learning to read and write was, to so many, laughable at best, an impossibility at worst. And plenty of people tried to dissuade Miss Packard and Miss Giles from founding this school. They said the South was too dangerous. They said that at the ages of 56 and 48, these women were too old.

But these two ladies were unmoved. As Miss Giles put it—and these are her words—they were determined to lift up "these women and girls who have never had a chance."

It's a story that has been told and re-told, enacted and re-enacted, in every generation since the day that Spelman first opened its doors.

In a time of black codes and lynching, this school was training African-American women to be leaders in education, in the health professions.

In a time of legalized segregation, this school was establishing math and biology departments and training a generation of black women scientists. (Applause.)

At a time when many workplaces were filled with not just glass ceilings, but brick walls, this school was urging black women to become doctors, and lawyers, engineers, ambassadors.

Now, that is the story of Spelman College: that unyielding presumption of promise, that presumption of brilliance, that presumption that every woman who enrolls at this school has something infinitely valuable to offer this world.

And ladies, that is now your story. That legacy is now your inheritance. And I've chosen that word—inheritance—very carefully, because it's not an entitlement that you can take for granted. It's not a gift with which you can do whatever you please. It is a commitment that comes with a certain set of obligations, obligations that don't end when you march through that arch today.

And that's really what I want to talk with you about this afternoon. I want to talk about the obligations that come with a Spelman education, and how I believe you all might fulfill those obligations going forward.

So let's go back again to those first 11 women in that church basement all those years ago. Their teachers started with nothing but a couple of Bibles, some notebooks and some pencils. When it rained, it got so damp in that church that grass started growing on the floor. Often, the stove was so smoky, and the light was so poor, that students could barely see their teachers.

But still, week after week, more women showed up to enroll. Some walked eight or nine miles each way. Many were older, in their 30s, 40s and 50s. Doesn't sound so old to me. (Laughter.) And often, they were ridiculed. But they kept coming.

One student, a woman named Mary Ann Brooks, simply stated—and these are her words: "I spoke of going to school, and people laughed at me and said 'You go to school! You too old! You're so old you'll die there.' But I told them it was just as good a place to die in as I ever wanted, and I knew Miss Packard and Miss Giles would bury me, so I just came right along." (Laughter and applause.)

Now, that spark, that spirit, that odds-defying tenacity, has defined the alumnae of this school from its very first graduating class.

I mean, think about one of my heroines, Marian Wright Edelman, class of 1960 (applause), working as a young civil rights lawyer down in Mississippi. Attorneys in judge's chambers refused to shake her hand. The sheriff locked the doors against her when she came to visit her clients in jail. She was always careful to leave the door open when she started her car in the morning. That way, if somebody had planted a car bomb, she had a chance of being injured rather than killed. But through it all, she continued to represent her clients. She continued to resist unjust laws with every fiber of her being.

Then there's Janet Bragg, class of 1925, who was determined to be a pilot. When she was barred from flying out of segregated airports, she worked with her flying school classmates and instructors to build their own airfield.

When she was rejected from the Women Air Force Service Pilots because of her race, she enrolled in a civilian training program instead.

And when she completed her training, but an instructor unfairly prevented her from receiving her license, she picked up and moved to Chicago, passed the exam, and became the first African-American woman to earn a commercial pilot's license. (Applause.) Of her experiences, she said: "There were so many things they said women couldn't do and blacks couldn't do. Every defeat to me was a challenge."

And for six generations, that is what Spelman women have done. They have seen every defeat as a challenge. Now, did they have moments of doubt, anxiety and fear? Did they have moments of despair when they thought about giving up, or giving in? Of course they did. We all do.

And I am no exception. I mean, some of you may have grown up like me, in neighborhoods where few had the chance to go to college, where being teased for doing well in school was a fact of life, where well-meaning but misguided folks questioned whether a girl with my background could get into a school like Princeton.

Sometimes, I'd save them the trouble, and raise the questions myself, in my own head, lying awake at night, doubting whether I had what it took to succeed. And the truth is that there will always be folks out there who make assumptions about others.

There will always be folks who try to raise themselves up by cutting other people down. That happens to everyone, including me, throughout their lives. But when that happens to you all, here's what I want you to do. I want you to just stop a minute. Take a deep breath, because it's going to need to be deep (laughter) and I want you to think about all those women who came before you, women like those first 11 students. (Applause.) Think about how they didn't sit around bemoaning their lack of resources and opportunities and affirmation.

I want you to think about women like Marian Wright Edelman and Janet Bragg. They didn't go around pointing fingers and making excuses for why they couldn't win a case or soar above the horizon. They were Spelman women with the privilege of a Spelman education. And instead of focusing on what they didn't have, they focused on what they did have: their intellect, their courage, their determination, their passion.

And with few advantages and long odds, with doors closed to them and laws stacked against them, still they achieved, still they triumphed, still they carved a glorious path for themselves in this world.

And graduates, every single one of you has an obligation to do the same. You have an obligation to see each setback as a challenge and as an opportunity to learn and grow. You have an obligation to face whatever life throws your way with confidence and with hope.

And don't ever let anyone get into your head, especially yourself, because if it's one thing I can promise you, it's this: With a Spelman education, you all have everything you need, right here and right now, to be everything you've ever wanted to be. (Applause.)

But let's be clear, the Spelman legacy isn't just about those first 11 women. And it's not just about the generations of students and alumnae who came after them. It's about everyone who believed in those women, it's about everyone who invested in those women, right from the beginning.

I mean, make no mistake about it, Miss Packard, Miss Giles, they were ambitious for their students. Even as they started their classes at a first-grade level, teaching the alphabet and basic arithmetic, they had big dreams. They were planning to build a full-scale liberal arts college for African-American women.

I mean, think about that. They could barely afford to keep their doors open. Their students could barely read or write. But already, they were planning to build something big, a college. And in those early years, they actually rejected an offer to merge with the Atlanta Baptist Seminary, the school that eventually became Morehouse. Yep, said, "No thank you, brothers!" (laughter and applause) because this move would have—may have solved all their financial problems. But they were afraid that a coed school—their students would be treated as second class citizens. And they weren't going to stand for that. No. (Applause.)

Then there was Father Quarles, the preacher who lent them his church basement. He undertook an arduous journey north to raise money for the school. And his last words to the students were: "I am going north for you. I may never return. But remember, if I die, I die for you and in a good cause."

And those words turned out to be prophetic. In the end, the harsh climate was too much, and he got sick and passed away not long after.

Miss Giles, Miss Packard, Father Quarles, they weren't the only ones who believed in these students. In those early years, thousands of dollars of donations poured in from the black community itself. I mean, these were folks who likely didn't have a dime to spare, digging deep into their wallets to support this school. See, that fierce devotion to the potential of others, that commitment to give even when you're barely getting by yourself, all of that is your legacy as well.

That is your mission now too. (Applause.) Your mission is to find those 11 women wherever in the world your journey may take you. Find those folks who have so much potential, but so little opportunity, and do for them what Spelman has done for you. Maybe it's a group of kids in your community. Maybe it's a struggling family at your church. And I'm not just talking about here at home. Maybe it's folks in a village or an inner city halfway around the world.

Wherever you go, I guarantee you that you will find folks who have been discounted or dismissed, but who have every bit as much promise as you have. They just haven't had the chance to fulfill it. It is your obligation to bring Spelman to those folks—to bring that same presumption of value and worth, to make that same kind of sacrifice, to be as ambitious for them as Spelman has been for you.

> *Your mission is to find those 11 women wherever in the world your journey may take you. Find those folks who have so much potential, but so little opportunity, and do for them what Spelman has done for you.*

And in so doing, I can promise you that you won't just enrich their lives, you'll immeasurably enrich your own lives as well.

All of you already know this from your own experiences here at Spelman. Over the past four years, you all have been serving your community in every way possible: tutoring kids, bringing meals to seniors, building homes, and so much more.

And I can tell you from my own experience just how rewarding it can be to make this kind of work the work of your careers. Back when I was sitting right where you are, I was certain that I wanted to be a lawyer. I knew it. So I did everything I was supposed to do. I got my law degree. Got a prestigious job at a fancy law firm. Had a nice big 'ol paycheck and was finally making a dent in my student loans. My friends were impressed. My family proud—and relieved. (Laughter.) By all appearances, I was living the dream.

But all the while, I knew something was missing, because the truth is, I didn't want to be up in that tall building, alone in an office writing memos. I wanted to be on the ground, working with the folks I grew up with. I wanted to be mentoring young people. I wanted to be helping families put food on the table and a roof over their heads. I wanted to be out there giving folks the same kind of chances that I had. (Applause.)

So much to the surprise of my family and friends, I left that secure, high-paying job and eventually became the executive director of a non-profit, working to help young people get involved in public service. I was making a lot less money—a lot— and my office was a lot smaller. But I woke up every morning with a sense of purpose and possibility. I went to work every day feeling excited (applause) because with every young person I inspired, I felt myself becoming inspired. With every community I engaged, I felt more engaged and alive than I'd felt in years.

Now, I'm not saying that you have to devote your entire career to public service, though I hope that many of you will. The private sector has all kinds of meaningful, satisfying opportunities. And there is nothing wrong with taking home a nice paycheck. And many of you will need that money to help pay off your student loans and support your families. That I know. And it is vitally important that you all rise to the highest ranks of every industry and of every profession. (Applause.)

But as you climb those career ladders, just remember to reach down and pull others up behind you. (Applause.) That's what so many folks have done for you all. And now it is your turn to repay the favor.

Now, juggling these obligations to yourself and to others won't be easy. And I know that along with the pride and joy you're feeling today, you may also be feeling some worry and some anxiety. Some of you may be worrying about getting a job or getting into grad school. Others may be wondering what it will be like to move back home with mom and dad again. And let me tell you there are plenty of moms and dads here who are wondering the same thing. (Laughter.)

But today, and every day going forward, I want you to remember one last legacy that Spelman has left you. It has left you each other.

I mean, look at all these beautiful, magnificent women beside you. (Applause.) It is breathtaking. (Applause.) Think of all the connections that you have, all those experiences that you've shared. The first time you set foot on the campus during Spelbound. Crying your eyes out together at the parting ceremony. Sweating through the night in those un-air-conditioned freshman dorms. (Applause.) Sounds pretty rough. (Laughter.) Maybe the alumni can help out with that. (Laughter and applause.) All those classes, convocations, Christmas concerts—ooh, and the late night conversations about some man. (Laughter.) You all know you were doing that. (Laughter.) You all are the keepers of each other's histories. And the bonds that you've formed here will nourish you and sustain you for the rest of your lives. Now, that is sisterhood. (Applause.)

And look at all these magnificent women around all of you—the alumnae of this institution who led you through that arch on Friday, cheering you on as you start your journey into the world.

I'm told that back in the depths of the recession in 2009, when many seniors here couldn't pay their tuition bills, President Tatum made an appeal to Spelman alumnae, parents and friends asking for help. And even though times were tough for everyone, enough gifts poured in to help 100 seniors graduate from Spelman that year. (Applause.) That is sisterhood. (Applause.)

And finally, think back over the years to all those who have made this day possible: Miss Giles, Miss Packard, Father Quarles, and so many others. Think about all those anonymous folks who were just barely getting by themselves, but still found a way to support this school. Those folks never had the chance to get an education themselves—never—but they were determined that other young people would. Even if it wasn't their daughters. Even if it wasn't their grand-daughters, because, see, what you all have to understand is that hope, that yearning, that wasn't just about themselves and their own families. It was about a vision for us as a people, and as a nation, where every child can develop every last bit of their God-given potential. (Applause.)

Graduates, you are their dream come true. You are the culmination of their sacrifice, of their longing, of their love. You are part of a glorious sisterhood—past, present and future. You have a diploma that will take you places you've never even dreamed of. (Applause.)

And no matter what obstacles you encounter, no matter what hardships you endure, all of you have that for life. No one can ever take that away from you.

And today, I want to end with some words from Tina McElroy Ansa, Spelman class of 1971. (Applause.) In one of her novels, she wrote, simply: "Claim what is yours. . . . You belong anywhere on this earth you want to."

And graduates, if you go out there and make that claim, if you reach back to help others do the same, then I am confident that you will lead lives worthy of your dreams, and you will fulfill that precious Spelman legacy that is now yours.

So congratulations, graduates, on all that you have achieved. I am so proud of you, all of you. We are so proud of you. Do big things. Thank you, and God bless.

About Michelle Obama

Born in 1964 on the South Side of Chicago, Michelle Obama, née Robinson, studied sociology and African American studies at Princeton University, graduating summa cum laude in 1985. After graduating from Harvard Law School in 1988, she joined the Chicago law firm Sidley & Austin. She then served as assistant commissioner of planning and development in Chicago's City Hall before becoming the founding executive director of the Chicago chapter of Public Allies, an AmeriCorps program that prepares youth for public service. She was named associate dean of student services at the University of Chicago in 1996, and developed the university's first community service program. In 2002, she began working for the University of Chicago Hospitals, first as executive director for community affairs and, beginning May 2005, as vice president for community and external affairs.

"Yes, And"

Jane Lynch

The Emmy– and Golden Globe–winning actress Jane Lynch proves as wise as she is funny in this May 2012 speech to the graduating class of Smith College. Lynch culls life lessons from improvisational theater, specifically the rule of "Yes, and," wherein a successful sketch is built by actors' embracing and expanding upon each others' improvisations. She explains that in an ever-changing world, a "Yes, and" philosophy allows individuals to move past negative situations by accepting them and making them their own. Lynch advices the graduates to forgo excessive planning, suggesting that plans prevent us from taking the chances that truly shape our lives.

I feel so important!

Thank you so much, President Christ, the Board of Trustees, distinguished alumnae, my fellow honorary degree recipients, parents and friends, and of course, all of you, the Smith College Class of 2012!

You are about to receive a piece of paper that proves to the world you are now fit to join the ranks of an elite and tremendously powerful group of game-changing women. Smith women have transformed cuisine, spearheaded social movements, created great literature and, in the case of my friend Piper, class of '92, even gone to prison! But damnit—when a Smithie goes to prison—she writes a clever and compelling book about it!

Just know, the fact that you sit here in a chair assigned to you, with your bright, shiny faces, looking gorgeous in caps and gowns, you've actually done far more than I was able to accomplish on my college graduation day back in 1982.

As a young person I was a victim of overwhelming angst and free-floating anxiety. I spent a great deal of my time running around like a chicken with its head cut off. This ongoing frenzy caused me to send in my graduation registration without a stamp or return address.

After my four mostly unfocused years as a solid "C" student at Illinois State University, in the aptly named Normal, Illinois, I sat where you now sit, hoping to God my name would be called and I would receive a diploma. I realized my postal booboo just as the envelope left my hand and dropped into the mailbox. Instead of figuring out a way to remedy this, I did what I have always done when I lack forethought and impulse control; I crossed my fingers and hoped for the best.

With my entire family out there in the audience, wearing a cap and gown I swiped when no one was looking, sharing a chair with my friend Jeannie Mahoney,

---

I held my breath and prayed to hear my name. They finished with the L's, and were on to the M's, when my heart sank. As Jeannie took her diploma from our dean, she whispered in his ear that my name had been left out. Gratefully, he called mine after hers. He didn't have a diploma for me but he did shake my hand. My parents, sitting way in the back, were none the wiser.

I know that none of you would have been so scattered and unfocused leading up to this day because you are the Smith Class of 2012. You are exceptional women, and if you were not you would not be here. I feel I know quite a bit about Smith women, because I married one of you. I know from living with Lara class of '91, and loving Lara class of '91, that the experience of attending this fabulous college is transformative. Your lives will take different paths, but you will always be Smithies.

You are the women of Smith. You are fiercely independent, wicked smart, trail blazing, uber confident and shockingly entitled. Like I told you, I live with one of you. I have no doubt you will continue with this legacy and you will change the world. And, we need you to, women of Smith College—now more than ever.

But in this moment, young ladies and Ada Comstocks, on this most auspicious of days, I want you to take a breath and reflect. Don't blow through this day, even if you are overwhelmed with family or just a little bit drunk. Take a breath. You have successfully completed a journey at an exceptional institution of learning and attention must be paid.

If I could do so much of my early life over, I would have taken more moments like this to breathe. I would have spent more time focusing on what was right in front of me, instead of recoiling from what is because it didn't look or feel exactly as I imagined it. I wouldn't have been forever trying to look around the corner to see "What's next, what's next?!"

I'd have taken in the beauty of the moment, and greeted everything in my life with a big "YES, AND." Which leads me to what I want to talk to you about today. And today is all about you. But just a little bit about me.

I was born a red-faced screaming malcontent with sparkling blue eyes and chubby cheeks. Along with this extra helping of angst, I felt alien in the world and in my own body, as I was sure I should have been a boy.

I spent most of my youth deeply disappointed so much of the time, because nothing ever looked or felt the way I imagined it should. I wanted to ride my bike with my shirt off all summer. I wanted to play little league baseball—I did not want to wear a dress or curl my hair. I was only happy with a clear blue sky, and I lived in Illinois where winter lasts until May and spring usually skips us altogether. If the day loomed cloudy, and it usually did, my poor mother would fear my lashing out at the weather for having let me down. I took everything so personally.

I lived my life this way for about 27 years, until my life stepped in with a huge lesson that I was just aware enough to notice.

At the time I fancied myself a serious actress; sketch comedy was not on my radar. Out of left field, I was hired for The Second City. For those of you who don't know, The Second City is a Chicago institution, and the improvisational breeding ground where Tina Fey, Amy Poehler, Rachel Dratch and Nia Vardalos along with some guys you might recognize, got their start.

There I was, a tightly wound young woman obsessed with process, rules, fresh out of grad school, I was a classically trained pain in the ass, frankly, engaging in improvisation: the creative equivalent of jumping off a cliff. An art where there are no rules, save one; it's called "YES, AND."

"YES AND" is the vital and only rule of improvisation. Never deny your fellow actor. You should be willing and able to accept whatever your fellow improviser throws at you. Use that as your jumping off point and expand it. "Heighten and explore," as we call it.

For instance, if I say to you "Stick 'em up!" and you say "That's not a gun, that's your finger!" We've got nowhere to go.

If I say "What a beautiful day" and you say, "No it's not, it's the middle of winter and it's snowing!" Where do we go?

Or I say "Come my darling, it's time for bed." And you say, "You're not my wife and put your pants back on!" Now what do I do with that? The scene is dead in the water and I'm literally caught with my pants down.

In order for our scene to go forward, we affirm what the other is saying, which is the "YES" part of our equation, and take it and build, the "AND" part of our equation.

In other words, in order for our lives to go forward, in order to engage fully in life, we need to be willing and able to accept what is right in front of us. Whatever it is, the good, the bad, the thrilling, the heartbreaking, every emotion, occurrence, event, person, place or thing, you will experience them all. That's the "YES" I'm talking about. And the acceptance and embrace of it with all your heart and doing something with it, that's the "AND." You accept influence and then you exert influence. You can't make a cloudy day a sunny day, but can embrace it and decide it's going to be a good day after all.

I learn through contrast. I had one of my first significant experiences of "NO, BUT" when I was a freshman in high school. I auditioned for and was cast as the king in a one-act version of the "Princess and the Pea" story called "The Ugly Duckling" (beginning a life-long pattern of playing roles originally intended for men). I'd known I wanted to be an actress right out of the chute and I was beside myself with excitement.

At the audition, I got huge laughs. At the first rehearsal, I didn't get the big laughs, I didn't get the love and I quit. I was devastated and so confused. I had no idea what I had done! My 14-year-old self had no idea how to process it. I had walked up to that which I had ached to do for as long as I could remember, and I don't think I go too far when I say, I came face to face with my destiny, and I walked away. Ya know why? Because it didn't feel like I imagined it should have felt. I didn't get the response, i.e., the big laugh, i.e., the big love like I expected. There was now a real possibility of failure and I quit. I was at this time unaware of the concept of "YES AND." Feeling the fear and doing it anyway.

As you travel through life, in these many years ahead, I guarantee that you will come upon countless times in which the last thing you're gonna want to say is "YES

AND." You will experience loss, heartache, the death of a loved one, you'll probably have to say goodbye to a lover, you'll experience rejection, maybe have to deal with a bad diagnosis. You'll age.

The trick isn't to avoid these times or pretend they're not happening; you can't. What you'll need to do is step up to them courageously and embrace them. Allow these experiences to permeate your being and weave them all into the fabric of your life. They will not only soften you and strengthen you, and you will open your heart to compassion. You will not be powerless in this. If you embrace what is happening, instead of denying it, you can make it your own. If life gives you lemons, grab it by the horns and drive. Yes I just mixed three metaphors, remember I was a "C" student.

As a younger person full of anxiety and fear, in desperate pursuit of keys to the kingdom, let me tell you what I did right. After I'd walked away from "The Ugly Duckling" my freshman year in high school, I would never let fear take me over again (at least in the acting department). Not that I would never feel fear again, I would just plow through it. I grabbed at almost every opportunity, maybe even some I should have left by the wayside.

This is not to suggest you should say "YES AND" to every opportunity presented to you.

Now, I know what you're thinking, "Jane, what about doing porno?" To which I say I am as surprised as you are that I was never offered that opportunity.

But would I have said yes to that? What if life gives us the opportunity to rob a bank, or a way to cheat on our taxes, or say it offers us several hours in a row of life with the Kardashians . . . hours that we can never get back?

To this I say: you can always trust that when you're coming from your highest self and from your heart, you'll know when you should say "YES AND," and when to engage the awesome power of "NO WAY."

Now, this "YES AND" way of life may not be the most natural thing to do for you Smith College Class of 2012 women sitting in front of me today. You're highly educated. You are so schooled in critical thinking it almost hurts to look at you. The point of your education is to get you to poke holes in theories, to question, to be loath to accept anything at face value. "YES AND" may not roll trippingly off your tongue, and into your life.

Your job is to honestly discern for yourself if you're saying "no" to an opportunity out of fear, or are you simply exercising good judgment.

For me, the hardest thing to get past was my need to plan. I thought I had to have a plan or a strategy to get where I wanted to go. From my earliest moments, I knew I wanted to be an actress. I had a driving, anxiety-filled ambition. Growing up in this concrete jungle of a suburb just south of Chicago, I had no idea how I would get there. "Just show me the road map or a manual. Or please, someone drop down from the heavens, take my hand and show me the way." I was ripe for a cult.

I took to rules, regulations and parameters in an effort to feel safe. While I waited for that clear plan of action, I would have at least an illusion of certainty in what has always felt to me to be an unsafe, unpredictable and ever-changing world.

It turns out I just had to be willing to take chances, look at what's right in front of me and greet everything with a big "YES AND," putting all of my heart into everything I do. My counsel to you, women of Smith College? Let life surprise you. Don't have a plan. Plans are for wusses. If my life went according to my plan, I would never ever have the life I have today.

> *My advice to you: live in the moment. Stay fluid and roll with those changes. Life is just a big extended improvisation. Embrace the ever changing, ever evolving world with the best rule I've ever found. Say 'YES AND.'*

You are obviously good planners, or you wouldn't be here. Stop it! Stop it now! Don't deprive yourself of the exciting journey your life can be when you relinquish the need to have goals and a blueprint.

I guess I am assuming you all are as terrified as I was of life, so you know that when you feel sick to your stomach, it's a good thing! It signals "Opportunity For Big Growth Ahead!" "Somethin's coming, somethin' good." Don't ignore the nausea. Step up to it.

At one point, I'd had a lean financial year, and performing "It's a Hard Knock Life" from Annie in my pantyhose had lost its charm. I was stuck creatively and professionally, I was in my late 30s, terrified that the parade was passing me by. The thought of writing a show by myself and for myself began to bubble up to the surface of my consciousness, making me very sick to my stomach.

So with a big "YES AND" and chutzpah I didn't even know I had, I created something where there had once been nothing for the very first time in my life.

On my own nickel, I rented a theater for eight consecutive Wednesday nights, wrote monologues for characters I had accessed from the deepest recesses of my psyche, and I created a one-hour romp (which I performed literally stinking of fear, at moments terrified and others, elated).

I was never more proud of myself, and it blew wide open the doors of my self-confidence. I emerged, in my humble opinion, an artist and a changed woman. I was now one poised for, and deserving of, the next level. I met Christopher Guest shortly thereafter and was cast in Best in Show. I was 40 years old, and I was finally in the game. I could never have planned this.

Other momentous occasions where my dreams were about to come true, and yet I wanted nothing more than to flee the scene:

Being offered the opportunity to host the Emmys.

Being asked to host "Saturday Night Live."

Being asked to give the Commencement speech at Smith College.

When my insides screamed "NO!!" I somehow got my mouth to say "YES AND."

Life is not all about work—and the scariest places to say "Yes And" are also the most rewarding . . . in a relationship.

Whoever you choose, your husband, wife or partner, will make you see more about yourself than any navel gazing in solitude could ever reveal.

And if the process isn't completely horrifying and frustrating, then you're not doing it right. This will be your most vulnerable place.

I put it off until I was almost 50. Your partner will inevitably see your soft underbelly. Shocking behavior you only read about will start to become your own. Your demon will rise up to righteously destroy your relationship in the guise of saving yourself from really seeing yourself. Your partner will say to you with all the tenderness that situation allows, "What the fuck?" You'll want to break up with yourself.

Don't be afraid of this horrible version of you! Face it, embrace it, coddle it, write it a poem, maybe it needs a hug. Shine the light of day on it. Unclaimed and unacknowledged, it's got the power and its darkest forces will have you enslaved! Accept its influence, mine it for its gold. Yep, sometimes saying "YES AND" is going to take everything you've got. But the payoff, trusting in love, is just incredible.

The day after I met my wife, I met my daughter. I don't really like kids; I'm a dog person. But you couldn't have designed a better kid for me. She's witty, wise beyond her years, she has a huge heart, and such patience with the frailties of human nature. I don't mean to make her sound like the Dalai Lama, but she is exceptional. One day you will meet your child; you may give birth to her, adopt her, she may just wander over or follow you home. We do "meet" them because they are born who they are. We don't make them, we welcome them. Nothing like knowing they are watching you will make you want to be your best self. Haden was 7 when I met her, she's now 10 and in eight more years we hope to be dropping her off right here.

Children also remind us that life is constantly changing and moving ever forward. It's true. It doth not stop. I really came to know this as I turned 40 years old. I'm just a late bloomer, folks. The big 4-0 was much anticipated. I resolved to have a party for myself and actually mark it, celebrate it. Say "YES AND" to it. So I turned 40 years old one day. And you know what happened? I turned 41. THEN, I turned 42! And it just kept on going, just like that, the number kept going up! Wait! Wait! Somebody press the pause button! I just got used to being 40! And it goes even faster as you get older. And the world keeps changing. My advice to you: live in the moment. Stay fluid and roll with those changes. Life is just a big extended improvisation. Embrace the ever changing, ever evolving world with the best rule I've ever found. Say "YES AND."

Accept the world for what it is, and at the same time, make it your own. I especially want you to make it your own. You are a particular variety of person, Ms. Smithie. You have spent the last four years in an environment that has encouraged you to be not just yourself, but your best self, your strongest self.

You will have many opportunities to embrace what the world has for you. I can't wait to see the ways in which you say "AND." Remember that Smith Woman entitlement I spoke of earlier? I'm counting on yours to ferociously guard the women's health care rights our sisters won for us years ago. I know you women of Smith will greet that fight with a big "YES AND," and any one who tries take them away from you with a huge "NO WAY."

In conclusion, I know you'll never forget your experience here and that you are a part of an incredible legacy. I'll be at a party with my wife, and she'll be meeting one person after another and if she by chance happens upon a fellow Smithie, both of their eyes will light up. They already share a profound connection; they've both had a unique and extraordinary experience. Today I become a Smithie! That same piece of paper that my wife and all of you toiled for years to get, I now get for handshake. I am so proud to be one of you.

Enjoy this day and thank you so much.

About Jane Lynch

Jane Lynch was born July 14, 1960, in Dolton, Illinois. She earned a BA from Illinois State University and an MFA at Cornell's graduate program for acting. After a period in New York, Lynch returned to Chicago and began work with the Steppenwolf Theatre and Second City touring companies. Her breakthrough to mainstream film occurred when Christopher Guest offered her a role in the hit movie Best in Show. *Following that success, Lynch continued to steal scenes with small parts in* A Mighty Wind *and* The 40-Year-Old Virgin, *and appearances on the television shows* Weeds, Arrested Development, Two and a Half Men, *and* The L Word. *In 2009 she landed a starring role in the comedy series* Party Down, *and, shortly after, began her celebrated role as Sue Sylvester on the hit show* Glee, *for which she received an Emmy Award and a Golden Globe. Lynch is additionally the author of an award-winning 1998 play,* Oh Sister, My Sister, *and a 2011 autobiography, titled* Happy Accidents. *She joins her partner, Lara Embry, as an honorary Smith graduate.*

"Four Truths"

Bob Woodruff

In an address to the new graduates of Boston College, television reporter Bob Woodruff shares four truths to live by that were reaffirmed for him in the wake of a near-fatal head injury sustained while reporting from Iraq in 2006. Woodruff suggests that cultivating a passion is the surest means of achieving both happiness and success. He encourages students to "exercise their faith" as a balm against life's troubles. Reminding students of the 2.3 million service members who have served in Iraq or Afghanistan, he urges the next generation to seize responsibility for the care of returning soldiers. Woodruff prompts his audience, in the face of life's unpredictability, to be affectionate with loved ones, and finally, insists that hardship and challenges are what recommit us to that which is truly important in life.

Thank you Father Keenan, and thanks to Father Leahy, trustees, faculty, students and family members.

I'm very honored to be here, even though I am fairly certain you won't remember a thing I say. When I graduated from Colgate University in 1983, my graduation speaker was Ted Koppel, a prominent journalist from the ABC News show *Nightline*. And I honestly cannot remember one thing he told us. Years later, when I had the chance to tell him that story, he told me that he couldn't remember his graduation speaker, let alone what he had said at my ceremony.

Now you may be asking yourself: who is this guy and why is he my graduation speaker?

I'm just a person with a story. I'm a person who has been where you are now—and I became a journalist because I fell in love with telling stories. Stories have the power to connect us as human beings. And they have the power to effect change.

So this is my story in a nutshell. I have an amazing family—a wife who is by far my better half; four terrific kids, one of whom goes to BC. I worked hard, I loved what I did and then the unexpected happened. I was critically injured by a roadside bomb while covering the war in Iraq.

I lost many things in that injury, but on balance I'd have to say that I gained many more.

By all rights I should have died on January 29, 2006. It is my "Alive Day," as it is referred to in the military—the day the nurses and doctors and medics brought me back despite all of the odds stacked against me. And if I had died that day, I can tell you this: Short of watching my children grow up, and meeting my grandkids, by that point in my life I had achieved all of the things that truly mattered. I had the love of a good woman, children who are the center of my world. I had reached what is considered the pinnacle of success in my career: co-anchor of *World News Tonight*, following in the footsteps of Peter Jennings. I had traveled the world and lived in enough other countries to understand how fortunate we are to be born in the USA.

Six years ago I was riding down a road in a tank outside Baghdad, when a 155 mm explosive device went off. Rock shrapnel hit my face, head and body, and the force of the explosion shattered my skull. I was not expected to live, and I was in a coma for 36 days. If I did survive, my prognosis was grim. One larger rock had cut across my neck and come to rest against the carotid artery on the other side. I was never expected to speak again, let alone be standing up here. I am a walking miracle and I am grateful for that every single day.

During and after my recovery, there were four truths that crystallized for me. They aren't vast wisdom and they are probably things you've heard before, but in the years since my injury my awareness of them has only sharpened. And so I share them with you today, in hopes that maybe you will remember at least one of them.

Number one: FIGURE OUT WHAT MAKES YOU HAPPY.

I was a lawyer in New York City when I met my wife. But it was 1987 and the economy was pretty grim. Sounds familiar, right? There were no mergers or deals happening and I was bored. I had studied Mandarin Chinese during law school and when I married Lee, we left for Beijing, China, in 1988, where I taught law to Chinese students.

The year that followed was a pivotal one. We would watch my students at the university begin to protest the communist regime, and the Tiananmen Square demonstrations blossomed. I took a job as a translator for CBS News, and when the tanks rolled into the Square and the Army began shooting at its own people, I witnessed the blood and the carnage.

Those moments on the Square changed the direction of my life. I fell in love with the idea of telling stories. I was hooked on journalism.

I found an entry level job in TV news and left the law and a nice salary behind. We qualified for food stamps in the state of California. We had a brand new baby and my wife supported us with her writing.

For the next 11 years we moved around the country to bigger and bigger TV markets, had three more kids and I continued to move up in my career. I was passionate about what I did. I learned something new every day. I worked hard, did whatever was asked or required, put in all the extra hours, kept my head down and the rest came. Figure out what engages you, what turns you on—because when you love what you do, happiness and even financial success can flow from that.

An education from BC is the perfect preparation for journalism and many other fields. There is no substitute for studying history, philosophy, theology, and literature. The kind of an education that you have received here will help you form the questions. And knowing how to ask questions is one of the most important tools in life, in every field.

Let me say that I do understand that not every single person gets to find passion in their job—for some people what they do is a vocation—but people find passion in other aspects of their life, whether it's playing music or writing books, building boats, cooking or running marathons. Whatever it may be, I urge you to find and feed a passion.

Number Two: EXERCISE YOUR FAITH.

You've had the opportunity here at BC to be exposed to faith in many forms. Everyone has a set of beliefs and they are calibrated in different measures. Some people don't believe in God, and that's their prerogative. But in what I've witnessed and experienced, having faith in something bigger than you can ease you through many things.

There are a lot of questions we can't answer. And faith never promises you that it has all the answers. It simply eases the journey. A battle with breast cancer, a parent's slow slide into Alzheimer's, the loss of a child, a husband kisses a wife goodbye and the World Trade Center falls. You will need faith in ways that may not seem important now, but at some point it will serve you well. Faith has the power to stop you from falling through the floor. Use it, explore it, tap into it from time to time and it will renew you in unexpected ways.

One of the memories I had when I woke up after five weeks in a coma was one that many other people have described who have had near-death experiences. I had fallen back in the tank and I remembered the sensation of floating above my body, looking down and seeing myself bleeding and being bathed in a white light. The light was warm and comforting. And I wanted to be there, but then I woke up hard on the floor of the tank. It was not my time, but the image of that light stayed with me, and to this day I am not afraid of death.

I'll share with you one other story about faith. It was when I was visiting the injured at Bethesda Naval Hospital. There was a young soldier, alone in his hospital room, who had his foot blown off and he was angry and in pain.

A nurse came in and she said "Henry, have you talked to God today?" And he grumbled a little and said "I don't believe in God." She turned to him, tucking in the sheet, making him comfortable, and she said, "Well, that's OK; I talked to him for you. He's got your back today." And you could see that soldier relax. He knew that someone else out there was including him in their prayers. Sometimes, just holding that hope for someone else is one of the greatest gifts you can give another human being.

Number Three: SERVE AND GIVE BACK.

Your education here at BC has emphasized service in many important ways. It is a part of the Jesuit tradition. As we sit here today and as you've spent the last four years pursuing your education, young men and women are crouched in a tank somewhere on a battlefield, serving our country. These are the people who raised their hands when their country asked them to go and whether or not you believe these wars are just or you vote left, right or center, you have to respect the fact that there are people willing to go into areas of conflict so that you can make that choice.

And when they come home, injured or different or looking for a job or a chance, it is up to America to welcome them home in our individual communities. Our government will not be able to care for them alone. It will fall on the 99% of us civilians who allow the less than 1% of us in the military to do the heavy lifting in warzones and hot spots while we enjoy life here.

As a journalist I had covered wars for many years. People asked me why I liked going to areas of conflict and one of the things that fascinated me is that in wars you see both the best and worst of human nature. I firmly believe that as long as there are Americans overseas willing to put their lives on the line for us back home, there need to be people willing to tell their story—and that of the Iraqis and Afghans.

> *But the big, awful thing that happened in my life can't define me. It only strengthened my love for so many things. It recommitted me to what's really important.*

Returning veterans and their families are facing enormous challenges when they return home from the battlefield. And more than 360,000 have returned home with some form of a brain injury. The need for employment, a record-breaking suicide rate and broken families are just a few of the issues they face. It will be up to your generation to ensure that we—as a country—take care of our own. This is simply what a great nation does.

My family and I got an inordinate amount of attention after my injury and it was our time to stand up—to use our voice and pulpit to remind America about the families making sacrifices every day. We saw firsthand how lucky we were; we had resources and loved ones and friends. We started a foundation to help our wounded veterans. Giving back—doing something way bigger than you or your family—feels good. I know that many of you already know that feeling and are engaged in service in multiple ways. So I urge you—when it's your turn, give back.

Number Four: GET VOCAL WITH FAMILY AND FRIENDS.

This last one is easy. The network of friends that you have hopefully made during your time here at BC will be an important gift throughout your life. These friends will support you and care for you, check in with you and be the webbing for the life you are about to launch. Your friends may change and morph over time—but I know that I could not have made the journey of my recovery without family and friends.

I hope today you get the chance to tell them that. Be vocal about it—tell your friends and your family at every opportunity how much they mean to you. Life is short. Life can change in an instant—I'm living proof of that—so don't be stingy with love or friendship.

Journalist David Brooks wrote a great book I urge you all to read called *The Social Animal*, and one of the passages that rang true for me was about how we prepare our children for life with tests and learning and information—but that one of the most important decisions you will ever make in life is something we don't exactly know how to prepare you for: who to be friends with and trust and love and spend your life with. In the end, those choices will be one of the most important indicators for your ongoing happiness and success. And knowing the kind of school that BC is, I know you have chosen well.

My injury changed many things. I lost the anchor chair at ABC News. I lost a photographic memory. I can't always find the word I want right at the moment I reach for it. That roadside bomb that changed my world forced me to reconfigure my life, in many amazing ways.

But the big, awful thing that happened in my life can't define me. It only strengthened my love for so many things. It recommitted me to what's really important. What counts isn't the title or the accomplishment. It's not a medal or an award. It is the people, my friends and family—the ones who have been and will be there for the long haul. So give your family a big hug today and thank them for helping you get to this place.

So, to the class of 2012: Congratulations for what you've done and all the amazing and wonderful places you are about to go. Go Eagles!

About Bob Woodruff

Bob Woodruff was born on August 18, 1961, in Bloomfield Hills, Michigan. He earned a bachelor's degree from Colgate University in 1983 and a law degree from the University of Michigan Law School in 1987. Having achieved fluency in Chinese during the course of his studies, he moved to Beijing in 1989 to teach law. In China, Woodruff worked for CBS News as an on-screen interpreter. After reporting on the Tiananmen Square protests, he left law and became a full-time correspondent, initially working for several local stations, and finally for ABC News by 1996. He succeeded Peter Jennings as co-anchor of ABC's weekday news broadcast in December 2005. A month later, Woodruff traveled to Baghdad with the intention of meeting with troops before President Bush's 2006 State of the Union address. On January 29, he was critically wounded when a roadside bomb struck his vehicle outside Taji, Iraq. For more than a year after his injury, Woodruff struggled with expressive aphasia, but recovered to return to air with ABC in February 2007. He now hosts Focus Earth with Bob Woodruff, *an ABC-produced newscast that focuses on environmental news, policy, and climate change. In 2007, he produced the documentary* To Iraq and Back: Bob Woodruff Reports, *which calls attention to the difficulties faced by veterans suffering from brain injuries when seeking treatment. Woodruff is also the founder of ReMIND, a foundation begun in 2008 to support American troops who have sustained "hidden" injuries of war.*

Memory and Ethics

Elie Wiesel

Drawing on the Bible, folk tales, and modern literature, writer and concentration camp survivor Elie Wiesel addresses the new graduates of Washington University, telling them that they should continue to look forward and not repeat the mistakes of the twentieth century, made violent by political and racist fanaticism. Wiesel affirms that every human life is worthy of respect, and encourages the graduates to maintain faith in the goodness of others and to take action against injustice.

Chancellor, Chairman of the Board of Trustees, members of the distinguished faculty, families, parents, grandparents and friends, and especially, of course, the graduating class:

I congratulate you together with my other fellow recipients of the honorary degree. What you have learned here should not stay only in memory, but you must open the gates of your own memory and try to do something with what you have learned.

I speak to you, of course, not only as a teacher, but also as a witness. And therefore I must maybe define myself. You should know that I am Jewish. Maybe you don't know it. But to me, to be Jewish is what? It's not exclusive—it's an opening. It is really as when the conductor here conducts his orchestra; he offers the person to sing or to play a certain part, a certain tune. And I offer my memory to you. You should know something about what is there, inside.

But what I say, that a Jew, the more Jewish he or she is, and the more universal is the message, I say that anyone else could say the same thing, whether as Protestant, Unitarian, Catholic, Buddhist or even agnostic. We must be before we give. We must shield and protect the identity, the inner identity that we have and that makes us who we are.

Now, the topic is memory. In the Bible, the expression is "Remember, don't forget." And when you study the text, you realize there is something wrong there. It's enough to say, "remember." Or it's enough to say, "don't forget." Why the repetition? It could mean, "Remember not to forget." It could also mean, "Don't forget to remember." I say that knowing one thing: that this is a very great university. I have been here before you were born, most of you. I have been here some 35 years ago or so. And so humbly I realize that it took the leaders of this university 35 years to invite me again.

Now, a story. A man is lost in the forest. And he tries to find the exit and fails. It takes him hours in night and day, and he's still lost in the forest. On the third day, he

Delivered May 20, 2011, at the Washington University commencement, St. Louis, Missouri, by Elie Wiesel. Copyright © 2011 by Elie Wiesel. Reprinted with permission. All rights reserved.

notices that someone else is in the forest. He runs to him and he says, "Ah! I'm so glad to meet you. Show me the way out." And he said, "I am like you—I am lost in the forest. One thing I can tell you: You see that road there? Don't go there. I have just come from there."

I belong to a generation that tells you that. Where you now can start your life, and you've of

> *... I believe that the human being—any human being of any community, any origin, any color—a human being is eternal. Any human being is a challenge. Any human being is worthy of my attention, of my love occasionally.*

course entered a lot of roads, cities, maybe new universities, and remember, there is something that you must remember: Don't go where I come from.

The 20th century was one of the worst centuries in the history of humankind. Why? Because it was dominated by two fanaticisms. Political fanaticism: capital, Moscow. Racist fanaticism: capital, Berlin. And therefore, that century has caused more deaths than any time before.

What do we know now? A new trend is hanging upon us, and the name is fanaticism. We must do whatever we can to, first of all, unmask. Second, to denounce. And, of course, to oppose fanaticism wherever it is. What is fanaticism? Perversion. You can take a beautiful idea—like religion in the Middle Ages—but fanaticism can turn it into something which is anti-human because a group of human beings decide that they know who is worthy of life, who is worthy of redemption.

And today, fanaticism has reached an even lower point in its development: the fanatic who becomes a suicide murderer. That is a kind of atomic bomb. A suicide murderer who becomes himself, and, in some cases, herself, a weapon! They do not want simply to die. For that, they could simply jump into the ocean. They want to kill innocent people mainly, including children, and therefore that is an option that you must resist in your own life.

What else have we learned? That we are not alone in this world. God alone is alone. Human beings are not. We are here to be together with others, and I insist on the others—which means, in some places, in some groups, they are suspicious of the other. Don't. I see the otherness of the other, which appeals to me. In fact it is the otherness of the other that makes me who I am. I am always to learn from the other. And the other is, to me, not an enemy, but a companion, an ally, and of course, in some cases of grace, a friend. So the other is never to be rejected, and surely not humiliated.

What else? I quote from the Bible, I continue, because after all that is my study—that's my upbringing. The greatest commandment, to me, in the Bible is not the Ten Commandments. First of all, it's too difficult to observe. Second, we all pretend to observe them. My commandment is, "Thou shall not stand idly by." Which means when you witness an injustice, don't stand idly by. When you hear of a person or a group being persecuted, do not stand idly by. When there is something wrong in the community around you—or far way—do not stand idly by. You must intervene.

You must interfere. And that is actually the motto of human rights. Human rights has become a kind of secular religion today. And I applaud it—I am part of it. And therefore wherever something happens, I try to be there as a witness.

One of my last dramatic visits was to Bosnia. I was sent by President Clinton as a Presidential Envoy. And I would go there, really, to those places in Bosnia, to speak with the victims. My interest is in the victims. And I would go literally from person to person, from family to family, from barrack to barrack, from tent to tent, asking them to tell me their stories. And they always began, but they stopped in the middle. Not one of the people I interviewed or interrogated ended the story. The story was usually about rape in the family, and murder, they were tortured, there was humiliation—no one finished the story! Because they all burst into tears.

And then I realized. Maybe that is my mission, as a teacher, as a witness: to finish the story for them. Because they were crying and crying and crying. And I felt like the prophet Elijah, when I sat down in private to do what I had to do. I said I'm going to collect their tears, and turn them into stories.

Now, you have already known something which I did not before I came here. This university is great not only because of its great faculty and its marvelous students, but also because it has a tradition. The commencement speaker should speak only for 15 minutes. I am sure they meant well because they felt sorry for you, graduates. You are waiting here patiently for the moment when the Chancellor will come and offer you the degree. So why should I expose you to torture, the torture of waiting?

I want you to know, with all that I have gone through in life: I still have faith in humanity. I still have faith in humanity. I have faith in language, although language was perverted by the enemy. I have faith in God, although I quarrel with Him a lot of the time. I don't know whether he feels upset or not, but I do. Why? Because I don't want to break the chain that links me to my parents and grandparents and theirs, and theirs, and theirs.

And furthermore, I believe that the human being—any human being of any community, any origin, any color—a human being is eternal. Any human being is a challenge. Any human being is worthy of my attention, of my love occasionally. And therefore I say it to you: When you are now going into a world which is hounded, obsessed with so much violence, often so much despair—when you enter this world and you say the world is not good today, good! Correct it! That's what you have learned here for four years from your great teachers. Go there, and tell them what you remember. Tell them that the nobility of the human being cannot be denied.

I'm sure you have learned French literature. I'm sure you have learned about Albert Camus, the great philosopher and novelist. In his famous novel, *The Plague*, at the end Dr. Rieux, who was the main character of the novel, sees a devastated city, thousands and thousands of victims from the plague. And this doctor at the end says, it's true, all that is true.

But nevertheless, I believe, he said, there is more in any human being to celebrate than to denigrate. I repeat: There is more in any human being to celebrate than to denigrate.

Let's celebrate. Thank you.

About Elie Wiesel

Born in 1928 in the town of Sighet, in what is now Romania, Elie Wiesel was sent, along with his family, to the German concentration and extermination camps. His parents and younger sister were killed there. Wiesel and his two older sisters survived. Liberated from Buchenwald in 1945 by the Allies, he was taken to Paris, where he studied at the Sorbonne and worked as a journalist. He published his first book, Night, *a memoir of his experiences in the concentration camps, in 1958. He has since written nearly forty volumes, some of them based on his experience in the camps. A New York resident and US citizen, Wiesel has served as a Yale University visiting scholar and a professor at the City College of New York. Since 1976, he has been the Andrew W. Mellon Professor in the Humanities at Boston University.*

"Bear Witness"

Billy Shore

Drawing on the wisdom of thinkers and writers from Mahatma Gandhi to Gwendolyn Brooks, Billy Shore urges the graduating class of Bronx Community College to know that they need not make the choice—offered in many commencement addresses—between doing well and doing good. He suggests that it is now possible to do both. He exhorts the graduates to see new things, to search their feelings, and to bear witness to the world about what they have seen and felt. Personal transformation powers social change, he says, asserting that in this simple but profound action, there is the possibility to change the world.

Thank you, President Berotte Joseph, and congratulations to each of you.

I intend to keep my comments concise for a variety of reasons including a sobering conversation I had with my seven-year-old son. Let's leave aside for a moment the improbability of my having a seven-year-old son. He's misbehaved with his baby-sitter and my wife Rosemary called me at work and said I had to come home right away so that we could talk to Nate about his character, and his purpose in life and the choices he makes. I went straight home and the three of us talked but it was mostly a monologue with Rosemary doing most of the monologuing. After she had the good sense to say: "Nate, do you in turn have anything you'd like to say to us?" And he looked us dead in the eye and said, "Thank you for your little presentation." To avoid evoking that reaction, I will say only three things to you this morning about my experiences and your opportunities, and then sit down.

First, as much as I appreciated that generous introduction, you should know that while everything that President Joseph said is true, that is not who I am. At least it is not, and of course could not be, all of who I am. Yes, it is true that I worked in government and started Share Our Strength and that we've raised more than $360 million, but that is only part of who I am.

I am also the son of a loving mother who died from a drug overdose before I'd completed my education. I was a principal architect of three losing presidential campaigns, one of which spent more than four years paying off its debts. And oh, after graduating law school I failed the bar exam. Twice. I tell you this not for sensationalism's sake or to gain sympathy, but to persuade you that no life, not even a successful life, perhaps especially not a successful life, is lived as an unbroken string of successes. And indeed the shortcomings, failures and even bad luck that are an inevitable part of being human need not hinder your success in the least if you know what to take from and do with them.

Whenever you think you know someone, try to remember that you usually only know what they have chosen to let you know, or what others have told you about him or her. You won't and can't know what they carry with them, what St. Exupery referred to when saying: "What's essential is invisible to the eye," and whether it has made them stronger or weaker, richer or poorer, better or worse. Being ever conscious of this may not make you more successful but it will make your life richer in immeasurable ways.

Second, as diverse as you are in your intellect, appetites, energies, appearance and ambition, you share in common three world-changing powers: to share your strength, to create community wealth and to bear witness.

Share Our Strength was built on the belief that everyone has a strength to share, sometimes a gift that you may take for granted but that can be deployed to benefit others. I'm talking about something more than writing a check once you are financially successful, or occasionally volunteering at a food bank or homeless shelter. I'm talking about giving of yourself, of your unique value added, as chefs have done by cooking at food and wine benefits or by teaching nutrition and food budgeting skills to low-income families. In the same way we have engaged authors, architects, public relations and marketing executives, and numerous others.

As a result we have helped to build the emergency food assistance network in the country, distribute 2.4 billion pounds of food, launched the No Kid Hungry campaign to end childhood hunger in the U.S. by ensuring that the 21 million kids who get a free school lunch also get breakfast, food stamps and other nutrition assistance to which they are entitled, and we've made a life and death difference in places like Haiti and Ethiopia.

What we are doing may sound good. But good is not good enough. Martin Luther King once said, "In this unfolding conundrum of life and history there is such a thing as being too late. Procrastination is still the thief of time. The tide in the affairs of men does not remain at flood, it ebbs."

To me these have always been more than eloquent words. I went to Ethiopia during the onset of a terrible famine there in 2000 and 2002 and met a 13-year-old girl at a school we were supporting, and where we were trying to build a hospital next door. Her name was Alima Dari and we stayed in touch for several years, exchanging letters and pictures. But one day a colleague of mine went to Ethiopia on a trip I couldn't make and I gave him a letter to give to Alima but then didn't hear from him for many days. He finally wrote to say "I hate to tell you this but Alima died of cerebral malaria. She's been misdiagnosed with tuberculosis and by the time they realized it was malaria and got her to Addis Ababa it was too late." And there again were Martin Luther King's words.

But you don't have to go all the way to Ethiopia to find and meet your Alima. Alima is in Boston, and in the Bronx, in Denver and Detroit, and wherever kids are at risk, vulnerable and voiceless. Despite our success there are still too many children for whom we are too late. The spectacular results we are getting in Arkansas have not found their way to Texas. The progress we've seen in Maryland, has not reached Mississippi.

As graduates you will soon be in a position to share your strengths and I hope that you will share at least some of them on behalf of an Alima somewhere in this community, our country or our world.

You graduate at a time when child poverty is at a near record high of 21 percent of all children in the U.S. (15 million kids living in homes that are below the poverty line.) Almost three million American kids live in "extreme poverty," in households with less than $2 a day per person, according to National Poverty Center at University of Michigan. Some urban areas face catastrophe, with as many as 67 percent of children living in a neighborhood of concentrated poverty. Forty-six million Americans are on food stamps for the first time in the history of the United States. And half of them are children.

> *Go somewhere you haven't been and see something you haven't yet seen. Look until you feel something and then tell someone what you've seen and felt. This is what it means to bear witness. This is what it takes to change the world.*

The failure to invest in at-risk kids early enough creates and perpetuates a cycle of poverty. And yet 2012 will be the second year in a row that Congress cuts appropriations for children.

America's national and economic security depends on human capital. And that security demands discussion of whether our school children are fed, fit, and ready to learn. Hunger and poverty are corrosive to our economic competitiveness. They handicap our schools. They impose huge costs on the health care system that you and I pay for. In short, hunger and poverty undermine and make more difficult our efforts to make health care and quality education a reality for all. There is no definition of the American Dream that includes one in five of our children suffering in poverty.

That is why we set out to fight a battle that, in the words of writer Jonathan Kozol, was big enough to matter but small enough to win, and could result in actually ending childhood hunger once and for all.

A second power that you share is the power to create a new kind of wealth called community wealth. When we created Share Our Strength we wanted to be a grant maker but not a re-grantor, we wanted to create new wealth rather than just redistribute wealth. Of the $360 million we've raised and spent at Share Our Strength, more than half comes not from charitable dollars but from corporate partnerships, cause-related marketing, licensing and other activities that essentially represent commerce. It requires a commitment to partnerships that are truly mutually beneficial and win-win. And we realized that most nonprofit organizations, in the course of pursuing their mission, create assets that have a marketplace value and can be leveraged into revenue generating opportunities.

An age-old issue expounded upon at moments like this is the choice you face between doing well and doing good, between creating wealth and serving the public interest. What I am here to tell you today is that for the first time in history, it is no longer a choice of one or the other, but an unprecedented challenge for your generation to create wealth to serve the public interest.

We tend to think of wealth in very personal terms, as something that enables us to have houses that are bigger and cars that are faster and vacations that are longer. But there is another kind of wealth that makes our streets safer and our schools better and our neighborhoods healthier. And you are in unique position to share your strength in ways that create such community wealth.

Finally, and perhaps most important, is the power to bear witness. Whether you graduated magna cum laude or by begging your instructors to pass you, each and every one of you has this gift in equal measure. The power to bear witness is the power to go, see, feel and share what you have felt.

I went to Ethiopia during a famine and to New Orleans right after Hurricane Katrina. Haiti. What I really wanted to do was to go and see for myself what had happened and how the victims were coping. I wanted to go and see and allow myself to feel things about what I'd seen, and then share what I'd felt. I had less of a sense that I could effect change than that I would be changed by the emotions—sadness, sympathy, despair, anger, outrage and ultimately hope—that are the inevitable response to such a situation.

Indeed I was moved and ended up bringing others to Ethiopia and New Orleans to share the experience and communicating to literally thousands about it.

Bearing witness has always been the essential prerequisite for changing society's most grievous conditions, for righting injustice, for reaching out to those in need. In the 21st century bearing witness is destined to become an even more powerful tool for advancing social change.

Technology today yields information at unprecedented speeds and quantities. But much of it—delivered via cable news, talk radio, the internet and other media—is devoted to faux drama that masquerades as relevant to our lives, like celebrity court trials. The irony is that real life-and-death dramas of enormous consequence surround us, on our street corners, in public schools, in the homes of new immigrants, across town and across the globe.

If history is a guide, we will experience successes and failures along the way in our quest to make the world a better place. There will surely be legitimate excuses on those occasions when we fail. But there are no excuses for not seeing or knowing how our fellow citizens live. Take the opportunity to do so in your own way and time. Go somewhere you haven't been and see something you haven't yet seen. Look until you feel something and then tell someone what you've seen and felt. This is what it means to bear witness. This is what it takes to change the world.

When something affects us powerfully we often say we have been moved. The literal implication is having started out in one place and ending up in another. In this way being moved means being transformed and personal transformation is what powers social change. It's what Gandhi meant when he said, "Be the change you want to see in the world."

By bearing witness you have the power to be a voice for the voiceless. You leave here today with a degree, and an education, and the support of a community, that gives you a voice. But you also leave with a choice. Will you raise that voice only on behalf of your own interests, or on behalf of others whose voices are not heard?

Third and finally, try to see the world whole and to let it see you that way, to see you for who you really are, as I have tried to do today. Not because it will always be attractive or appealing, but because in the long run you really don't have a choice. People will figure it out anyway.

Most often when we stand where I am standing we share what my wife Rosemary calls our on-stage life. But of course we all have back stage lives as well. And as Rosemary understood long before I did, we will live longer and healthier if our front stage and back stage life are one and the same, if you live an undivided life. It is the richest blessing I can wish for each of you.

I hope that as citizen leaders you will succeed where our political leaders have failed. On the airplane that brought me here I looked down at the farms and factories, at the small towns and schools where children were taught that Presidents and Congress, governors and mayors act on their behalf no matter which class they belong to. From that vantage point America looks fertile and full of possibility. But our leaders no longer see the whole, as one can from this vantage point. They have instead narrowed their vision to see only what is small and advantageous in the short-term. As a result they perpetuate the smallness, the narrowness and the division. By such actions they are choosing to follow rather than to lead. The only remedy is for others to lead, for citizens and community organizations and businesses to act not on behalf of a class, but on behalf of a country. As graduates today you not only have that opportunity, but that responsibility. And you can do so by sharing your strength, creating community wealth, and bearing witness.

No one spoke more eloquently about the need to share our strengths than the poet Gwendolyn Brooks, who wrote:

> We are others harvest
> We are each other's business
> We are each other's magnitude
> And bond.

I have learned that these words are true. Whether you are a banker on Wall Street or a baker on Arthur Avenue we are each other's harvest. Whether you are an engineer or an educator, we are each other's harvest. Whether you design video games for next year or cathedrals that last centuries, we are each other's harvest.

Thank you and congratulations.

About Billy Shore

Bill Shore is the founder and executive director of Share Our Strength, a nonprofit organization that works to end childhood hunger in America. Shore is also the chair of Community Wealth Ventures Inc., a for-profit subsidiary of Share Our Strength that offers strategy and implementation services to foundations and nonprofit organizations. From 1978 through 1987, he served on the senatorial and presidential campaign staffs of former US senator Gary Hart (D-CO). From 1988 to 1991, Shore served as chief of staff for former US senator Robert Kerrey (D-NE). Shore has been an adjunct professor at New York University's Stern School of Business, and he is currently an adviser for the Reynolds Foundation Fellowship program at the John F. Kennedy School of Government at Harvard University, Cambridge, Massachusetts.

"The Fourth Instinct"

Arianna Huffington

In a speech honoring the 2011 graduates of Sarah Lawrence College, journalist Arianna Huffington affirms her faith in the next generation's ability to bring positive change to an admittedly chaotic world. The source of her faith is the graduates themselves, who she believes possess unprecedented creativity, connectedness, and compassion. Huffington espouses empathy over competition and wisdom over IQ, reminding the audience that failure and perseverance are necessary components of success. She warns graduates not to wait for solutions from Washington, encouraging them to shape the world for themselves.

President Lawrence, Board of Trustees, members of the faculty, proud parents, family, and friends, and above all the graduating class of 2011, I'm deeply honored and grateful that you have invited me to be a part of such a seminal moment in your lives. The fact that I have two daughters in college—one a senior next year, the other a sophomore—makes this all the more meaningful for me.

This is the most magical, incredible place. I was here last night for dinner at the president's beautiful home, and I met an alum who had been here together with her mother—at the same time! No, they did not share a room. I met a trustee who is a second generation man in this college. I met a student graduating today who is leaving for Paris and has already written her memoir. There were surprises around every corner, and as you can imagine, I did not want to leave.

You are very lucky to have President Lawrence, a James Joyce scholar, at the helm of your school. Actually, it's a little known fact that my original idea when I launched The Huffington Post in 2005 was to call it Huffington's Wake. It was going to be full of puns and allusions to Greek mythology. And it was going to have a blog by Leopold Bloom and Stephen Daedalus. Nobody was actually going to read it, but everyone was going to pretend to have read it.

So . . . you made it! Congratulations! And I know it doesn't matter, and it's not as important as everything else, but you look amazing!

If you look at the world you are graduating into, it's a split screen world. And depending on what part of the screen you are looking at, you will have a dramatically different perception of what the world looks like . . . and it will alter everything you think about the present—and especially about the future.

On one half of the screen: the old world is exploding in a pre-scientific, almost medieval eruption of irrationality and anger, where nothing can be known for certain, facts don't matter, and truth can be nullified by assertion.

It's a world in which the head of the IMF, who was on course to become president of France, is arrested on charges of attempted rape; a world in which the former governor of California had to admit to having a child with his housekeeper ten years ago. (As an aside, don't these stories make you long for more women leaders? When was the last time a woman leader was accused of rape?)

It's also a world in which we have 70 percent of people in this country who think we are on the wrong track. In which the American Dream is fading, with almost 25 million Americans unemployed or underemployed. And in which for the first time, total outstanding student loan debt will be higher than total credit card debt—going over $1 trillion. And the percentage of young adults moving back in with mom and dad has jumped to a staggering 34 percent.

And it's also a world in which we have senators and presidential candidates who don't believe in evolution and who think that global warming is a myth . . . a world in which politicians don't just have their own set of ideas but their own set of facts.

But there is another world, and that's the world you're creating. While the media are obsessing over Donald Trump's presidential run or Kim Kardashian's latest boyfriend, your generation is busy creating another world. On this part of the split screen there is an explosion of creativity, innovation, empathy, and compassion. You are the most connected and engaged generation in history. And you are asking the big questions and contemplating the cosmic riddles about why we're here and what life is really about.

In the 1990s I wrote a book called *The Fourth Instinct*, which explored the instinct that takes us beyond our first three—our impulses for survival, sex, and power—and drives us to expand the boundaries of our caring to include our communities and the world around us. That instinct is just as vital as the other three but we rarely give it the same kind of attention.

Which is unfortunate because these days—and especially since the economic meltdown—the role empathy plays in our lives has only grown more important. In fact, in this time of economic hardship, political instability, and rapid technological change, empathy is the one quality we most need if we're going to survive and flourish in the 21st century.

Just before he died, Jonas Salk defined the transition we're in as moving from Epoch A (based on survival and competition) to Epoch B (based on collaboration and meaning). During this seismic shift in our world, in which values are changing, the most important thing that we are missing is not IQ, but wisdom. That's why I love your school's motto—Wisdom With Understanding. Because nothing matters as much.

Wherever you look in the world, there are brilliant leaders in business, media, and politics making terrible decisions every day. What they're lacking is not intelligence but wisdom. Because leadership, after all, is seeing the icebergs before the Titanic hits them.

In the third century, before even Twitter existed, the philosopher Plotinus described three different sources of knowledge: opinion, science, and illumination.

Illumination—or wisdom—is precisely what we most need today. Part of wisdom is recognizing that there is a purpose to our life that may not be immediately obvious as our life unfolds. Things—especially the biggest heartbreaks—often only make sense as we look back, not as we are experiencing them.

I remember, for example, in my 20s, when I fell in love with a man whom I had not met. I fell in love with his writing. His name was Bernard Levin, and he was writing for the London *Times*. I would literally cut out his columns, underline them, and learn them by heart. When I finally met him, I was petrified and tongue-tied. Nevertheless, he invited me to dinner, and I prepped for the date not by going to the hair dresser but by reading everything he was writing. I read every detail about Northern Ireland. Of course, Northern Ireland never came up on the date . . . and we ended up being together for seven years. Then I hit 30 and I desperately wanted to have children. He wanted to have cats. So I did something that I was terrified to do: I left the man I deeply loved. And basically everything that's happened in my life—my children, my books, The Huffington Post, the fact that I'm here speaking in front of you today—is because a man wouldn't marry me.

Remember that, okay? In life, the things that go wrong are often the very things that lead to other things going right. Or as Max Teicher, who is graduating today, put it to me last night: he was bumped from an art class he really wanted to be in because there were already too many kids enrolled, but because of that he ended up in a philosophy class he really loved. So, to quote Max, "By getting unlucky, I actually got lucky."

A key component of wisdom is fearlessness, which is not the absence of fear, but rather not letting our fears get in the way. I remember one of the low points in my life, when my second book was rejected by 37 publishers. By about rejection 25, you would have thought I might have said, "Hey, you know, there's something wrong here. Maybe I should be looking at a different career."

Instead, I remember running out of money and walking, depressed, down St. James Street in London and seeing a Barclays Bank. I walked in and, armed with nothing but a lot of chutzpah, I asked to speak to the manager and asked him for a loan. Even though I didn't have any assets, the banker—whose name was Ian Bell—gave me a loan. It changed my life, because it meant I could keep things together for another 13 rejections.

And then I got an acceptance. In fairytales there are helpful animals that come out of nowhere to help the hero or heroine through a dark and difficult time, often helping them find a way out of the forest. Well, in life too, there are helpful animals disguised as human beings—like Ian Bell, to whom I still send a Christmas card every year. So, very often, the difference between success and failure is perseverance. It's how long can we keep going until success happens. It's getting up one more time than we fall down.

Of the many things my mother taught me—including the delightful notion that "Angels fly because they take themselves lightly"—the one that's proved most useful in my life is the understanding that failure is not the opposite of success, it's an integral part of success.

And that means not letting the fears in our heads get in our way. Not letting that voice of doubt, which I call the obnoxious roommates living in your heads, have the last word. Because, as Montaigne said, "There were many terrible things in my life, but most of them never happened."

I work with great engineers every day, creating amazing apps. But I think what we really need is a killer app that gauges the state of our mind, body, and spirit and automatically offers the exact steps we need to take to realign ourselves and course correct. Call it a GPS for the soul.

I love the tradition at Sarah Lawrence in its early women-only days of "productive leisure." Students occupied themselves each week with activities such as gardening, crafts, tap dancing, observing stars and French conversation.

The notion of productive leisure is more important than ever in our hyper-connected, always-on world. I call it unplugging and recharging.

> *So as you are leaving this beautiful campus behind, please don't wait for leaders on a white horse to save us. Instead, turn to the leader in the mirror. Tap into your own leadership potential because the world desperately needs you. And that means daring to take risks and to fail, as many times as it takes, along the way to success—and, more important, to re-making the world. And to do it all with more balance, more joy, more sleep, and more gratitude.*

When my mother died, I realized that she and I had been different in one key way: She lived in the rhythm of a timeless world, a child's rhythm; I lived in the hectic, often unnatural rhythm of the modern world. While I had the sense every time I looked at my watch that it was later than I thought, she lived in a world where there were no impersonal encounters, where a trip to the farmer's market happily filled half a day, where there was always enough time for wonder at how lovely the rosemary looked next to the lavender. In fact, going through the market with her was like walking through the Louvre with an art connoisseur—except that you could touch and smell these still lifes. It would be a real blessing if you can integrate that timeless rhythm into your hectic, everyday lives.

As Nicholas Carr wrote, "there needs to be time for efficient data collection and time for inefficient contemplation, time to operate the machine and time to sit idly in the garden." There's not a lot of garden left in the world you're heading into—so, when you find it, stop and savor the stillness. Do not miss your life by multitasking.

A key, and often-overlooked aspect of recharging is also one of the most obvious: getting enough sleep. There is nothing that negatively affects my productivity and efficiency more than lack of sleep. After years of burning the candle on both ends, my eyes have been opened to the value of getting some serious shuteye.

And in the macho boys' club atmosphere that dominates many offices, women too often feel they have to overcompensate by working harder, longer, and later. In fact, lack of sleep has become a sort of virility symbol. I was once out to dinner with a guy who kept bragging about how he only needed four hours of sleep a night. I wanted to tell him that he'd be much more interesting if he'd gotten five.

Sleep and productive leisure can be keys to tapping into our wisdom—as is making our lives about something more than ourselves.

In a study on the roots of altruism, psychologist Dr. Ervin Staub analyzed men and women who had risked their lives during World War II to protect Jews hiding from the Nazis. "Goodness," he wrote, "like evil, often begins in small steps. " Small steps that frequently lead to much larger commitments—and can have ever-widening positive reverberations through our communities.

But of course it seems that all of you have already discovered this at Sarah Lawrence, with many of you serving in many different ways: at the Early Childhood Center, at a "Right to Write" prison program, at an art exhibition in the Yonkers public library, doing theater outreach in public schools, working on affordable housing and with the homeless, etc, etc. And I would love to invite all of you to write on The Huffington Post about what you're doing, because it inspires others and puts the spotlight on the good that's being done.

Marketers, who pride themselves on being ahead of the curve, are already tapping into our growing collective desire to do good. I was sitting in a hotel room the other night, when a commercial grabbed my attention. It began with somber piano music, followed by a voice-over: "Millions of people," it said, "everyone out for themselves. . . can this really be the only way?" We then see images of various people doing the right thing, helping someone push-start a broken down car, tired firefighters after fighting a blaze. The commercial ends with the tag line: "Here's to doing the right thing." And do you know what that commercial was for? Chivas whiskey.

If Chivas whiskey feels that altruism is a good way to sell scotch, you know there's something in the zeitgeist.

This moment in history demands that we stop waiting on others—especially others living in Washington—to solve the problems and right the wrongs of our times. So as you are leaving this beautiful campus behind, please don't wait for leaders on a white horse to save us. Instead, turn to the leader in the mirror. Tap into your own leadership potential because the world desperately needs you. And that means daring to take risks and to fail, as many times as it takes, along the way to success—and, more important, to re-making the world. And to do it all with more balance, more joy, more sleep, and more gratitude. Thank you so much.

About Arianna Huffington

Arianna Huffington, née Stassinopoulos, was born in Athens, Greece, in 1950, and studied economics at Cambridge College, in England, where she led the Cambridge Union debating society. Huffington began writing in the 1970s under the mentorship of journalist Bernard Levin. She moved to New York in 1980, at the age of thirty, where she published books on artists Pablo Picasso and Maria Callas. Huffington became a household name after she campaigned for her then-husband Michael Huffington's

1994 bid for senator of California. In the late 1990s, Huffington's politics swung from right to center, and she ran as an independent candidate in the 2003 California recall of Governor Gray Davis. Huffington is currently a regular panelist on Both Sides Now with Huffington and Matalin, *a nationally syndicated weekend radio program, and she heads the Detroit Project, a public-interest lobbying group for alternative fuels. She founded the news website The Huffington Post in 2005.*

"The Importance of Saying 'Yes'"

David Evans

David Evans, speaking to the graduating class of the College of Design at North Carolina State University, makes an impassioned case for the value of designers' work. A photographer, video producer, and graduate of the college, he describes the winding path that his career has taken, and asserts that he never would have planned the unlikely and extremely rewarding path that he has been able to pursue in life had he not accepted offers that have been given him when he, as he puts it, heard the universe whispering to him.

Thank you, thank you so much.

What a privilege to share the stage with you again, Dean Malecha. Thank you so much for this wonderful honor. It means the world to me that I'm still involved with the College of Design after all these years. My education here truly shaped my career and indeed my life.

And congratulations to all of you. I was sitting where you were once, so I know how hard you worked to get here. It's such a pleasure to be here today to celebrate this milestone with you. It's a big deal and you should all be wildly proud of yourselves.

For many of us, this path chose us, not the other way around. We were called to it because we know at our core that there is deep substance in design. Sure, we swoon over couture, and we can get giddy about a new typeface . . . museums, cathedrals and skyscrapers can make our knees buckle in awe of their mass and materials.

But we also believe that there is power in what we do. That we leave behind the clues that history will know us by, and that we play a powerful role in shaping the contours of the future.

People live, eat, work, love, raise families, worship, study, celebrate and grieve in our buildings. They are informed by our layouts, by our websites, by our graphics, and they are entertained by our animations, and our films. They declare their identities by wearing the clothing we fashion for them, and they listen to music, climb mountains, and perform surgery using the products we create and improve upon.

You wield profound influence. You honestly *can* change the world. And with all the goings on here in North Carolina that have put the state in the spotlight this week, I'd say there's never been a better time to roll up our sleeves and fight harder for justice through the ideals we embody.

Now, you've just received your diplomas. I'm sure a lot of you already have jobs lined up, or you've figured out a plan to get one. Some of you already have 5-year plans,

10-year plans. Some of you probably even have retirement plans. And that's great. In fact, I'm blown away by so many of you who I've met and the plans you've told me you have. The world needs creative people in stable positions. No doubt about it.

But I imagine—in fact I really *hope*—there are some of you sitting here today with absolutely no plans whatsoever. (Parents, please save your jeers and rotten tomatoes for the end of the presentation . . . it gets worse.)

Because I don't believe that everyone needs a plan, or that having one is even the surest route to success. I've never had a plan. I don't have one now.

Don't get me wrong. Not having a plan is not the same thing as not being prepared. And all of you have just checked that box; you're incredibly prepared. And not having a plan is not the same thing as having no ambition, or not wanting to accomplish great things.

But not having a plan is one way to make yourself available when the universe whispers that it has something special for you, and it frees you up to say yes when the universe plots random dots on the map of your life that you may only connect years or decades later.

I'd like to share just a couple of stories of how not making plans and leaving myself available to say yes plotted insanely random dots for me that I'm only now seeing the connections between.

I just got back from Madagascar a couple of weeks ago where I was directing a documentary. It may be the best project I'll ever work on. And it's all because I said yes, and moved to Venezuela in 1992. Say what? . . . Venezuela? . . . Madagascar? What's the connection? Try to pay attention because this is a little hard to follow. And that's kind of my point.

In 1992, I had a good start on a successful career as an art director in a big ad agency in Washington, D.C., when I happened to see an employment ad in a trade magazine. It said "Come work in Venezuela." I really didn't even know where Venezuela was exactly, but something in me recognized that this ad was speaking to me, and only to me. I had no doubt that I would get that job, and that I would soon be in Venezuela, wherever that was. But I had no idea that this would also be the first in a long series of random dots that have connected to draw a beautiful, if zig-zagging map of my life so far.

My first visit to Venezuela after being offered that job didn't turn out so well. I flew down to make sure I would like the place enough to accept the job. After I met my new colleagues in Caracas, I flew to the interior of the country to see if there was anything cool to photograph.

See, I already loved photography. And I had even dropped off my photo portfolio once at National Geographic a few years before. They returned my images with a note from the editor who had reviewed my work. I'll paraphrase: "Dear David. You suck." So I had let that dream go a long time ago, but it didn't stop me from doing what I loved. I still took photographs and the potential to take photographs guided many of my decisions.

Anyway, while I was in the interior of Venezuela, I managed to get trapped behind rebel lines for a week during an attempted coup d'etat. Burning buses, bodies in the street, I never knew if it was the good guys or the bad guys pointing their guns at me. It was just an awful mess. But you know? After things calmed down, I ended up accepting the job anyway. Something told me to make myself available, that the risk could be worth the reward. So I said yes. Everyone I knew thought I was insane and I couldn't really argue with them.

I went to Caracas on a one-year contract as creative director for a large agency. I ended up staying for three years. I met Max, a famous Venezuelan architect who became my friend, and he introduced me to the Andes and to the ancient farmhouse he was renovating high up in a cloud forest. His adobe house and primitive folk art collection turned everything I thought I knew about aesthetics on its head. Little did I know how much else it would change for me.

As I was about to leave Venezuela, Max said, "¿Sabes que, David? There is a small property for sale just down the mountain. It has a couple of mud shacks on it. If you bought it, I would design and manage the renovation for you as a favor." Now it's a much longer story than that how I came to own the property, and it was probably owing at least partly to the altitude and maybe a little bit to the moonshine we were sipping, but I was pretty sure I heard something whispering to me that I should keep myself available, that I should take this risk. So I said, "yes."

So now it's 1996, and I'm back in D.C. freelancing as a graphic designer to pay for the renovation of my mud shacks in the Venezuelan Andes, where I would disappear to for weeks, collecting folk art like a man possessed, and taking photographs.

Back in D.C., I was designing a brochure for National Geographic Television and they offered me a position running their design department.

Now, for all I've just said to you about saying yes, I didn't hear the universe whispering to me this time and I said no. And I said no twice. And I said no a third time. It's not that I was such a hotshot that I could turn my nose up at a place like National Geographic. But like I told the executive offering me the job, "The truth is Kathie, I have a house in Venezuela, and right now I'm committed to collecting folk art and taking photographs while I finish the renovations."

"You're a photographer?" she asked. "You have a home in the Andes?" Well, the truth was I had exactly one published photograph . . . in the 1983 Windhover at NC State. And my "home in the Andes" was more of a construction site infested with scorpions, but "well, yeah," I said, "more or less, I, um, I guess that's mostly sort of correct . . . sure." She took some of my photos with her and came back with an offer that included plenty of vacation time for me to travel, and also to put me in charge of their photography department. I didn't hear any whispering this time, it was more like a scream. And I didn't just say yes, but "WHOA! Yes!"

That job led to all kinds of experiences. I helped launch an international cable television network, and since I was the boss of the photo department, I gave myself photography assignments all over the world. My second published photograph? It was in *National Geographic* magazine.

We'll get to Madagascar soon, I promise. I told you it was complicated.

I left National Geographic after 6 years, but I continued my relationship with them. My work with National Geographic got my photographs a lot of attention. So

I decided to give up graphic design and just pursue photography. I'd recaptured my first dream of being a photographer because I'd never given up my love of photography even though I'd been doing other things to make money.

If you hold onto the thing you love and find ways to make it important sometimes good things can happen.

Of course, that also means taking risks. And not just the kind that mean getting shot at in strange countries. Giving up graphic design, which had been my bread and butter involved a risk. But somehow I knew that now was the time to go all-in on photography. Doing that was scary because I had no idea what would happen, but it also seemed exactly the right thing.

So being available to say yes when the universe whispers also means being willing to take risks. But if all of you weren't already risk takers, you wouldn't be here in the first place. After all design isn't the safest career choice you could have made.

Here's something else. Being open when the universe whispers also means being open to making new friends. Friends are also part of the story because they will often help you in unexpected ways. But making friends is different from networking, which is purposeful and plan-driven. Making friends is random and meaningful on its own.

So here's how a random dot led to a random friend of mine. Because I had a house in Venezuela, a colleague at National Geographic recommended me to his former boss Jimmy Carter, to be an election monitor for The Carter Center during elections in Venezuela. That led to another election mission with President Carter in Ethiopia. And because I'd been to Ethiopia, National Geographic sent me on a photo assignment to central Africa. It was there that I met Lindy, a videographer traveling with the expedition. During the month we worked together, camping in the Sahara, he mainly just yelled at me; "Hey photo guy, get the hell out of my shot!" He and I would eventually work together on lots of assignments all over the world and he's become a good friend. Remember Lindy; he comes up again in a second.

Another random dot and another friend: I was photographing a cooking show being filmed in a private home in Washington, when I met and became friends with the home's owner, Dan, who had just started his new position at the United Nations Foundation.

Because of my background with National Geographic Television, and my experience in Africa, the United Nations Foundation asked me to produce some video about fighting child marriage in Ethiopia. I had never really produced a video quite like this one, and I could end up looking pretty stupid if it didn't go well. But sure . . . I heard that whispering again. And I said "Yes, I'll take that risk."

> *So being available to say yes when the universe whispers also means being willing to take risks. But if all of you weren't already risk takers, you wouldn't be here in the first place. After all design isn't the safest career choice you could have made.*

When I went to Ethiopia to produce that video, The Global Fund to Fight AIDS, Tuberculosis and Malaria was holding their board meeting in the same hotel where I was staying in Addis Ababa. The elevator door opened and there stood Dan from the United Nations Foundation and Todd, who I knew from the Bill and Melinda Gates Foundation. Turns out, both he and Dan sat on the board of the Global Fund. The next day, I learned they wanted to create and fund a new "Storytelling Committee," and asked me to direct a video about their work. It would be a risky adventure visiting AIDS, TB and malaria clinics in prisons, slums, and houses of prostitution in some of the poorest places on earth, and it would consume the better part of a year to finish it. But I heard that whisper again and I said "Yes. I'll do it."

There's so much more to that story too, but we've all got someplace to be, so I'm going to try and wrap this up.

The film focused on the empowerment of the underserved, especially empowering women, and the film was a tool that helped The Global Fund raise billions of dollars, which in turn helped them save millions of lives. It also won a bunch of awards, which is also pretty gratifying. So no, I'm not *all* about noble causes . . . I really like awards, too. I admit it.

But causes *are* important, of course. It goes back to that idea of using our designs and our art to make a difference. And in fact when the universe whispers to people like us, one reason I think we listen is because the whisper also connects us with our values, with the things we believe in.

One final random dot: A friend from my now-distant days at National Geographic introduced me to someone looking for a documentary film director. The subject was about how global markets for folk artists empower women in the developing world.

Folk art. Empowering women. In the developing world.

Now, I may not be the only person with that very specific set of experiences, but I don't think there can be many of us. The project had my name on it, and 18 months after that conversation, Lindy and I were off to Madagascar to make a film about folk art silk weavers. We hope to use this film as a pilot to raise funds for a 3-year project about folk artists all over the world.

So, let's connect these random dots: Moving to Venezuela in 1992 led me to collect folk art, and it got me a job at National Geographic Television. Working at National Geographic Television allowed me to fulfill my dream of being a photographer and introduced me to filmmaking. It also connected me with Bill & Melinda Gates, the United Nations Foundation, the Carter Center, and The Global Fund. All of which combined to get me an amazing assignment in Madagascar doing a film about folk art, something I really love, and which may end up being the most important project I'll ever do.

No plan in the world could have resulted in all of this.

But wait, the random dots are still connecting, and a pretty important connection was made just a couple of days ago.

Remember Lindy? Who I met in central Africa and who was with me a couple of weeks ago in Madagascar? While we were traveling together last year on a project—I can't remember if we were in Germany, Brazil, or Japan—I told him about my husband Sam's hearing impairment, and how we were having trouble getting insurance to pay for expensive cochlear implant surgery. Lindy says, "Dude, call my brother, he's one of the nation's foremost cochlear implant surgeons and he might be able to help." Sam and I met with Lindy's brother in New York two days ago, and Sam is now scheduled to receive his implant 10 days from now, all paid for by his insurance. All because I listened when the universe whispered to me and I said yes, and moved to Venezuela in 1992.

So that's it. Make a plan if that's what makes you comfortable. But if you don't have a plan, don't worry, just make yourself available, and try to hear the universe when it speaks to you, especially about things you love and believe in. And then always . . . *always*, say "YES."

Thank you and congratulations.

About David Evans

David Evans is a creative director, executive producer, and photographer whose work focuses on such topics as international development, sustainability, global health, education, cultural anthropology, scientific research, and philanthropic advocacy. He has worked with organizations such as the National Geographic Society, the Bill & Melinda Gates Foundation, the United Nations Foundation, the Global Fund, the Smithsonian Institution, and the Discovery Channel. Evans's background includes executive branding, marketing, and creative positions with firms including DDB Needham Worldwide, Ogilvy & Mather Worldwide, and National Geographic Television.

2

Debate on the Congressional Floor

(Getty Images)

In the summer of 2012, many of the major issues that would dominate the political race, including the Affordable Care Act, the DISCLOSE Act, and tax cuts for the middle class, were debated on the congressional floors. Senator Bernie Sanders (I-VT) would challenge Senate Republicans and Democrats to respond to Americans' anger at congressional stalemates over fixing the economy.

Floor Statement on the DISCLOSE Act

Senator John McCain

Senator John McCain (R-AZ), a longtime champion of campaign finance reform, argues for a healthier system of disclosure than what he sees in the DISCLOSE Act, then under review in the Senate. He decries the overall excessive influence of money on politics. The senator argues that the bill is slanted to require more disclosure of political giving from one side and less from the other. Specifically, he argues that unions are given preferential treatment, and asserts that the Democratic sponsor of the bill has no Republican cosponsor, unlike the 2002 McCain-Feingold Act, cosponsored by Democrat Russ Feingold.

Mr. President, here we are with 41 months of over 8 percent unemployment in America, and the national defense authorization bill is languishing in the shadows while we continue to have this debate and, obviously, there is no doubt in most people's minds that—with the full knowledge of the sponsors of this legislation that it will not pass—it is obviously for certain political purposes.

I oppose cloture on the motion. My reasons for opposing this motion are simple, even though the subject of campaign finance reform is not. In its current form, the DISCLOSE Act is closer to a clever attempt at political gamesmanship than actual reform.

By conveniently setting high thresholds for reporting requirements, the DISCLOSE Act forces some entities to inform the public about the origins of their financial support, while allowing others—most notably those affiliated with organized labor—to fly below the Federal Election Commission's regulatory radar.

My colleagues are aware that I have a long history of fighting for campaign finance reform and to break the influence of money in American politics. Regardless of what the U.S. Supreme Court may do or say, I continue to be proud of my record because I believe the cause to improve our democracy and further empower the citizens of our country was and continues to be worth fighting for.

But let's be clear. Reforms that we have successfully enacted over the years have not cured all the public cynicism about the state of politics in our country. No legislative measure or Supreme Court decision will completely free politics from influence peddling or the appearance of it. But I do believe that fair and just reforms will move many Americans, who have grown more and more disaffected from the practices and institutions of our democracy, to begin to get a clearer understanding of whether their elected representatives value their commitment to our Constitution more than their own incumbency.

Delievered July 17, 2012. Remarks made on the Senate floor by John McCain.

For far too long, money and politics have been deeply intertwined. Anyone who has ever run for a Federal office will assure us of the fact that candidates come to Washington not seeking wisdom or ideas but because they need help raising money. The same candidates will most likely tell us they are asked one question when they announce they are going to seek office. Unfortunately, it is not how they feel about taxes or what is their opinion of the role of government. No, the question they are asked is: How are you going to raise the money? Couple that sad reality with the dawn of the super PAC spending from corporate treasuries and record spending by big labor and one can easily see a major scandal is not far off, and there will be a scandal, mark my words. The American people know it and I know it.

Reform is necessary, but it must be fair and just and this legislation is not. I say that from many years of experience on this issue.

A recent *Wall Street Journal* article by Tom McGinty and Brody Mullins, titled "Political Spending by Unions Far Exceeds Direct Donations," noted that organized labor spent about four times as much on politics and lobbying as originally thought—$4.4 billion from 2005 to 2011. According to the *Wall Street Journal*'s analysis, unions are spending far more money on a wider range of political activities than what is reported to the Federal Election Commission. The report plainly states:

> **The same candidates will most likely tell us they are asked one question when they announce they are going to seek office. Unfortunately, it is not how they feel about taxes or what is their opinion of the role of government. No, the question they are asked is: How are you going to raise the money?**

This kind of spending, which is on the rise, has enabled the largest unions to maintain and in some cases increase their clout in Washington and state capitals, even though unionized workers make up a declining share of the workforce. The result is that labor could be a stronger counterweight than commonly realized to "super PACs" that today raise millions from wealthy donors, in many cases to support Republican candidates and causes.

The hours spent by union employees working on political matters were equivalent in 2010 to a shadow army much larger than President Obama's current re-election staff, data analyzed by the *Journal* show.

The report goes on to note:

Another difference is that companies use their political money differently than unions do, spending a far larger share of it on lobbying, while not undertaking anything equivalent to unions' drives to persuade members to vote as the leadership dictates. Corporations and their employees also tend to spread their donations fairly evenly between the two major parties, unlike unions, which overwhelmingly assist Democrats. In 2008, Democrats received 55 percent of the $2 billion contributed by corporate PACs and company employees, while labor unions were responsible for $75 million in political donations, with 92 percent of it going to Democrats.

The traditional measure of unions' political spending—reports filed by the FEC—undercounts the effort unions pour into politics because the FEC reports are mostly based on donations unions make to individual candidates from their PACs, as well as spending on campaign advertisements.

Unions spend millions of dollars yearly paying teams of political hands to contact members, educating them about election issues and trying to make sure they vote for union-endorsed candidates.

Such activities are central to unions' political power: The proportion of members who vote as the leadership prefers has ranged from 68 percent to 74 percent over the past decades at AFL-CIO-affiliated unions, according to statistics from the labor federation.

Additionally, according to a February 22, 2012, *Washington Post* article, titled "Union Spending for Obama, Democrats Could Top $400 million in 2012 Election," AFSCME reportedly expects to spend $100 million "on political action, including television advertising, phone banks and member canvassing, while the SEIU plans to spend at least $85 million in 2012."

With that analysis, combined with the $1.1 billion the unions reported to the FEC from 2005 to 2011, and the additional $3.3 billion unions reported to the Labor Department over the same period on political activity, the need for equal treatment of political advocacy under the law becomes readily apparent. I repeat, the need for equal treatment of political advocacy under the law becomes readily apparent.

Given the strength and political muscle behind all these figures, it is easy to understand why disclosure may sound nice, but unless the treatment is completely fair, taking into account the diverse nature and purpose of different types of organizations, disclosure requirements will likely be used to give one side a political advantage over another. That is just one of the flaws of the bill before us today.

The DISCLOSE Act would have little impact on unions because of the convenient thresholds for reporting. But it would have a huge effect on associations and other advocacy groups. From my own experience, I can state without question that real reform—and, in particular, campaign finance reform—will never be attained without equal treatment of both sides. A half dose of campaign finance reform will be quickly—and rightly—labeled as political favoritism and will undermine future opportunities for true progress. Furthermore, these sorts of games and measures will only make the American people more cynical and have less faith in what we do.

The authors of this bill insist it is fair and not designed to benefit one party over the other. Sadly, the stated intent doesn't comport with the facts. The DISCLOSE Act is written to burden labor unions significantly less than the other groups. In the United States, there are roughly 14 million to 16 million union members, each of whom is required to pay dues to its local union chapter. Historically, these local union chapters send a portion of their revenues up to their affiliated larger "international" labor unions. And while each union member's dues may be modest, the amounts that ultimately flow up to the central political arms are vast. The DIS-CLOSE Act protects this flow of money in two distinct ways: Number one, organizations that engage in political conduct are only required to disclose payments to it that exceed $10,000 in a 2-year election cycle, meaning the local union chapter will not be required to disclose the payments of individual union members to the union even if those funds will be used for political purposes.

What is the final difference between one $10,000 check and 1,000 $10 checks? Other than the impact on trees, very little. So why should one be free from having to disclose its origin?

Number two, the bill exempts from the disclosure requirements transfers from affiliates that do not exceed $50,000 for a 2-year election cycle. As a result, unions would not have to disclose the transfers made to it by many of its smaller local chapters. Given the contrast between union and corporate structures, this would allow unions to fall beneath the bill's threshold limits. For local union chapters, this anonymity is probably pretty important because, among other effects, it prevents union chapter members from learning how much of their dues payments are being used on political activities.

While the exemptions outlined in the DISCLOSE Act may be facially applied to business organizations and associations, it is apparent to me the unions' unique pyramid-style, ground-up, money-funneling structure would allow unions to not be treated equally by the DISCLOSE Act. Unlike unions, most organizations do not have thousands of local affiliates where they can pull up to $50,000 in "affiliate transfers."

I have been involved in the issue of campaign finance reform for most of my career. I am proud of my record. I am supportive of measures which call for full and complete disclosure of all spending in Federal campaigns. I reaffirmed this commitment by submitting an amicus brief to the U.S. Supreme Court regarding campaign finance reform along with the author of the DISCLOSE Act. This bill falls short. The American people see it for what it is: Political opportunism at its best, political demagoguery at its worst.

My former colleague from Wisconsin, Senator Feingold, and I set out to eliminate the corrupting influence of soft money and to reform how our campaigns are paid for. We vowed to be truly bipartisan and to do nothing which would give one party a political advantage over the other. The fact is this gives one party an advantage over the other.

I say with great respect to the Senator from Rhode Island, the way I began campaign finance reform is I found a person on the other side of the aisle who was willing to work with me, and we worked together on campaign finance reform. The Senator from Rhode Island and the sponsors of this bill have no one on this side of the aisle. By not having anyone on this side of the aisle, the Senator from Rhode Island has now embarked on a partisan enterprise.

I suggest strongly to the sponsors of the bill—if they are serious about campaign finance reform and about curing the evils going on now—they approach Members on this side of the aisle and make sure our concerns about the role of labor unions in this financing of political campaigns are addressed as well.

It is too bad—it is too bad—that Members on that side of the aisle are now orchestrating a vote which is strictly partisan in nature when they know full well the only way true campaign finance reform will ever be enacted by the Congress is in a bipartisan fashion. This is a partisan bill, and I am disappointed we are wasting the time of the Senate on a bill—and on a cause that is of utmost importance, in my view—in a partisan fashion.

About John McCain

Born August 29, 1936, in the Panama Canal Zone, John McCain graduated from the United States Naval Academy in 1958. He became a naval aviator and, during the Vietnam War, was shot down while on a bombing mission over Hanoi. He spent the years 1967 until 1973 as a prisoner of war, suffering repeated torture. He retired from the Navy as a captain and moved to Nevada in 1981, where he entered politics, serving two terms in the US House of Representatives, beginning in 1982. He was elected to the Senate in 1986, where he has served ever since. He is perhaps best known for the McCain-Feingold Act of 2002, which sought to limit the influence of money in political campaigns. He ran unsuccessfully for president on the Republican ticket in 2008, losing to Barack Obama.

The American People Are Angry

Senator Bernie Sanders

In a lengthy and passionate address on the Senate floor, Senator Bernie Sanders (D-VT) explains why "the American people are angry." Sanders indicts Wall Street for gambling with America's money and lambasts the government for failing to create meaningful regulations, even as those who caused the so-called Great Recession continue to gamble with Americans' money. He bluntly opposes those who argue that benefits for various constituencies should be cut to address the nation's debt while supporting two lengthy and costly wars that were not supported with tax hikes—for, he says, the first time in American history.

Madam President, the American people are angry because they are living through the worst recession since the Great Depression. Unemployment is not 8.2 percent; real unemployment is closer to 15 percent. Young people who are graduating from high school and college are going out into the world, and they want to become independent and create jobs. There are no jobs. There are workers out there—and I am sure you know them—who are 50, 55 years old who intended to work out the remainder of their work lives, and suddenly they got pink slips and their self-esteem was destroyed. They will never have another job again, and they are worried about retirement security.

What the American people are angry about is that they understand they did not cause this recession. Teachers did not cause this recession. Firefighters and police officers, who are being attacked daily by Governors all over this country, did not cause this recession. Construction workers did not cause this recession. This recession was caused by the greed, recklessness, and illegal behavior of the people on Wall Street.

What these people on Wall Street did was spend billions of dollars trying to deregulate Wall Street, and they got their way. Five billion dollars in 10 years is what they spent. And then they were able to merge investment banks with commercial banks with insurance companies, and they got everything they wanted. They said: Get the government off the backs of Wall Street. They got it. The end result was that they plunged this country into the worst recession since the Great Depression.

Four years after the financial crisis caused by JPMorgan Chase, Bank of America, Goldman Sachs, and the other huge financial institutions, one might have thought that perhaps they learned something, that maybe the lesson of the great financial crisis was that you cannot continue to maintain the largest gambling casino in the history of the world. But apparently they have not learned that lesson. They are back at it again. We have recently seen the $2 billion or $3 billion gambling losses at JPMorgan Chase.

Delivered June 27, 2012. Remarks made on the floor of the House of Representatives by Bernie Sanders.

What we need from Wall Street if we are going to put people back to work is investment in the productive economy. Small and medium-sized businesses all over this country need affordable loans, and that is what financial institutions should be doing. They should be helping us create jobs, expand businesses, not continuing to engage in their wild and exotic gambling schemes.

When we talk about why the American people are angry, they are angry because they understand that Wall Street received the largest taxpayer bailout in the history of the world. But it was not just the $700 billion that Congress approved through TARP. As a result of an independent audit that some of us helped to bring about in the Dodd-Frank bill, we learned that the Federal Reserve provided a jaw-dropping $16 trillion in virtually zero-interest loans to every major financial institution in this country, the central banks all over the world, to large corporations in America and, in fact, even wealthy individuals. What the American people are saying is that if the Fed can provide $16 trillion to large financial institutions, why can't they begin to move to protect homeowners, unemployed workers, and the middle class of this country?

The American people are looking around them. They are angry not just because unemployment is high, they are angry not just because millions of people have lost their homes and life savings, they are angry because they understand that the middle class of this country is collapsing, poverty is increasing, while at the same time the people on top are doing phenomenally well. The taxpayers bailed out Wall Street, and Wall Street recovers, Wall Street does well, but now we have kids in this country graduating college deeply in debt, can't find a job, and we have older workers losing their jobs, and people are saying: What is going on in America?

I believe the American people ultimately are angry because they are looking at this great country—a country for which many of our veterans fought and died—and what they are seeing is this Nation is losing its middle class, losing its democratic values, and, in fact, is moving toward an oligarchic form of government, where a handful of billionaires control the economic and political life of this Nation.

In the United States today, we have the most unequal distribution of wealth and income since the 1920s. You are not going to see what I am talking about now on Fox or NBC or CBS, but it is important that we discuss this issue because it is one of the most important issues facing America.

Today, the wealthiest 400 individuals in America own more wealth than the bottom half of America, 150 million people—400 to 150 million. Today—and this is really quite amazing—the six heirs to the Walmart fortune—the Walmart company started by Sam Walton, his children—one family now owns more wealth than do the bottom 30 percent of the American people. One family owns more wealth than the bottom 30 percent or 90 million Americans. Today, the top 1 percent owns 40 percent of all of the wealth in America. The top 1 percent owns 40 percent of all the wealth in America.

What do we think the bottom 60 percent of the American people own? I ask this question a lot around Vermont. I have a lot of meetings. I say that the top 1 percent owns 40 percent, and people say: That is not good, but we understand that.

Then I ask: What about the bottom 60 percent?

Maybe they own 15 or 20 percent, they say.

The answer is that they own less than 2 percent—less than 2 percent. So you have the bottom 60 percent of the American people owning less than 2 percent of the wealth, and the top 1 percent owns 40 percent of the wealth.

Here is another astounding fact. We don't see it much in the media and many colleagues don't talk about it too often, but, incredibly, the bottom 40 percent of the American people own three-tenths of 1 percent of the wealth in this country.

I know we have some of my colleagues coming up and saying: Look, not everybody in America is paying taxes. You have millions of people not paying any taxes.

> *Sheldon Adelson, who is only worth $20 billion—he is kind of a pauper—is willing to spend what it takes to buy the government. If we look at it, that ain't a bad deal. If someone is worth $50 billion and they spend $1 billion or $2 billion, they can buy the U.S. Government. That is a pretty good investment, and that is what they are about to do.*

No kidding. Well, they don't have any money. All of the money is on the top.

According to a new study from the Federal Reserve, the medium net worth for middle-class families dropped by nearly 40 percent from 2007 to 2010, primarily because of the plummeting value of homes. That is the equivalent of wiping out 18 years of savings for the average middle-class family.

I have talked about distribution of wealth. That is what you accumulate in your lifetime. Let me say a word about income, which is what we earn in a year. The last study that was done on income distribution was done recently. This is what it told us, and this is literally quite hard to believe. The last study on income distribution showed us that between the years 2009 and 2010, 93 percent of all new income created in the previous year went to the top 1 percent.

Ninety-three percent of all the new income created between 2009, 2010—the last information we had—went to the top 1 percent, while the bottom 99 percent had the privilege of enjoying the remaining 7 percent. In other words, the wealthiest people in this country are becoming phenomenally wealthier, the middle class is disappearing, and poverty is increasing.

When we talk about an oligarchic form of government, what we are talking about is not just a handful of families owning entire nations, we are also talking about the politics of the nation. As a result of this disastrous Citizens United decision, which is now 2 years of age—one of the worst decisions ever brought about by the Supreme Court of this country and a decision they just reaffirmed a few days ago with regard to Montana—what the Supreme Court has done is to say to the wealthiest people in this country: OK. You own almost all the wealth of this Nation. That is great. Now we are going to give you an opportunity to own the political life of this Nation, and if you are getting bored by just owning coal companies and casinos and manufacturing plants, you now have the opportunity to own the U.S. Government.

So we have people such as the Koch brothers and Sheldon Adelson—the Koch brothers are worth $50 billion. That is what they are worth. They are worth $50 billion and they have said they are prepared to put $400 million into this campaign to defeat Obama, to defeat candidates who are representing working families. Sheldon Adelson, who is only worth $20 billion—he is kind of a pauper—is willing to spend what it takes to buy the government. If we look at it, that ain't a bad deal. If someone is worth $50 billion and they spend $1 billion or $2 billion, they can buy the U.S. Government. That is a pretty good investment, and that is what they are about to do.

On the one hand, we have a grossly unequal distribution of wealth in income. These guys control the economy. We have the six largest financial institutions in this country that have assets equivalent to two-thirds of the GDP of America—over $9 trillion—and these six financial institutions write half the mortgages and two-thirds of the credit cards in America. That is a huge impact on the economy. But that is not enough for these guys. The top 1 percent own 40 percent of the wealth—not enough for these guys. Now they have the opportunity to buy the U.S. Government.

So that is where we are. In my view, working families all over this country are saying enough is enough. They want this Congress to start standing for them and not just the millionaires and the billionaires who are spending unbelievable sums of money in this campaign. It seems to me what we have to do is start listening to the needs of working families—the vast majority of our people—and not just the people who make campaign contributions.

I know that is a very radical idea. I do know that. But it might be a good idea to try a little bit to reaffirm the faith of the American people in their Democratic form of government. We could let them know just a little bit that maybe we are hearing their pain—their unemployment, their debt, the fact they are losing their houses, the fact they do not have any health care, the fact they can't afford to send their kids to college. Maybe, just maybe, we ought to listen to them before we go out running to another fundraising event with millionaires and billionaires.

I do know, however, that is a radical idea. So let's talk about what we can actually do for the American people. In the midst of this terrible recession, where real unemployment is closer to 15 percent if you include those folks who have given up looking for work and those people working part-time when they want to work full time, we know the fastest way to create decent-paying jobs is to rebuild our crumbling infrastructure.

I see the Senator from Minnesota has taken the chair and is now presiding, and I don't know about Minnesota, but I do know in Vermont many of our bridges are in desperate need of repair, our roads are in need of repair, and our rail system is falling further and further behind Europe and China. We have water systems that desperately need repair, wastewater plants, and we have schools that need repair. We can put millions of people back to work making our country more competitive and more efficient by addressing our infrastructure crisis. Let's do it.

It is beyond my comprehension why we can't even get a modest transportation bill. I know Chairwoman Boxer and Senator Inhofe are working on a modest transportation bill, but we can't even get that through the House. In fact, we have to do a lot more than that, but at least they are making the effort.

At a time when we spend some $300 billion a year importing oil from Saudi Arabia and other foreign countries, at a time when this planet is struggling with global warming and all the extreme weather disturbances we see, and the billions of dollars we are spending in response to these extreme weather disturbances, we need to move toward energy independence. We need to reverse greenhouse gas emissions. In other words, we need to transform our energy system away from fossil fuel into energy efficiency and into sustainable energies, such as wind, solar, geothermal, and biomass. When we do that, we also create a substantial number of decent-paying jobs.

By the way, in the midst of a very competitive global economy, what we should not be doing is laying off teachers and childcare workers. We should be investing in education, not laying off those people who are educating our kids.

I know there is a lot of discussion on the floor with regard to the national debt—almost $16 trillion—and the deficit—over $1 trillion. That is a serious issue and we have to deal with it. But my view is a little different than many of my colleagues in terms of how we deal with it.

I think most Americans understand the causation of the deficit crisis; that is, President Bush went to war in Iraq and he went to war in Afghanistan, and he just forgot something. We all have memory lapses, don't we? We go shopping and we forget to buy the milk or the bread. He had a memory lapse. He forgot to pay for those wars—a couple trillion dollars' worth. He forgot to pay for them. To all of our deficit hawks out here, all those folks who say we have to cut food stamps, we have to cut education, we have to cut health care—oh, two wars, $2 trillion, $3 trillion, $4 trillion? Hey, no problem, no problem at all.

For the first time, as I understand it, in the history of this country, we went to war—which is an expensive proposition—and at the same time not only did we not raise the money to pay for the war, we went the other way and decided to give huge tax breaks, including to the wealthiest people in this country. We spent trillions going to war and we gave tax breaks to the wealthiest people in this country. That begins to add up. That is called creating a deficit.

Then, on top of that, because of the greed and the recklessness and illegal behavior on Wall Street, which drove us into this recession—and when you are in a recession and people are unemployed and small businesses go under, less revenue is coming into the Federal Treasury. If we are spending a whole lot, less revenue is coming in, so you have a deficit crisis.

Some of my Republican friends say—and some Democrats say—maybe we should have paid for the war. Yes, you are right. Maybe we shouldn't have given those tax breaks to the rich. Maybe you are right. But be that as it may, we are where we are and we need deficit reduction and we know how to do it. We are going to cut Social Security.

My friends back home, when you hear folks talking about Social Security reform, hold on to your wallets because they are talking about cuts in Social Security—nothing more, nothing less. I don't know about Minnesota, Mr. President, but in Vermont no one has heard of the concept of chained CPI. I have asked them, and they do not know what chained CPI is, which is what they are trying to pass here. It is this belief—and senior citizens back home will start laughing when I say this— that COLAs for Social Security are too high. Seniors back home are scratching their heads, saying: Wait. We just went through 2 years when my prescription drug costs went up, my health care costs went up and I got zero in COLA and there are people in Washington—Republicans, some Democrats—who think I got too much in COLA? What world are these people living in? That is the reality.

So some of the folks here want to pass something called a chained CPI, which, if it were imposed—and I will do everything I can to see it does not get imposed— would mean seniors between the ages of 65 and 75 would lose about $550 a year. Then, when they are 85 and they are trying to get by on $13,000 or $14,000 a year, it will cost them about 1,000 bucks a year. That is what some of our colleagues want to do—virtually all the Republicans want to do it and some Democrats want to do it as well. I am going to, as chairman of the Defend Social Security Caucus, do everything I can to prevent that.

They also want to cut Medicare and Medicaid. We have 50 million people without any health insurance at all, we have people paying huge deductibles, Medicaid covering nursing home care, and they want to cut Medicare and Medicaid. They have the brilliant idea, some of them, that maybe we should raise the retirement age for Medicare from 65 to 67. Tell me about somebody in Minnesota who is 66 and is diagnosed with cancer, and if we do what the Republicans want us to do in the House, which is to create a voucher plan for Medicare, we would give that person a check for, I don't know, $7,000, I think, or $8,000, and we would say: Go out to the private insurance market, anyone you want, here is your $7,000 or $8,000—remember, they are suffering with cancer—and go get your insurance. I guess that would last them maybe 1 or 2 days in the hospital is what it would do. But that is the Republican plan.

I agree that deficit reduction is a real issue, and I think we have to deal with it. But we are not, if I have anything to say about it, going to deal with it on the backs of the elderly, the children, the sick, the poor, and the hungry. The way we deal with deficit reduction in a responsible way, in a fair way, is to look to the billionaires in this country who are doing phenomenally well and make the point that Warren Buffett made, that there is something a little absurd about millionaires and billionaires today, in the midst of the deficit crisis, paying the lowest tax rates they have paid in decades. Yes, we are going to have to ask the wealthiest people in this country to start paying their fair share of taxes.

I saw a piece in the paper the other day which was quite incredible. Rich people, apparently, are giving up their citizenship. They are leaving America and going abroad. These great lovers of America who made their money in this country, when we ask them to start paying their fair share of taxes, start running abroad. We have 19-year-old kids who have died in Iraq and Afghanistan who went abroad not to escape taxes; they are working-class kids who died in wars. Now the billionaires want to run abroad in order to avoid paying their fair share of taxes. What patriotism; what love of country.

We have to deal with deficit reduction, but we don't have to cut Social Security, we don't have to cut Medicare, we don't have to cut Medicaid, and we don't have to cut education. We can ask the wealthiest people, the millionaires and billionaires, to start paying their fair share of taxes. We can end these outrageous corporate loopholes Senator *Conrad* talked about. He showed a picture of a building in the Cayman Islands where there are 18,000 corporations using the same postal address in order to avoid paying their taxes. We are losing about $100 billion a year. We have large corporations making billions, and paying, in some cases, nothing in taxes. That is the way to get to deficit reduction, not on the backs of people who are already hurting.

We are at a very difficult moment in American history. We are in the process of losing the great middle class. We are seeing more of our people being poor. We are seeing savage attacks being waged against the elderly in terms of cuts in Social Security and Medicare, attacks against those who get sick in terms of going after Medicaid and Medicare.

I think what the American people are saying is enough is enough. This great country belongs to all of us. It cannot continue to be controlled by a handful of billionaires who apparently want it all.

I cannot understand why people who have billions of dollars are compulsively driven for more and more. When is enough enough? How many children in this country have got to go hungry? How many people have got to die because they don't go to a doctor because you want to avoid paying your taxes? That is not what America is about. That is not what people fought and died to create.

We have a fight on our hands. The job of the Senate is to represent the middle-class working families of this country, all of the people, and not just the superrich. I hope we can begin to do that.

About Bernie Sanders

Born in 1941 in Brooklyn, New York, Senator Bernie Sanders is a self-described Democratic Socialist. He is the junior senator from Vermont. He earned a bachelor's degree in political science from the University of Chicago in 1964, after which he spent time on a kibbutz in Israel before moving to Vermont in 1971. After several unsuccessful runs for office, he worked as the director of the nonprofit American People's Historical Society. He was elected mayor of Burlington, Vermont, in 1981, holding the mayoralty until 1989. In 1990 he won a seat in the House of Representatives, where he served until 2007, when he was elected to the Senate.

The Middle-Class Tax Cut Act

Senator Carl Levin

Taking aim at what he describes as faulty assumptions and misleading statements, Senator Carl Levin (D-MI) speaks out against the Republican Party's proposals to cut taxes for the wealthy in the belief that this will spur economic growth. In fact, he argues, the targeted tax cuts for the country's most affluent citizens under President George W. Bush coincided with extremely slow growth of the economy.

Madam President, many of our Republican colleagues argue that we can't extend tax relief for middle-class families unless we also extend tax cuts for the wealthiest. They argue without tax cuts for the wealthiest 2 percent, we will harm job creators and slow the economy. Their arguments rely on faulty assumptions, mistaken beliefs, and misleading statements. Let's get to the facts.

It is a fact that every American taxpayer would receive a tax cut under our bill on the first $250,000 of their income. It is a fact that compared to the middle-class tax cut act now before us, the plan the Republicans have put forward would increase the deficit by $155 billion. It is a fact that the bill Republicans have put forward, despite their professed support for tax cuts, would raise taxes on the middle class by failing to extend the 2009 tax cuts for middle-class families, including the American opportunity tax credit and credits that help families with children.

What is unfolding on the Senate floor now is the culmination of a rigid Republican adherence to tax cuts for the wealthy as the supreme goal of public policy. Republicans have demonstrated a willingness to risk government shutdowns. They have demonstrated a willingness to risk grave economic damage, to risk rising taxes on the vast majority of Americans in pursuit of their highest priority: lower taxes on the wealthiest 2 percent of us. They want to risk all of that in service to an idea that has already proved a failure.

When historians look back at the Republican dedication to the tax cuts for the wealthy, they will find it remarkable that so many fought so long and so hard to go back to a failed policy. Income for the typical American family peaked in the year 2000, not coincidentally just before the Republican tax-cuts-for-the-wealthy mania reached its zenith.

A June study by the Federal Reserve found that the average middle-class family's net worth had fallen by 40 percent from 2007 to 2010. In 2010, the bottom 99 percent of income earners reaped just 7 percent of total income growth while 93 percent of all growth flowed to the top 1 percent.

As David Leonhardt of the *New York Times* reported on Monday:

Delivered July 24, 2012. Remarks made on the Senate floor by Carl Levin.

The top-earning 1 percent of households now bring home about 20 percent of total income, up from less than 10 percent 40 years ago. The top earning 1/10,000th of households—each earning at least $7.8 million a year, many of them working in finance—bring home almost 5 percent of income, up from 1 percent 40 years ago.

> *But the Republican emphasis on policies that are more and more generous to the wealthiest have utterly failed to spark economic growth or create the jobs we need. Their experiment failed.*

Perhaps this vast accumulation of wealth would arguably be acceptable if it had resulted in faster economic growth that produced new jobs and helped average Americans prosper. Indeed, since the time of President Reagan, America has been told that the rising tide lifting up the wealthy would lift all boats, and that the benefits would trickle down to all Americans. Our Republican colleagues today argue that we must continue the President Bush tax cuts for the wealthy or risk harm to the "job creators."

But the Republican emphasis on policies that are more and more generous to the wealthiest have utterly failed to spark economic growth or create the jobs we need. Their experiment failed.

The Bush tax cuts coincided with the slowest rate of job growth in American history. Economic growth, even before the financial crisis, nearly sent our economy into depression and was woefully short by historic standards.

The failure of the Bush policies to spur economic growth and job creation underlies the failure of another promise from supporters of tax cuts for the wealthy, the promise that those cuts would pay for themselves. Republicans backing the tax cuts of 2001 and 2003 painted those grand scenarios that grow so rapidly that it would yield increased tax revenue. But instead of growing Federal coffers, we got a flood of red ink.

So the policy of tax cuts for the wealthy failed as a fiscal policy. It added to our deficit. It failed as an economic policy, coinciding with weak growth and economic output and job creation, and it failed as a vital test of public policy in a democratic society because it failed the fairness test. Instead, it facilitated massive accumulations of wealth for a fortunate few while most Americans have struggled just to tread water.

Yet our Republican colleagues persist in their pursuit of their failed policy—persist, in fact, to the point that they are willing to force a tax increase on more than 90 percent of taxpayers and potentially send our economy tumbling back into recession in adherence to that failed policy.

We are not arguing against this policy of tax cuts for the wealthiest because we seek to denigrate success or to stoke class warfare, as some Republicans allege. We are arguing against these policies because they are broken, they have failed, and they are unfair. We should reject them lest they do even more harm. We should reject the Republican pursuit of tax cuts for the wealthy at all costs, every other consideration be damned. We should allow middle-class families to keep a few of their hard-earned dollars and pass the Middle Class Tax Cut Act. At a minimum we should vote tomorrow to overcome the filibuster threat and proceed to debate this singularly important issue.

About Carl Levin

Born in Detroit, Michigan, in 1934, Carl Levin graduated from Swarthmore College in 1956 and Harvard Law School in 1959. He entered private practice in Detroit soon after graduating. He served as assistant attorney general and general counsel of the Michigan Civil Rights Commission beginning in 1964. He was elected to the Detroit City Council in 1969. He has served as a senator from Michigan since 1979. He has served on the Armed Services Committee since 1997.

The Health-Care Decision
of the Supreme Court

Senator Mike Enzi

Senator Mike Enzi, a Republican from Wyoming, expresses his regret over the Supreme Court ruling that upheld the Affordable Care Act as constitutional, stating that the real problems in the American health-care system are only made worse by the law. Referring to the fifty states as laboratories for democracy, he cites some state-level approaches that have reined in costs and improved health-care delivery, asserting that reform does not have to come from the federal government. He also deplores what he describes as the act's divisiveness, saying that it is a sure harbinger of trouble when a bill cannot get bipartisan support.

Madam President, it is disappointing that the Supreme Court has upheld the constitutionality of the new health care law. Just because it is constitutional doesn't mean it is the best policy, the perfect policy, or even good policy. And just because the Court upheld the law does not change the fact that the American people have overwhelming concerns about it—not all of it but a lot of it.

In fact, the Court affirmed that the new health care law is a massive tax increase on the American people. Congress must get serious about fixing our broken health care system. We can start by changing this misguided health care law that has divided the American people and failed to address rising health care costs. Congress should work together to make commonsense, step-by-step health reforms that can truly lower the cost of health care. I was pleased to see that the Supreme Court narrowed the Medicaid expansion because States can't afford them. Hard-working Americans are still struggling in this anemic economy and need real action to make health care more affordable.

Reforms do not have to start here in Washington. Our Nation's States are laboratories of democracy and can play a significant role in addressing the health care crisis in America. Governors are in a special position to understand the unique problems facing their States, and fixing health care, like most problems facing our Nation, cannot be a one-size-fits-all solution. Efforts underway by Indiana Governor Mitch Daniels provide a great example of what different States are working on. He is moving forward with the Healthy Indiana initiative, which is an affordable insurance program for uninsured State adults aged 19 to 64.

Outside Washington, some health insurance companies have already stated they will adopt several reasonable provisions to lower health care costs. These include allowing young adults to be covered until age 26 while on their parent's plan, not

---

Delivered June 28, 2012. Remarks made on the Senate floor by Mike Enzi.

charging patients copays for certain care, not imposing lifetime limits, and not implementing retroactive cancellation of health care coverage. They said they would do that regardless of how the Supreme Court case came out.

One of the most effective ways Congress can address the rising costs of health care is to focus on the way it is delivered as part of the Nation's current cost-driven and ineffective patient care system. America's broken fee-for-service structure is driving our Nation's health care system further downward, and tackling this issue is a good start to reining in rising health care costs. What is fee for service? This method of payment encourages providers to see as many patients and prescribe as many treatments as possible but does nothing to reward providers who help keep patients healthy. These misaligned incentives drive up costs and hurt patient care.

> *Reforms do not have to start here in Washington. Our Nation's States are laboratories of democracy and can play a significant role in addressing the health care crisis in America.*

The new health care law championed by President Obama and congressional Democrats did very little to address these problems. The legislation instead relied on a massive expansion of unsustainable government price controls found in fee-for-service Medicare. If we want to address the threat posed by out-of-control entitlement spending, we need to restructure Medicare to better align incentives for providers and beneficiaries. This will not only lower health care costs, it will also improve the quality of care for millions of Americans. In the health care bill, we took $500 billion out of Medicare and put it into new programs. Then we appointed an unelected board to suggest cuts that can be made, and the only place left for cuts are providers, hospitals, home health care, nursing homes, and hospice care. I don't think that is where we want to be cutting Medicare.

Shifting the health care delivery system from one that pays and delivers services based on volume to one that pays and delivers services based on value is an idea that unites both Republicans and Democrats. We have been mentioning a number of simple steps that can be taken while Congress weighs the larger fixes needed for preventive care. We can encourage insurers to offer plans that focus on delivering health care services by reducing copays for high-value services and increasing copays for low-value or excessive services. Consumer-directed health plans provide another avenue for linking financial and delivery system incentives and have the potential to reduce health care spending by $57 billion a year. Bundled payments will support more efficient and integrated care. All of these options have already been utilized by a number of private sector firms with great success. The Federal Government should be willing to support viable reforms where it is needed, but also refrain from handcuffing innovative private sector designs with excessive regulations or narrow political interests.

Our Nation has made great strides in improving the quality of life for all Americans, and we need to remember that every major legislative issue that has helped transform our country was forged in the spirit of compromise and cooperation. These qualities are essential to the success and longevity of crucial programs such as Medicare and Medicaid. But when it comes to health care decisions being made in Washington lately, the only thing the government is doing is increasing partisanship and legislative gridlock. I wish to leave the Senate with some words of wisdom from one of our departed Members, and that is Senator Daniel Patrick Moynihan, a Democrat from New York, who served in this body. He said in 2001, shortly before he retired:

> Never pass major legislation that affects most Americans without real bipartisan support. It opens the door to all kinds of political trouble.

Senator Moynihan correctly noted that the party that didn't vote for it "will criticize the resulting program whenever things go wrong." More importantly, he predicted the measure's very legitimacy will be "constantly questioned by a large segment of the population who will never accept it unless it is shown to be a huge success."

That is a quote from Daniel Patrick Moynihan, former Senator.

Truer words were never spoken. We have seen each of these scenarios play out over the past 2 years as the new health care law polarized the Nation. I hope this distinguished body has the courage to learn from our mistakes, because our Nation needs health care reform, but it has to be done the right way. Providing Americans with access to high-quality affordable health care is something I am confident Democrats and Republicans should be able to agree on.

Two-and-a-half years ago, a Democratic President teamed up with a Democratic-led Congress with only Democratic votes to force a piece of legislation on the American people that they never asked for and that has turned out to be as disastrous as predicted. How so? Amid an economic recession, a spiraling Federal debt, and accelerating increases in government health spending, they proposed a bill that has made the problems worse.

Americans were promised lower health care costs. They are going up. Americans were promised lower premiums. They are going up. Most Americans were promised their taxes wouldn't change. They are going up. Seniors were promised Medicare would be protected. It was raided to pay for a new entitlement instead. Americans were promised it would create jobs. The CBO predicts it will lead to nearly 1 million fewer jobs. Americans were promised they can keep their plan if they liked it, yet millions have learned that they can't. And the President of the United States himself promised up and down that this bill was not a tax. That was one of the Democrats' top selling points, because they knew it would never get passed if they said it was a tax. The Supreme Court spoke today. It said it is a tax.

This law was sold to the American people under deception. But it is not just that the promises about this law were not kept, it is that it has made the problems it was meant to solve even worse. The supposed cure has proved to be worse than the disease.

We pass plenty of terrible laws around here that the Court finds constitutional. We need to do some commonsense, step-by-step reforms that protect Americans' access to the care they need, from the doctor they choose, and at a lower cost. That is precisely what I am committed to doing.

The American people weren't waiting on the Supreme Court to tell them whether they supported this law. That question was settled two-and-a-half years ago. The more the American people have learned about this law, the less they have liked it.

Now that the Court has ruled, it is time to move beyond the constitutional debate and focus on the primary flaws of this law because of the colossal damage it is doing and has already done to the health care system and to the economy and to the job market, which needs to be turned around. There are things that need to be done and can be done.

About Mike Enzi

Enzi was born on February 1, 1944, in Bremerton, Washington. Enzi and his family moved to Thermopolis, Wyoming, shortly after his birth. He earned an accounting degree in 1966 at George Washington University and a master's degree in retail marketing in 1968 at the University of Denver. He served in the Wyoming Air National Guard from 1967 until 1973. In 1969, Enzi and his wife moved to Gillette, Wyoming, where they started their own small business, NZ Shoes. In 1974, he was elected to the first of his two four-year terms as mayor of Gillette. He served on the Department of the Interior Coal Advisory Committee from 1976 until 1979. He has also served as a state representative, elected three times beginning in 1987, and a state senator from 1991 to 1996. Enzi is also the cofounder and chair of the US Air Force Caucus for the US Senate.

The Affordable Care Act

Senate Majority Leader Harry Reid

In the remarks made by Senator Harry Reid to the US Senate regarding the Affordable Care Act, he speaks specifically about the law's implications for American women. He begins by pointing out that insurance companies previously charged women higher premiums just for being women—he specifically points to the high cost of contraception and other women's preventative health care such as mammograms, which has meant that, as he puts it, being a woman constituted a "preexisting condition." Reid points out that his wife was diagnosed with breast cancer that developed quickly between scheduled mammograms in order to buttress his argument that increased preventive care for women should be a top priority.

Mr. President, I am going to spend a few minutes talking about the Affordable Care Act. I wonder how many people on the Republican side today are going to talk about Obama Care. If they do, they should be in a very positive state. We know that as a result of this bill, the Affordable Care Act, people are getting or soon will get a rebate. One of the things we did—led by Senator Franken and others—was make sure that 80 percent of the money paid for premiums goes to patient care and any amount that doesn't has to be refunded to the patients. That is in the process now. In the month of August, all those moneys will come back in a significant amount to Americans who, in effect, are part of programs that spend too much on salaries for bosses.

Also, we are going to talk a little bit today about what this Affordable Care Act does for women in America. As I said, I am going to speak very briefly, but we are going to have people come—as soon as I and the Republican leader finish—to talk about good things in this bill for women. I will touch on them very briefly.

There is no question this bill that was signed by President Obama is a landmark piece of legislation. It signaled an end to insurance company discrimination among many but especially against those who are ill, those with a preexisting condition, and especially against women.

As a result of this bill we passed, being a woman is no longer a preexisting disability in America. For many years, insurance companies charged American women higher premiums. Why? Because they are women. For years, American women have unfairly borne the burden of the high cost of contraception as well. Even women with private insurance often wind up spending hundreds of dollars more each year for birth control. Today, women of reproductive age spend two-thirds more out of their own pockets for health care costs than men, largely due to the high cost of

Delivered July 31, 2012. Remarks made on the Senate floor by Harry Reid.

birth control. But starting tomorrow—Wednesday of this week—new insurance plans must cover contraception and many other preventive health services for women. How much? No additional pay at all. Under health care reform, about 47 million women, including almost 400,000 women in Nevada, will have guaranteed access to those additional preventive services without cost sharing.

Ending insurance company discrimination will help millions more women afford the care they need when they need it. It will restore basic fairness to the health care system.

Many on the other side downplayed the importance of these benefits or fought to repeal them altogether. It is hard to comprehend but true. Forcing American women to continue struggling with the high price of contraception has very real consequences. Every year millions of women in the United States put off doctors' visits because they can't afford the co-pay and millions more skip pills or shots to save money.

It is no mystery why the United States has one of the highest rates of unintended pregnancies of all industrialized nations. Half of all pregnancies in America are unplanned. Of those unintended pregnancies, about half wind up in abortion. Increasing access to contraception is the most effective way to reduce unintended pregnancies and reduce the number of abortions, but the high cost is often a barrier.

That is why, in 1997, Olympia Snowe and I began a bipartisan effort to prevent unintended pregnancies by expanding access to contraception. It has not been an easy path, but we did make a start. As part of this effort, we helped pass a law ensuring Federal employees access to contraception. It was a big issue. That was 15 years ago or more. It is an issue that is still important, but we started it, and I am very happy about that. Olympia Snowe was terrific to work with.

When this benefit took place in 1999, premiums did not go up one single dime because neither did health care costs—not one penny. It was rewarding to note that a pro-life Democrat and pro-choice Republican were able to confront the issue with a practical eye rather than a political eye. It is unfortunate that over the last 15 years an idea that started as a common-ground proposal has become so polarizing in Congress. The controversy is quite strange when we consider that almost 99 percent of women have relied on contraception at some point in their lives, and many have struggled to afford it. The Affordable Care Act will ensure that insurance companies treat women fairly and treat birth control as any other preventive service.

Prior to Senator Snowe and me doing this, anything a man wanted they got. Viagra, fine; we will take care of that. Anything a man wanted they got—but not a woman. The law doesn't just guarantee women's access to contraception, it assures their access to many other lifesaving procedures as well.

Thanks to the health care bill—the Affordable Care Act—insurance companies are already required to cover preventive care such as mammograms. For a person who is able to have a mammogram, it is lifesaving. Most people in the Senate know my wife is battling breast cancer. She had a mammogram in December and in August discovered a lump in her breast. Think of what would have happened if she had waited 1 year because she couldn't afford that mammogram. Frankly, the thought of it is very hard for me to comprehend because even though she had that mammogram in December, she had found it and was in stage 3 of breast cancer. It has been very difficult. What if she waited an extra year? Many people wait a lot longer than an extra year.

Colonoscopies save lives. I was talking to one of my friends in the Senate who is going to have his done. They do it every 5 years. It takes at least 10 years for polyps to develop into cancer, and some polyps develop into cancer if they are not taken out. People need to have this done.

Blood pressure checks, childhood immunizations without cost sharing is part of what is in this bill. It used to be a bill; now it is the law.

Starting tomorrow—again, Wednesday of this week—women will no longer have to reach in their pockets to pay for wellness checkups. They can do screening for diabetes, HPV testing, sexually transmitted infection counseling, HIV screening and counseling, breastfeeding support, domestic violence screening and counseling. That is all in the law starting tomorrow. All women in new insurance plans will have access to all forms of FDA-approved contraception without having to shell out more money on top of their premiums. Ending insurance company discrimination will help millions more women afford the care they need when they need it. It will restore basic fairness to the health care system. Sometimes the practical thing to do is also the right thing to do, and that is what the legislation we worked so hard to pass is all about. It is about doing the right thing for everyone. Today we are going to focus on women.

About Harry Reid

Harry Reid was elected senator of the state of Nevada in 1986, and has served as the majority leader in the US Senate since January 2007. He previously served as senate minority leader and minority whip and majority whip. Before becoming a senator, Reid, who is a Mormon, represented Nevada's First Congressional District, acted as Nevada's twenty-fifth lieutenant governor, and served as chair of the Nevada Gaming Commission.

The Paycheck Fairness Act

Senator Debbie Stabenow

Senator Debbie Stabenow expresses her support for the Paycheck Fairness Act in an impassioned statement given on the Senate floor on June 5, 2012. She begins by referring to the history of the United States as a political haven for individuals seeking equal opportunity. She then presents statistical facts about income inequality in the United States and further inequality in her home state of Michigan. To back up the statistics and show her support for equal pay for equal work, Stabenow presents seven examples of women working in her state who earn less than their male colleagues doing the same job.

Mr. President, first, let me say thank you to the champion. We have just been hearing from the champion, not only in the Senate but in the Congress, on so many issues that have led to empowerment for women and equality for all people to have a chance to succeed in our economy. Certainly, whether it is preventive health for women or the Paycheck Fairness Act, I thank Senator Mikulski for leading the way and being the person we look to. I am proud to stand with Senator Mikulski on the floor of the Senate.

Since our founding, our country has been a destination for those who seek equal treatment and equal opportunity. Across the world, America is known as the land of opportunity. I am very proud we have that label. Our hard work and ingenuity built the country, brick by brick, city by city. My home State of Michigan was right in the middle of it—building the tools, the vehicles that built our country and that, frankly, built the middle class of our country. Those looking for new opportunity, those with entrepreneurial spirit have always been welcome here in America.

People still make the journey to this country in search of a better life. We tell the world that everyone has equal opportunity, that if they put in just as much hard work as their neighbor, they will earn a decent living and be able to provide for their family. But that is only half true. Everyone can work hard, everyone can be successful, but for some reason it is acceptable that women do not need to be paid as much as men for the exact same work. This is unacceptable. That is what this legislation is all about.

Nationally, women make 77 cents for every $1 a man makes for the exact same job. In Michigan, the numbers are even worse. Women make 74 cents on every $1 for the exact same job. I received countless letters from constituents describing how this affects their lives and their families' lives. Teresa from Detroit is a single mom with two daughters. One daughter is in college. Teresa tries to help her out as much as she can, but she gets paid less than her male coworkers for doing the same work so it is tough.

Delivered June 5, 2012. Remarks made on the Senate floor by Debbie Stabenow.

Pamela from Romulus, Michigan, is the sole breadwinner in her house, supporting her husband who is a disabled Vietnam veteran and their children. She works at a corporation and took over a man's job. Then the company changed the title so they could pay her less.

Craig from Lowell wrote in to tell me his story. By the way, this is a common story in Michigan over the last number of years. He lost his job in 2008 because of the recession. His wife had to support their entire family of four. The family had to go on food assistance, something they never thought in their wildest dreams they would have to do because Craig's wife has been working at the same company for 23 years but has not gotten a raise in the last 4 years and makes several dollars an hour less than her male counterparts.

> *Women in Michigan make 74 cents for every dollar a man earns for the exact same job. There are so many families in Michigan struggling right now. It should not be harder on them just because the primary bread-winners are women.*

Melissa from Ann Arbor is the sole breadwinner in a family of four. She figured out if she were paid the same as her male colleagues, she would take home an extra $1,000 a month after taxes. She said that $1,000 would make her family more stable and let Melissa and her husband take her children on trips, give them new opportunities, allow them to be enrolled in sports and save for retirement—that extra $1,000 a month.

Cheryl from Okemos has had to take a second job just to make as much as her male counterparts at her day job, and it has cut down on how much time she can spend with her family. She has a second job just so she can make as much as her colleagues who work one job—she has two jobs. The tradeoff for her is as a mom spending less time with her family. She is able to feed and clothe their children, but she says she is missing out on watching them grow up—also a very important value we talk about all the time on the floor of the Senate, in terms of values for families.

Linda from South Lyon wrote about her lifetime of being discriminated against just because she is a woman. Over her career she has consistently made less than men in the same industry with the same job description. One executive even told her he only hires women because they work harder and he can pay them less. They work harder, but he should not be able to pay them less.

Sandra from Marshall has worked as an engineer at the same company for 28 years. She has been rated as one of the company's best performers. Despite this, she has never risen to the level where she earns bonuses and a better pension—a level in her company that is dominated by men.

She has countless people she has hired and trained and watched them pass her by. These stories are real.

Jennifer, from the west side of Michigan, is a university teacher and athletic coach. She was the head coach of a varsity women's team and taught six classes. She saw men in the same position make more money while they taught fewer classes.

She watched them receive tenure with master's degrees while she was required to work toward a Ph.D. to be eligible for the same tenure. She was denied tenure despite good performance evaluations. Yet a male assistant coach at the university was given tenure without a Ph.D. because he had a family. These are real stories.

This is about families, economic opportunities, and security for families. America is known as the land of opportunity, and people still make the journey to our great country in search of a better life. Everyone has an equal chance to work hard and everyone can be successful, but not everyone gets the same opportunity to be successful.

Women in Michigan make 74 cents for every dollar a man earns for the exact same job. There are so many families in Michigan struggling right now. It should not be harder on them just because the primary breadwinners are women. It is just not right.

Middle-class families need economic security, and that is why we need the Paycheck Fairness Act. We have made strides to move forward. This is not complicated. It is not rocket science. It is very simple. This is about equal pay for equal work. We talk the talk all the time. It is time to walk the walk and to pass this bill.

About Debbie Stabenow

Born in 1950 in Gladwin, Michigan, Debbie Stabenow earned a bachelor's degree in 1972 and a master's degree in social work in 1975 from Michigan State University. She served in the Michigan House of Representatives from 1979 to 1990; she was the first woman to preside over that body. She served in the Michigan State Senate from 1991 to 1994. Elected to the US House of Representatives in 1996, she served two terms. She was elected to the United States Senate in 2000, becoming the first woman to represent the state of Michigan. Currently she is chair of the Senate Agriculture, Nutrition, and Forestry Committee.

Dark Money Donors, Show Yourselves

Representative Raúl Grijalva

Representative Raúl Grijalva warns that large corporations and powerful lobbyists have hijacked our political system with what he calls "dark money donations." He gives the example of the National Federation of Independent Business (NFIB), an organization that received multimillion-dollar donations to support its efforts to block the Affordable Care Act. The congressman says that the NFIB, which is not obligated to disclose the identities of its members and the sources of its money, represents the interests of large corporations over the interests of US citizens.

Mr. Speaker, money has taken over our political process. Big corporations and high-rolling political schemers tell us everything is still mom and apple pie, and there's nothing to worry about.

But some of us have seen the effects of these hidden million-dollar dark money donations. We've seen the ads that tell you what to think and who to vote for, without telling you who's talking. We've seen the multimillion-dollar lawsuits that help elite corporate interests, without explaining who's paying the bill. We've seen more and more elections bought and paid for by the only people who can afford it. And those people are not us.

It's time to start naming names and asking why these people won't tell us who they are. We must start to fight back and ask them what they have to hide.

A front group called the National Federation of Independent Business is suing to block the Affordable Care Act. The president of the group says he's doing this to help small businesses. When I and my colleague Representative *Keith Ellison* wrote him a letter, asking him who his members are, he refused to answer. We asked him who gave him several recent million-dollar-plus donations that have helped fund the lawsuit; he refused to answer. We asked him why Karl Rove's Crossroads GPS political group gave him $3.7 million just when he initiated the lawsuit; he refused to answer. And he thinks that's good enough. Well, it's not.

NFIB has never liked answering questions. In 2006, according to an article in the *Nashville Scene*, the organization claimed 600,000 member businesses nationwide. Today on its Web site, it claims about 300,000. But when we asked NFIB to disclose where its money comes from, instead of providing us the courtesy of a written response, the group told the press that its membership has been growing by leaps and bounds since the lawsuit began. It described shrinking by 50 percent as big, new expansion, and it said new members had made small donations that covered the cost of this complex lawsuit before the Supreme Court.

Delivered June 27, 2012. Remarks on the floor of Congress by Representative Raúl Grijalva of Arizona's Seventh Congressional District.

In other words, NFIB won't tell us the truth about who it represents or how big it is. What does it have to hide?

Our democracy has always been about people. It's been about individuals and families making choices about who represents their interests. It's about what kind of country we want to live in, not about what kind of country the very wealthy want to choose for us.

Today, as we prepare for the Supreme Court ruling on the Affordable Care Act, millions of Americans with preexisting health conditions, with sick children, with long-term medical needs, and with no insurance stand together on one side. A front group with bottomless pockets that won't explain its motives sits on the other.

> *Democracy is not for sale, and an election should not be an auction. I'm proud to be on the floor today and say that I am on the side of people that want disclosure, want fair elections, and are tired of the influence of dark money in our collective democracy.*

Mr. Speaker, this is not what our democracy is supposed to be about. Our Founding Fathers did not believe wealth makes a man more important than his neighbor. They didn't believe money is more important than the dignity of the individual. They didn't believe that any company or any organization is entitled to a special set of rules. And they certainly didn't believe that an incorporated business entity is the same thing as a human being.

There is no reason we have to accept the choices that the very, very wealthy few in this country are making for the rest us. Today we stand up to be counted, and we demand that dark money donations come to light; that anyone who wants to influence our democracy step forward and state his name for the record and be honest and transparent with the American people.

Democracy is not for sale, and an election should not be an auction. I'm proud to be on the floor today and say that I am on the side of people that want disclosure, want fair elections, and are tired of the influence of dark money in our collective democracy.

I challenge those front groups to "put up" or "shut up." Tell us who's funding you and what you really want. It's about 4 months and a little more time until America elects a new Congress and a President. Let the voters decide. They know where I stand. And we want these front groups to tell us where they stand, where they get their money, who they are, and who they represent.

The American people in this great democracy of ours should make the choice whether we like it or not. The influence by a very few secretive groups that are fronting for others should not be the ones that decide who represents the American people, who will run this country, and who will set the priorities for this country.

About Raúl Grijalva

Born in 1948 in Tucson, Arizona, Raúl Grijalva earned a bachelor's degree in sociology from the University of Arizona. In 1974, he was elected a member of the Tucson

Unified School District, serving until 1986. From 1975 to 1986, Grijalva was the director of the El Pueblo Neighborhood Center, and in 1987, he served as assistant dean for Hispanic Student Affairs at the University of Arizona. He was a member of the Pima County Board of Supervisors from 1989 to 2002, serving as chair for the last two years. He has served as a democratic Representative of Arizona's Seventh Congressional District since his election in 2003.

Fiscal Responsibility

Senator Dianne Feinstein

Speaking on the Senate floor on September 10, 2012, Senator Dianne Feinstein (D-CA) speaks out against the budget proposal put forth by Representative Paul Ryan (R-MI), who was already a rising star in the Republican Party before being selected as Mitt Romney's running mate for the 2012 presidential campaign. Feinstein reviews the Ryan budget and summarizes its provisions, including a tax cut for the wealthy, the elimination of spending on domestic programs, the conversion of Medicare into a block-grant fund, and the repeal of the Affordable Care Act. She cites analyses by the Tax Policy Center and the Congressional Budget Office to paint a bleak picture of what the Ryan budget would mean for seniors and the middle class, who, she argues, would be adversely affected.

Mr. President, I rise today to speak about the budget proposed by Congressman Paul Ryan, which has been approved twice by the House of Representatives.

The Ryan budget, which is purported to be a measure of fiscal responsibility, is in fact an attempt to rewrite the social contract in this country while at the same time adding to the national debt.

Let me explain. There are four major components of the Ryan budget.

The first is another round of tax cuts for the wealthy. According to the non-partisan Tax Policy Center, the Ryan tax plan would add an additional $4.5 trillion to the Nation's debt. That is on top of the staggering cost of the Bush tax cuts.

Second, the Ryan budget would virtually eliminate spending on domestic programs, imposing debilitating funding cuts for education, air quality, roads, bridges, railways, national parks, first responder programs and a host of other vital national interests.

Third, this budget ends Medicare as we know it and converts Medicaid into a block-grant program with capped funds. The Ryan budget endangers our two most vital sources of health care services for seniors, the poor and those with disabilities.

Finally, the budget repeals the health reform law, reducing the solvency of Medicare and eliminating critical consumer protections.

The tax proposal in the Ryan budget is especially troubling. According to the Tax Policy Center, the Ryan budget would mean a tax windfall of $265,000 a year for millionaires.

At the same time, the middle class and working poor would see few if any benefits.

The Ryan tax plan is very similar to that of Mitt Romney. Both plans would substantially reduce tax rates on the wealthy, and both are supposedly paid for by closing unspecified tax loopholes.

Delivered September 10, 2012. Remarks made on the Senate floor by Dianne Feinstein.

The Tax Policy Center has already analyzed Mitt Romney's plan. In order to substantially lower tax rates and remain revenue neutral, the Romney plan would have to eliminate so many tax credits and deductions that it would actually raise taxes on the middle class.

To make matters worse, the Ryan budget does not stand up to scrutiny. This is a question of basic arithmetic.

How do you reduce the national debt while at the same time handing massive tax cuts to the wealthy?

Congressman Ryan already took one option off the table—reducing the Defense Department budget. In fact, his budget proposes to spend even more money on defense, money the Pentagon does not even want.

That leaves deeper cuts to domestic programs and entitlement spending as the only remaining options. And it is important to note that Congressman Ryan refuses to specify what those cuts would be—because they would be so painful to so many Americans.

Let me be candid: The Ryan budget is just another salvo in the war against the middle class and working poor.

Medicare in particular would be savaged by the Ryan budget.

Beginning in 2023, his budget ends the traditional guaranteed benefits structure of Medicare, instead offering vouchers to purchase either a private health insurance plan or traditional Medicare.

According to the Congressional Budget Office, that means new Medicare beneficiaries would pay $1,200 more out of pocket by 2030 and $5,900 more by 2050. Experts say the Ryan budget would also likely lead to reduced access to health care and diminished quality of care for beneficiaries.

Essentially, seniors would be forced to purchase more expensive care with less.

Consider that in 2010, half of all Medicare beneficiaries had incomes of less than $21,000 and you can see why this proposal is so dangerous.

The Center for American Progress estimates that if the Ryan budget were to pass, someone who is 54 years old today would face increased costs of $59,450 during retirement. Someone who is 29 years old today would spend $331,000 more over the course of their retirement.

I would also note that the Ryan budget includes $700 billion in Medicare savings the exact same amount that was included in the health reform law he seeks to repeal.

The difference is that rather than applying those savings to lower costs and increased benefits for seniors, the Ryan budget diverts those savings to even more tax breaks for millionaires and billionaires.

Speaking of Congressman Ryan's desire to repeal health reform—his efforts to unwind that law, which has been upheld by the Supreme Court, would add tens of millions of Americans to the ranks of the uninsured, it would eliminate critical consumer protections, and it would hasten the insolvency of Medicare by 8 years.

House Republicans want to put insurance companies back in the driver's seat, able to charge higher rates based on gender and deny coverage to people with preexisting conditions. They would remove protections that guarantee children the right to health insurance.

American families would again be at risk for bankruptcy because of costly illnesses like cancer. More than 12 million Californians would once again face lifetime limits on their health coverage.

The budget would reopen the prescription drug "doughnut hole," forcing 5.2 million seniors to once again dip into their pockets to cover the full cost of prescription drugs.

In California, 3.4 million seniors would be forced to pay more for preventive services, such as cancer screenings and mammograms, meaning fewer seniors would have access to these services.

Let me be clear: the health reform law extended the life of Medicare by 8 years. In addition to forcing seniors to pay more for services, the Ryan budget would place the Medicare Trust Fund on a track for insolvency by 2016.

Medicaid is another big loss in the Ryan budget. He would change Medicaid from a State-Federal match program to a block grant program, including dangerous funding caps. Millions more of the most at-risk Americans would become uninsured or underinsured because of this budget.

Medicaid spending would be slashed by $810 billion over 10 years, a 22 percent cut.

This would jeopardize health care for nearly 7.3 million Medi-Cal beneficiaries in California, many of whom would see reduced eligibility, coverage of fewer services and increased out-of-pocket expenses.

Low-income pregnant women who depend on Medicaid could be dropped from the program, a threat to the health of both mother and baby.

Let me be candid: The Ryan budget is just another salvo in the war against the middle class and working poor.

It would mean more tax cuts for the wealthy at the expense of investments in our future, it would lead to greater numbers of uninsured and it would demolish some of the most vital safety net programs in the Nation.

Let's set aside the politics and get to work on real solutions for the country.

About Dianne Feinstein

Born Dianne Emiel Goldman in San Francisco in 1933, Dianne Feinstein earned a bachelor's in history from Stanford University in 1955. She was elected to the San Francisco Board of Supervisors in 1969 and served nine years. After she was elected president of the board in 1978, San Francisco Mayor George Moscone was assassinated, along with supervisor Harvey Milk, and Feinstein succeeded to the mayoralty. Elected twice in her own right, she remained in office until 1988. She has served as Democratic Senator from California since 1992. From 2007 to 2009, she chaired the Senate Rules and Administration Committee. In 2009, she became chair of the Caucus on International Narcotics Control and the Senate Select Committee on Intelligence.

Republican Intransigence and Obstruction

Representative Steny Hoyer

Speaking on the floor of the House of Representatives, House Democratic Whip Steny Hoyer blasts Congressional Republicans for what he calls a tactic of "obstruct, delay, and walk away." In a debate about tax cuts for the middle class, he says, Republicans have insisted on a tax cut for the nation's wealthiest 2 percent, one which Hoyer asserts would add $10 trillion to the nation's deficit. He cites Republican obstruction on the Violence Against Women Act, the farm bill, postal reform, the highway bill, FAA reauthorization, and others. In each case, he argues, Republicans have blocked legislation to appease the extreme right wing of their party.

Mr. Speaker, this week's middle class tax cut debate is unfortunately an unnecessary sequel to December's fight over extending payroll tax cuts. Republicans campaigned on a pledge to seek bipartisan solutions to our pressing challenges, but when faced with a bipartisan agreement in December of last year, they chose to walk away. Unfortunately, they appear ready to do so again. When it comes to extending tax cuts to the middle class, Democrats and Republicans agree; both believe we ought to do so. So we have agreement. That agreement has been reflected in a Senate-passed bill, Mr. Speaker, as you know.

So with millions faced with the uncertainty of whether their taxes will go up next year, why haven't we acted? This should be an easy vote for an overwhelming majority of Members to say, Let's extend these tax cuts we agree on, and then debate what we don't agree on. It should be easy. But the Republicans, Mr. Speaker, are continuing to do what they do so often, have done best this Congress—obstruct, delay, and walk away.

In December, by holding hostage an extension of the payroll tax cuts for 98 percent of our taxpayers, Republicans walked away from the middle class. They walked away from their responsibility to seek compromise on job creation and economic recovery. They walked away from negotiations over deficit reduction, setting up the dangerous sequester that now looms at the end of the year. The sequester exists because Republicans pursued a policy of placing the Nation's debt at risk.

Today, sadly, they are walking away from the middle class and working families once more, demanding their way or nothing on tax cuts. No tax cuts for the middle class, they insist, without an additional tax break for the upper 2 percent of income earners. In other words, we agree on 98 percent. We don't agree on 2 percent. Rather than doing that which we agree upon for 98 percent of the American taxpayers, we will hold them hostage until we get agreement on the 2 percent. Of course if we

Delivered August 1, 2012. Remarks made on the floor of the House of Representatives by Steny Hoyer.

agree on the 2 percent, it will add a trillion dollars over 10 years, if followed for 10 years, to our deficit and debt.

Republicans' plan of tax cuts for the wealthy hasn't worked before, and it won't work now. Under President Reagan and both Presidents Bush, deficits climbed.

Democrats want to return to the successful policies we had under President Clinton, when we had the most successful economy, 4 years of balanced budgets, and 4 years in which we did not increase the national debt.

> *I say to my friends on the Republican side of the aisle, Mr. Speaker, we've had many opportunities to work together this year to address our challenges, but each time our Republican colleagues have walked away.*

I say to my friends on the Republican side of the aisle, Mr. Speaker, we've had many opportunities to work together this year to address our challenges, but each time our Republican colleagues have walked away. In doing so, they broke a central promise in their pledge to America—that is, the promise to let the majority work its will.

We could have extended the payroll tax cuts without a fight. We could have found a big and balanced solution to deficits. And we could be voting today on a tax cut extension for 100 percent of Americans who make up to $200,000. Or, if they're a couple, $250,000. But in each case, Mr. Speaker, Republicans moved not towards the center but to the right to placate the extreme wing within their party.

Yesterday, Mr. Speaker, Representative Richard Hanna of New York, a Republican, said this about his party in Congress:

"I have to say that I am frustrated by how much we—I mean the Republican Party—are willing to give deferential treatment to our extremes in this moment of history."

The gentleman from New York went on to say:

"We render ourselves incapable of governing when all we do is take severe sides. If all people do is go down there and join a team, and the team is invested in winning and you have something similar to the shirts and the skins, there's not a lot of value there."

Congressman Hanna in this instance is right. Republicans have been unable to govern. Again and again, this Republican House has received compromise bills from the Senate but has been incapable of agreeing to legislation or passing a version that could become law.

That was true on transportation. It's true on the farm bill, and it's true on Violence Against Women. And it's true on this tax bill. Examples include, as I've said, Violence Against Women and the farm bill, postal reform, the highway bill, FAA reauthorization, and many others. Instead of focusing on winning politically, they ought to be concerned about governing effectively.

They could learn much from our outstanding Olympic athletes. In team sports like soccer and basketball, athletes who normally compete against each other at home have come together as one team, Team USA. They've won gold; they've been successful. We could be as well if we came together as Team USA.

Those athletes may harbor rivalries most of the time. They may not be used to working together. And they all know that when the cauldron is extinguished, they'll once again wear different colors. But right now in London, they're all wearing red, white, and blue, and they've set their differences aside to achieve victory together. We ought to follow their example. Republicans ought to follow their example.

We have a chance today to be one team and make possible what we agree ought to happen. Again, we agree on 98 percent of the proposal. Let's agree on that, and agree to debate that on which we don't agree. So I say to my Republican friends, stop walking away from the middle class and start working with us to get things done on their behalf.

Let me quote someone I don't usually quote, Newt Gingrich, when he was Speaker of this House when we were considering a compromise that he and President Clinton had agreed to, and so many of his Republicans colleagues, Mr. Speaker, as you may remember, opposed Newt Gingrich's efforts. He said:

"I would say for just a minute, if I might, to my friends who were asking for a 'no' vote, the 'perfectionist caucus.'"

He concluded his remarks in urging them to vote for a compromise agreement:

"So the question is: Can we craft a bill which is a win for the American people because it is a win for the President and a win for the Congress? Because if we cannot find a way to have all three winning, we do not have a bill worthy of being passed."

The President has indicated he will not sign the Republican bill, and the Senate won't pass the Republican bill. But again, my friends, Mr. Speaker, as you know, we have agreement on 98 percent, and we are hung up because we don't have agreement on the other 2 percent.

Speaker Gingrich went on:

"Now, my fine friends who are perfectionists, each in their own world where they are petty dictators, could write a perfect bill."

And he concluded:

"In a free society, we have to have give and take. We have to be able to work."

Mr. Speaker, Americans must lament the fact that they see their Representatives agreeing on 98 percent of a proposition and will not pass it. They will not pass it because the perfectionist caucus has promised in many respects to one individual American we will not raise taxes ever. We won't pay for what we buy, even if we think it's important.

Mr. Speaker, both parties have an opportunity today to stand up and reflect agreement and do something positive for the American people, do something positive for the American economy, do something positive to grow jobs in America. Do something that will give certainty and confidence to the overwhelming majority of Americans, who will say that Congress can work.

It can, as families understand they must do every day, reach compromise, come together, reason with one another and give and take, as Speaker Gingrich said.

Let us hope, Mr. Speaker, that we reflect the best in us today, not the worst, not the confrontational inclination, but the inclination to come together, to make America better and to make sure that the American people, who are working hard every day, don't see a tax increase on January 1 as a result of a "perfectionist caucus" unwilling to compromise, unwilling to pass an already-passed Senate bill that will give 98 percent of Americans confidence that they will not receive any tax increase on January 1.

What a good thing that would be for America, for the American people, and for the American economy. Let's work together. America expects us to do that, and that's what we ought to do.

About Steny Hoyer

Born in 1939 in New York City, Representative Steny Hoyer serves Maryland's Fifth District. He graduated from the University of Maryland in 1963 and earned a law degree from Georgetown University Law Center in 1966. That year, he won a seat in the Maryland State Senate, and in 1975, he became the youngest president of that body in history. He served on the Maryland Board of Higher Education from 1978 until 1981. He was elected to the US House of Representatives in 1981 and has served since, currently acting as House Minority Whip. He was the House Majority Leader from 2007 to 2011.

"Let the Tide Rise for All Boats"

Representative Mike Kelly

Representative Mike Kelly of Pennsylvania received a rare standing ovation for his July 2012 speech to the House of Representatives, in which he urges his fellow Congress members to vote in favor of H.R. 4078, a bill drafted by Arkansas Representative Tim Griffin, proposing a freeze on federal regulatory action until the national unemployment rate falls below 6 percent. Excessive federal regulation, he asserts, increases production costs, discouraging business expansion and the creation of jobs, while saddling consumers with high prices. Kelly envisions an America that not only participates in, but dominates the world economy, and he insists that halting cumbersome government mandates is the surest way to make this goal a reality. He reminds the House that jobs are not created for Republicans or Democrats, but Americans, and that if excessive regulation is curtailed, Americans of all stripes will benefit.

Mr. Speaker, in 2011, we came to this House for one reason, and it was a motion to recommit. We recommitted to the people of the United States that we were going to change the way business was done in this town. This motion to recommit is a joke. This is ridiculous.

Let me tell you about what it's like to be in the real world and not inside the Beltway. I operate a business that my father started back in 1953, after being a parts picker in a General Motors warehouse, going to fight the war, and coming back home. I called our body shop manager today, Jason Sholes. He's been with me for 26 years. I said to Jason, "I need to know the cost of tape, Jason." He goes, "What are you talking about, Mike?" I said, "In our body shop, when people wreck their car and bring their car in, I know we have to use a lot of tape." He said, "Oh, my goodness. Has the cost of tape gone crazy. We use two types of tape, Mike. We use green tape. Green tape is the tape we use when we have to use water on a job, and we have to make sure that he tape sticks, and that's up to $4 a roll."

I said, "Tell me about the other tape." He said, "The other tape is yellow tape." I said, "Tell me about the yellow tape." He said, "That's when we're going to paint a car, and we don't have to use the green tape. The yellow tape is a little less expensive. It's only $2 a roll. But, Mike, I've got to tell you that we're spending $160 a month on tape, and it's really making me wonder about whether I'm doing the right thing."

I said, "Jason, we're spending about $2,000 a year on green and yellow tape?" He said, "Yes, we are." I said, "Jason, do you know what the cost of red tape?" He goes, "I have no idea. We don't use red tape." I said, "Yes, we do. It's $1.75 trillion." That's the cost of red tape.

Delivered July 25, 2012. Remarks made to the House of Representatives by Mike Kelly.

> *The jobs we are talking about are not red jobs or blue jobs; they're red, white, and blue jobs. ... If you want this country to thrive and not just survive, then please start playing the game by the rules and stop this ridiculous mockery of what it is that we do here in this town.*

I called my friend Don Shamey at NexTier Bank. I said, "Don, we've know each other since we were kids. Our wives know each other, and our kids grew up together. We do a lot of things together. I've done business with you for 40 years. You're right across the street from me. Don, tell me about the new regulations." He said, "Mike, if you take a look at it, there's 1,100 pages now that are the definition of whether you're a qualified borrower or not." I said, "It only took 1,100 pages for the government to determine what the definition of a qualified borrower is? Are you kidding me? Do you mean to sit here and say that you are serious?"

We renovated a ballpark in my hometown with a guy named Tom Burnatowski, a veteran. It took us a couple of million dollars to renovate our ballpark. The day we were going to open up, I got a call at the dealership where he said, "Mike, could you come down." I said, "Why? What's going on?" He said, "We're having trouble with the occupancy permit." I went down to see. I said, "What's the problem?" He said, "Come into the men's room. Let me show you what the problem is. "I said, "You know, we have 1,500 people that want to come and see the opening ball game." He said, "But we've got a major problem. The mirrors in the restroom are a quarter of an inch too low. So you can't possibly open that ballpark."

You want to know the price of regulation? You want to talk about the thousands and thousands of pages that we put on the backs of the job creators? You want to talk about creating jobs in America? When you want to see a Nation that doesn't want to participate but wants to dominate in the world market, then let them rise. Take the heavy boot off the throat of America's job creators and let them breathe.

The jobs we are talking about are not red jobs or blue jobs; they're red, white, and blue jobs. They are not Democrat jobs or Republican jobs or independent jobs or libertarian jobs; they are American jobs. If you want this country to thrive and not just survive, then please start playing the game by the rules and stop this ridiculous mockery of what it is that we do here in this town. We are so out of touch with the American people.

Do you know what all this does? It adds layer after layer of cost, and that cost is ultimately paid for by the American consumer. You want to have more revenues? Then let the tide rise for all boats. Let us be able to not only survive, but to thrive.

This is not a left or right issue, this is an American issue. I urge my colleagues on both sides of the aisle to rise today and vote for H.R. 4078. Let's let America get back to work.

About Mike Kelly

Representative Mike Kelly was born on May 10, 1948, in Pittsburgh. Raised in Butler, Pennsylvania, he attended the University of Notre Dame on football and academic scholarships before returning to his hometown, where he has lived for the past fifty-three years. In Butler, Kelly worked at his father's Cadillac dealership, taking ownership of the company in the mid-1990s and expanding it to include Hyundai and Kia franchises. He has served on multiple boards related to Hyundai, Kia, and Cadillac businesses in Pennsylvania and the Eastern United States, and was the secretary and treasurer of "Hope on Wheels," a Hyundai initiative donating to child cancer research. Kelly was a Butler City councilman before winning a seat in the House of Representatives for Pennsylvania's Third Congressional District in 2011. He serves on the Oversight and Government Reform Committee, the House Committee on Foreign Affairs, and the Education and Workforce Committee.

3

A Decade after 9/11

One World Trade Center is reflected in one of the memorial pools at the National September 11 Memorial at the World Trade Center site in New York before a ceremony marking the 10th anniversary of the attacks on the trade center, Sunday, September 11, 2011.

Joy Cometh in the Morning

President Barack Obama

In his speech commemorating the tenth anniversary of the terrorist attacks of September 11, 2001, President Barack Obama reflects on the devastating events of 9/11 and their effect on the decade that followed. He traces the nation's journey from shock, fear, and mourning to resilience, recovery, and repair, contending that this journey has ultimately strengthened the American union. With references to past struggles our nation has faced, from the Civil War to the Great Depression to the Cold War, President Obama asserts that each trial makes American democracy more durable and more perfect. Americans, he holds, have learned from 9/11 to honor the past while guarding infinite hope for the future.

The Bible tells us—"weeping may endure for a night, but joy cometh in the morning."

Ten years ago, America confronted one of our darkest nights. Mighty towers crumbled. Black smoke billowed up from the Pentagon. Airplane wreckage smoldered on a Pennsylvania field. Friends and neighbors; sisters and brothers; mothers and fathers; sons and daughters—they were taken from us with heartbreaking swiftness and cruelty. On September 12, 2001, we awoke to a world in which evil was closer at hand, and uncertainty clouded our future.

In the decade since, much has changed for Americans. We've known war and recession; passionate debates and political divides. We can never get back the lives we lost on that day, or the Americans who made the ultimate sacrifice in the wars that followed.

Yet today, it is worth remembering what has not changed. Our character as a nation has not changed. Our faith—in God and each other—that has not changed. Our belief in America, born of a timeless ideal that men and women should govern themselves; that all people are created equal, and deserve the same freedom to determine their own destiny—that belief, through test and trials, has only been strengthened.

These past ten years have shown that America does not give in to fear. The rescue workers who rushed to the scene; the firefighters who charged up the stairs; the passengers who stormed the cockpit—these patriots defined the very nature of courage. Over the years we have also seen a more quiet form of heroism—in the ladder company that lost so many men and still suits up to save lives every day; the businesses that have rebuilt; the burn victim who has bounced back; the families that press on.

Delivered September 11, 2011, in Washington, DC, by President Barack Obama, on the tenth anniversary of the terrorist attacks of September 11, 2001.

Last spring, I received a letter from a woman named Suzanne Swaine. She had lost her husband and brother in the Twin Towers, and said that she had been robbed of "so many would-be proud moments where a father watches their child graduate, or tend goal in a lacrosse game, or succeed academically." But two of her daughters are in college, the other doing well in high school. "It has been ten years of raising these girls on my own," Suzanne wrote. "I could not be prouder of their strength and resilience." That spirit typifies the American family. And the hopeful future for those girls is the ultimate rebuke to the hateful killers who took the life of their father.

These past ten years have shown America's resolve to defend its citizens, and our way of life. Diplomats serve in far off posts, and intelligence professionals work tirelessly without recognition. Two million Americans have gone to war since 9/11. They have demonstrated that those who do us harm cannot hide from the reach of justice, anywhere in the world. America has been defended not by conscripts, but by citizens who choose to serve—young people who signed up straight out of school; guardsmen and reservists; workers and business-people; immigrants and fourth-generation soldiers. They are men and women who left behind lives of comfort for two, three, four, or five tours of duty. Too many will never come home. Those that do carry dark memories from distant places, and the legacy of fallen friends.

> *More than monuments, that will be the legacy of 9/11—a legacy of firefighters who walked into fire and soldiers who signed up to serve; of workers who raised new towers, citizens who faced down fear, and children who realized the dreams of their parents. It will be said of us that we kept that faith; that we took a painful blow, and emerged stronger.*

The sacrifices of these men and women, and of our military families, reminds us that the wages of war are great; that while their service to our nation is full of glory, war itself is never glorious. Our troops have been to lands unknown to many Americans a decade ago—to Kandahar and Kabul; to Mosul and Basra. But our strength is not measured in our ability to stay in these places; it comes from our commitment to leave those lands to free people and sovereign states, and our desire to move from a decade of war to a future of peace.

These ten years have shown that we hold fast to our freedoms. Yes, we are more vigilant against those who threaten us, and there are inconveniences that come with our common defense. Debates—about war and peace; about security and civil liberties—have often been fierce. But it is precisely the rigor of these debates, and our ability to resolve them in a way that honors our values, that is a measure of our strength. Meanwhile, our open markets still provide innovators with the chance to create, our citizens are still free to speak their minds, and our souls are still enriched in our churches and temples, our synagogues and mosques.

These past ten years underscore the bonds between all Americans. We have not succumbed to suspicion and mistrust. After 9/11, President Bush made clear what we reaffirm today: the United States will never wage war against Islam or any religion. Immigrants come here from all parts of the globe. In the biggest cities and the smallest towns, in our schools and workplaces, you still see people of every conceivable race, religion and ethnicity—all of them pledging allegiance to one flag; all of them reaching for the same American dream—e pluribus unum, out of many, we are one.

These past ten years tell a story of resilience. The Pentagon is repaired, and filled with patriots working in common purpose. Shanksville is the scene of friendships forged between residents of that town, and families who lost loved ones there. New York remains a vibrant capital of the arts and industry, fashion and commerce. Where the World Trade Center once stood, the sun glistens off a new tower that reaches toward the sky. Our people still work in skyscrapers. Our stadiums are filled with fans, and our parks full of children playing ball. Our airports hum with travel, and our buses and subways take millions where they need to go. Families sit down to Sunday dinner, and students prepare for school. This land pulses with the optimism of those who set out for distant shores, and the courage of those who died for human freedom.

Decades from now, Americans will visit the memorials to those who were lost on 9/11. They will run their fingers over the places where the names of those we loved are carved into marble and stone, and wonder at the lives they led. Standing before the white headstones in Arlington, and in peaceful cemeteries and small-town squares in every corner of our country, they will pay respects to those lost in Afghanistan and Iraq. They will see the names of the fallen on bridges and statues; at gardens and schools.

And they will know that nothing can break the will of a truly United States of America. They will remember that we have overcome slavery and Civil War; bread lines and fascism; recession and riots; Communism and, yes, terrorism. They will be reminded that we are not perfect, but our democracy is durable, and that democracy—reflecting, as it does, the imperfections of man—also gives us the opportunity to perfect our union. That is what we honor on days of national commemoration—those aspects of the American experience that are enduring, and the determination to move forward as one people.

More than monuments, that will be the legacy of 9/11—a legacy of firefighters who walked into fire and soldiers who signed up to serve; of workers who raised new towers, citizens who faced down fear, and children who realized the dreams of their parents. It will be said of us that we kept that faith; that we took a painful blow, and emerged stronger.

"Weeping may endure for a night, but joy cometh in the morning."

With a just God as our guide, let us honor those who have been lost; let us re-dedicate ourselves to the ideals that define our nation, and let us look to the future with hearts full of hope. May God bless the memory of those we lost, and may God Bless the United States of America.

❖

About President Barack Obama

Barack H. Obama was born on August 4, 1961, in Honolulu, Hawaii. After studying political science and international relations at Columbia University, Obama worked as a community organizer in Chicago until 1988, when he entered Harvard Law School. While at Harvard, Obama served as the first African American president of the Harvard Law Review. Graduating in 1991, Obama returned to Chicago and worked as a lecturer of constitutional law at the University of Chicago. In 1996, he was elected as a member of the Illinois State Senate, where he served for eight years and, in 2004, he was elected to the US Senate to represent Illinois, where he served for four years. He resigned from the Senate on November 8, 2008, after being elected as the forty-fourth and first African American president of the United States. In 2009, President Obama was awarded the Nobel Peace Prize for his work in international cooperation and diplomacy.

Al-Qaeda after Bin Laden: Implications for American Strategy

Brian Michael Jenkins

In his testimony presented to the House Armed Services Committee on June 22, 2011, senior adviser at the RAND Corporation and terrorism expert Brian Michael Jenkins assesses the threat currently posed by al-Qaeda and draws conclusions about what it means for American counterterrorist strategy. He begins by detailing the five phases of al-Qaeda's development. Jenkins concludes that most recently, al-Qaeda has seen a rapid decentralization and diffusion of power, a direct result of the death of leader Osama bin Laden. He holds that, although al-Qaeda presently does not have the ability to mount another attack on the scale of the attacks of September 11, 2001, threats still exist from local insurgencies. This decentralized "do-it-yourself terrorism" poses a new threat because it is both cheaper to carry out and harder to prevent. Thus, as al-Qaeda evolves, so too must American strategy. Stressing international cooperation, Jenkins ultimately asserts that we must turn away from the idea of a permanent war on terror while accepting the inevitable responsibility of remaining permanently vigilant.

There is remarkably little consensus among analysts about the threat now posed by al Qaeda. Some view al Qaeda as a spent force, its demise hastened by bin Laden's death. Others point to al Qaeda's still active field commands, in particular al Qaeda in the Arabian Peninsula (AQAP); the spread of its ideology, especially on the Internet; its determination to acquire and employ weapons of mass destruction; and the still difficult situations in Afghanistan and Pakistan.

Al Qaeda is many things. It is an ideology of violence. It is the inspiration for a global terrorist campaign. It is a tiny army in Afghanistan. It is a loose collection of autonomous field commands and allies in North Africa, the Middle East, and South and Southeast Asia. It is a communications network. Increasingly, it is the conveyer of individual discontents. A thorough assessment would have to examine each component and aspect of its activities.

The Five Phases of Al Qaeda's Campaign

We are currently in what might be called the fifth or "post–bin Laden phase" of al Qaeda's campaign.

Phase I – Preparing for war. The first phase began with al Qaeda's formation in 1988 and includes Saudi Arabia's rejection of bin Laden's offer to mobilize an army of mujahadeen instead of American forces to protect the kingdom, along with

Delivered June 22, 2011. Remarks made before the House Armed Services Committee by Brian Michael Jenkins.

an angry bin Laden's subsequent efforts in the early 1990s to rebuild the Afghan network.

Phase II – Escalating to 9/11. The second phase began in 1996 with Osama bin Laden's declaration of war on the United States and al Qaeda's escalating centrally directed terrorist operations, culminating in the 9/11 attacks.

Phase III – A counterproductive terrorist campaign. The third stage began with the American attack on Afghanistan, dispersing al Qaeda's training camps and putting its leaders on the run. Nevertheless, al Qaeda's international terrorist campaign continued, with spectacular attacks in Indonesia, Kenya, Tunisia, Morocco, Egypt, Jordan, Turkey, Spain, and the United Kingdom. These attacks, however, provoked crackdowns by local governments, which largely destroyed local jihadist networks.

Meanwhile, America's invasion of Iraq in 2003 opened up another front for al Qaeda, which it exploited with a brutal terrorist campaign aimed primarily at other Muslims in an effort to provoke civil war.

But al Qaeda's wanton violence against civilians and Muslims alienated Muslim communities. In Iraq, even Sunni Muslims turned on al Qaeda—a key turning point in the war. With American reinforcements and a crucial change in counterinsurgency strategy, the Iraqi insurgency began to subside.

Phase IV – Individual jihad and do-it-yourself terrorism. The fourth phase, which began in 2007, saw al Qaeda's recession. During this period, it failed to carry out any significant terrorist attacks outside of Iraq or Afghanistan. Its central command became increasingly dependent on affiliates, allies, and homegrown terrorists to continue its global campaign. Algerian terrorists declared themselves to be part of al Qaeda, while AQAP found new sanctuary in Yemen. AQAP launched several attacks which failed but were nonetheless alarming. Meanwhile, the Taliban, recovered from its defeat in 2001, returned to Afghanistan and expanded its influence throughout the country, compelling the United States to send additional troops.

The death of bin Laden—23 years after al Qaeda's official founding, 15 years after his declaration of war on America—marks the end of this fourth phase.

Phase V – Al Qaeda post–bin Laden. The trajectory of al Qaeda cannot be predicted. However, some general observations are possible.

An Appreciation of the Current Situation

We have made considerable progress in the past ten years. Al Qaeda's operational capabilities clearly have been degraded. Its leadership has been decimated, its tiny army scattered. It has not been able to launch a major terrorist operation in the West since 2005. But we have not dented its determination to continue its campaign.

The death of bin Laden does not end al Qaeda's global terrorist campaign. The reported elevation of Ayman al-Zawahiri as al Qaeda's leader suggests that bin Laden's focus on attacking the United States will continue after his death.

Al Qaeda after bin Laden is likely to be even more decentralized, its threat more diffuse. While he was alive, bin Laden was able to impose a unanimity of focus on his inherently fractious enterprise. No successor will speak with bin Laden's authority. Al Qaeda could become a collection of autonomous field commands, presided over by a central command, united only in its beliefs.

The devastating September 11 attacks were an exceptional event, unprecedented in the annals of terrorism, with far-reaching consequences. Al Qaeda expected its terrorist campaign to inspire jihadist groups worldwide to take up arms. It failed to do so. Instead, al Qaeda turned to indiscriminate slaughter of Muslims, which provoked widespread anger and rejection, although among some young Muslims in the West, brandishing al Qaeda sympathies is an act of defiance—like wearing a Che Guevara T-shirt.

Al Qaeda today has far less capability to mount another attack on the scale of 9/11, although caution is in order. Small groups can still be lethal. In 2006, terrorists inspired by al Qaeda's ideology plotted to bring down airliners flying across the Atlantic. Before that, in 1995, a small group of terrorists, then still outside of al Qaeda's orbit, plotted to bring down 12 airliners flying across the Pacific. Had the terrorists succeeded in either case, the numbers of casualties would have rivaled those of 9/11.

Al Qaeda survives by embedding itself in local insurgencies. It has joined such insurgencies in Afghanistan, Iraq, Algeria, Somalia, making itself part of a larger enterprise into which it can inject its ideology. However, these insurgencies have their own trajectory. Al Qaeda is the beneficiary, not the originator of political violence. Regardless of al Qaeda's fate, the insurgencies are likely to go on.

Decades of internal war and weak national institutions in Afghanistan, Yemen, and Somalia guarantee continued conflict. Pacifying these distant turbulent frontiers in order to preserve public safety at home will be an enduring mission.

The revolutions in Tunisia and Egypt and ongoing challenges to Arab autocracies demonstrate the irrelevance of al Qaeda's ideology and terrorist methods. However, al Qaeda benefits from the chaos and the distraction of government, and if these revolutions are crushed or produce no political change, al Qaeda will find new recruiting space. There are also fears that the ultimate beneficiaries of the upheavals will be well-organized Islamist parties, which, although not violent, hold views nearly as extreme as these of al Qaeda. This would not be good news for al Qaeda, but neither would it be good news for the United States.

Al Qaeda's communications have expanded and improved. The movement's leaders have always believed that communications are the most important aspect of its activities. The number of its websites has increased. The number of English language jihadist sites has increased. Al Qaeda publishes a slick online magazine that appeals to an audience of young males. Its American-born spokesmen understand and speak to their audience in easily understood terms.

Al Qaeda has embraced individual jihadism and do-it-yourself terrorism. Its communicators have argued that organization is not necessary: individual jihad is possible and preferable—it is cheap to wage and harder to thwart. This is a change from al Qaeda's initial centralized strategy, and it reflects current realities. Do-it-yourself terrorism goes a step further, accepting that even failed terrorist attempts cause alarm and force governments to devote disproportionate resources to security. The objective is to bankrupt America's already weakened economy. Ultimately, al

Qaeda hopes to turn this audience of online jihadists into the real thing. Thus far, it hasn't worked. Al Qaeda's virtual army remains virtual.

Al Qaeda's exhortations to join its violent jihad have thus far yielded meager results among American Muslims. Between 9/11 and the end of 2010, 176 persons were identified as providing material support to jihadist terrorist groups, attempting to join terrorist fronts abroad, or plotting to carry out terrorist attacks in the United States. Authorities have found no terrorist undergrounds, no armies of sleeper cells. Many of those identified were Somalis, a special case that may be explained more by intense nationalism following Ethiopia's invasion of Somalia than by jihadist ideology. Overall, converts to Islam account for a disproportionate percentage of the homegrown terrorists, suggesting that radicalization and recruitment to terrorism is an individual rather than a community phenomenon.

Few American jihadists have been self-starters. Of the 32 plots to carry out terrorist attacks in the United States, only 10 had anything resembling an operational plan. Six of these were FBI stings. Provided with the means, these self-proclaimed jihadists were demonstrably willing to kill. On their own, only three plots got as far as carrying out an attack; authorities intercepted the fourth. Only two attacks, both carried out by lone gunmen, succeeded. This level of terrorist violence contrasts with the level in the 1970s, when there were 50 to 60 terrorist bombings a year in the United States.

Implications for Counterterrorist Strategy

This is an appropriate time for a review. Ten years of counterterrorism and counterinsurgency offer historical perspective and hard-earned knowledge of the threat we confront as a nation. As al Qaeda has evolved, so must American strategy. This cannot be a linear, sequential strategy. Instead, we should talk about strategic principles.

We must accept great uncertainty about what may happen in the next decade—there will be surprises. If on this date ten years ago, I, with far more prescience than I can claim, had accurately predicted the events of the following decade—the 9/11 attacks; the American invasions of Afghanistan and Iraq; America's longest war, with 100,000 American troops still in Afghanistan and another 40,000 still in Iraq; a wave of revolutions sweeping across North Africa and the Middle East; NATO aircraft bombing Libya—you would have dismissed me as an imaginative novelist.

Al Qaeda and its affiliates remain the primary target of America's counterterrorist campaign; efforts to destroy it must be relentless. Although weakened, the jihadist movement still poses a threat. Historically, al Qaeda has shown itself to be resilient, organizationally flexible, and opportunistic. It remains determined to bring down the United States. Left unmolested, it will find new sanctuaries from which to pursue its campaign. Its complete destruction is also a matter of justice that will serve as an object lesson for other groups that may contemplate attacking America.

International cooperation must be preserved. War-weariness, economic constraints, and the death of bin Laden may erode the unprecedented worldwide cooperation among intelligence services and law enforcement organizations that has succeeded in reducing al Qaeda's capability to mount large-scale attacks. It is crucial that this cooperation be preserved.

How things turn out in Afghanistan remains critical to the future trajectory of the conflict. Although some argue that America need not wage endless war in Afghanistan in order to destroy al Qaeda, it is hard to see how civil war in the country or a Taliban takeover would serve U.S. objectives. Al Qaeda would almost certainly find a less hostile environment there.

Creating a national army and police force in Afghanistan able to effectively secure the country will take longer than the United States is likely to be willing to sustain current troop levels. A drawdown of American forces is necessary, but arbitrary timetables that dictate the pace of withdrawal could encourage the Taliban to wait us out while discouraging our Afghan allies. Abandonment of Afghanistan would be dangerous. Guaranteeing a stable unified democratic Afghanistan, free of political violence is not achievable. We should examine ways we can reconfigure our effort. The development of local and tribal Afghan defense forces can be accelerated to help fill the gap. These are within Afghan tradition, but require supervision to ensure their effectiveness and prevent abuses. An overall peace settlement with the Taliban seems unrealistic. Instead, talks can encourage local accommodations and reconciliation. Talking does not end the fighting. It is a component of the contest.

> *In sum, we have greatly reduced al Qaeda's capacity for large-scale attacks, but the terrorist campaign led by al Qaeda may go on for many years. It is fair to call it a war, without implying that, like America's past wars, it must have a finite ending. But it is time for fundamental and thoughtful review of our effort.*

Large commitments of American ground forces should be avoided. The American armed forces have gained tremendous experience in combating insurgencies, but Americans have also learned that counterinsurgency and nation-building can be costly and require open-ended commitments. The challenge is how to deprive al Qaeda and its allies of safe havens without the United States having to fix failed states.

Counterterrorism has framed much of U.S. foreign policy for nearly a decade. Whatever new governments emerge in the Middle East, the issue of terrorism will not likely be at the top of their agenda. Counterterrorism cannot be the single note of America's diplomacy.

We cannot seek or invent an artificial end to the war on terrorism. This is not a finite wartime effort followed by demobilization. We may be chasing al Qaeda for decades. While rejecting the idea of permanent warfare, we must accept the notion of eternal vigilance.

What we do at home and abroad must be sustainable. It is premature to dismantle the structure we have constructed for security, but the government should be very cautious about adding new security measures. Extraordinary security measures almost invariably become permanent features of the landscape. Efforts should focus on developing less burdensome and more efficient ways to maintain current security levels. We should also move toward risk-based security rather than pretending that we can prevent all attacks.

Public expectations of security must be realistic. The nine years and nine months since 9/11 represent the longest passage of time without a major terrorist attack on an American target abroad or at home since the late 1960s, with the exception of the tragic shooting at Fort Hood. Americans have come to expect that authorities will prevent all terrorist attacks and react with outrage and anger when even a failed attempt occurs. This is not realistic. Even unsuccessful al Qaeda attacks could succeed in undermining our economy if we respond to each with self-injurious security investments and protocols.

The threat of homegrown terrorism is real but should not be exaggerated. The paucity of jihadist recruits suggests that America remains a tolerant nation where immigrants successfully assimilate into the everyday life of our communities and the nation as a whole. America's Muslims are not America's enemies.

Domestic intelligence collection is essential, especially as al Qaeda places more emphasis on inspiring local volunteers to take action. Local police are frontline collectors. The Muslim community is not being picked on. This is not indiscriminate surveillance simply because people are Muslims. The nature of the threat determines the social geography of the collection effort. In response to criminal and terrorist threats in the past, immigrant diasporas and domestic ethnic groups have been the targets of intelligence efforts. Ku Klux Klan violence in the 1960s focused intelligence efforts on certain southern white communities. Anti-Mafia investigations focused on the Italian community. No apologies are necessary. At the same time, community policing to build trust and open lines of communication are critical to reducing radicalization and preventing terrorist attacks.

In sum, we have greatly reduced al Qaeda's capacity for large-scale attacks, but the terrorist campaign led by al Qaeda may go on for many years. It is fair to call it a war, without implying that, like America's past wars, it must have a finite ending. But it is time for a fundamental and thoughtful review of our effort. America's current troop commitments abroad cannot be sustained, nor can we eliminate every vulnerability at home. We have gone big. We need to go long.

About Brian Michael Jenkins

Born in 1942 in Chicago, Illinois, Brian Michael Jenkins is an expert on terrorism and senior adviser to the president at the RAND Corporation, a nonprofit research organization that provides objective analysis and problem-solving services to the private and public sectors. At age nineteen, Jenkins joined the United States Army and served in the Dominican Republic and in Vietnam. He is the author of Will Terrorists Go Nuclear? *(2008) as well as many articles on the subject of terrorism. Under President Clinton, Jenkins was appointed to the White House Commission on Aviation Safety and Security. He has served as an adviser on the National Commission on Terrorism from 1999 to 2000 and was appointed to the US Comptroller's Advisory Board in 2000.*

Strength in Resilience

Secretary of State Hillary Rodham Clinton

In this speech, delivered in New York City at the 2011 Voices of September 11th Luncheon, Secretary of State Hillary Clinton commemorates the tenth anniversary of the 9/11 attacks and the opening of the September 11 Memorial and Museum at Ground Zero. Clinton praises the efforts of the Voices of September 11th, a nonprofit organization with the goal of promoting resilience and a sense of community among those deeply affected by the terrorist attacks of September 11, 2001. Clinton commends the organization's activism, but warns that the fight against terrorist ideology will be a long-term effort, as the ultimate victory will not be in the death of terrorist leaders, but in making those leaders irrelevant. This victory, she contends, will be rooted in the resilience of the American people, resilience such as that demonstrated so gracefully by members of the Voices of September 11th organization, who have been able to channel grief into activism.

I am honored indeed to be here with all of you, and I thank you so much, Mary, and I thank each and every one of you who have been part of what Voices of September 11th has meant to families and also to our nation. I had the privilege this morning of spending about an hour and a half down by the memorial and meeting with and talking to and listening to a lot of the families who were seeing it for the first time.

Like many of them, I had resisted going before it was complete, because I didn't want to see something still in process; I wanted to see it finished. And like many of them, I had looked at the pictures of the plans and I couldn't quite envision what it would look like. And I came away this morning so grateful, because the memorial provides a place for people to come to reflect, to remember, to be close to their loved one. And so many this morning said to me that it was an enormous comfort.

I am convinced that many of the actions, the reforms, the changes that we have taken in our country in the last 10 years are due, in large measure, to the Voices of September 11th families. And many of you turned your grief into a commitment on behalf of those you lost and on behalf of the nation that mourned with you.

I know Mary had an idea in her mind that she wanted to be active after losing her 24-year-old son Brad. But as she just confessed, I don't think she fully grasped what that would mean. People rank what they're most afraid of, and even today at the top of the list public speaking is the number one fear. And there was Mary and Beverly and others who were stepping forward who had never given a thought to being on a public stage speaking to hundreds, even thousands, of their fellow citizens.

Delivered September 11, 2011, in New York, New York, by Secretary of State Hillary Rodham Clinton.

But in this case, it was absolutely essential, and I thank you for being willing to do that, Mary. And we all grieve Beverly's loss, who started this organization with you.

I remember Mary telling me in those early meetings that she wanted to ensure that nobody else had to walk in her shoes. And family members began asking the questions about what happened and why. And when the Voices of September 11th was founded, you carried through with your questions by being the catalyst behind the creation of the 9/11 Commission. It was family members who began poring over the details of skyscraper security, radio interoperability, government reform. And you didn't take no for an answer, and for that, again, I am grateful.

Some of you had a time when you had to ask yourself why, what, and who, me. Somebody else needs to do this, you perhaps thought. Somebody else needs to take the leadership in trying to get the answers. And you looked around and realized that, really, it had to be you. Those of us who were in public service at the time stood ready to help, but I am convinced that we would not have succeeded without your perseverance and your persistence.

As a senator, I was proud to bring your cause to Congress, to represent victims and families. And the work is not finished. There are still specific tasks coming out even 10 years later. The continuing need for medical care for those who were on the pile—they still need our support. As the members of the 9/11 Commission just made clear recently, many of their recommendations still need to be enacted.

As we commemorate the opening of the memorial, we know that we still have work to do to bring all those who were part of attacking us to justice. But I can tell you it was a particular satisfaction for me, as a former senator of New York, to be in the team in the Obama Administration that made sure bin Laden was brought to justice. (Applause.)

As I have said and as President Obama has said, we will not rest until all those who were part of planning and facilitating the attacks are similarly brought to justice. We are capturing and killing terrorists. We are disrupting cells and conspiracies. And as the 9/11 Commission asked us to, we are breaking down the bureaucratic silos inside the Executive Branch and working across the whole of government.

We do have to recognize that we are engaged in a long-term struggle to face down and defeat the murderous ideology that continues to incite violence around the world. And while we will never give up our right to use military force as needed, we have to use every tool in our arsenal.

I gave a speech Friday at John Jay College outlining the many efforts that we are undertaking. I can tell you that the State Department and the United States Agency for International Development that are under my authority are working to blunt the drivers of extremism. We are putting a decade's worth of lessons to work to launch targeted efforts to undermine terrorist recruitment. We are working along with a coalition of other nations to choke off the illicit financing networks that pay for terrorist training camps, the propaganda and the operations. We are building the capacity of other nations to deal with terrorist threats that they face before they challenge the people of those countries or us. We are training thousands of police and anti-terrorism officials across the globe, and we are creating new forums for

nations to deepen our counterterrorism cooperation.

Our diplomats are out in the
field and in cyberspace exposing al-
Qaida's hypocrisy and brutality, and
the enormous toll it has inflicted,
above all, on Muslims. Even though
the United States, thankfully, has
not experienced another attack
since 9/11, London has, Madrid
has, Mumbai has, Islamabad has,
Jakarta, Bali—other places continue

> *Our struggle against terror-ism is rooted in our strengths as a society, and one of those strengths is resilience. Resilience has been a theme of this organization. How does one nurture it? How does one create it where it is absent?*

to be attacked. And we want to make sure that every person understands that these
violent extremists are not representing any religion. They are representing evil and
nihilism, and they need to be stopped by all people.

We don't just want to capture and kill terrorist leaders. We want to make them
irrelevant. We want to prevent them from attracting new recruits. We want to end
the attraction they have for young people.

Now, we're making progress, but this weekend's threats are one more reminder
that we still face danger and we have to stay vigilant. We have to keep our eye on
what we are fighting against, but we also have to remember what we are fighting for.
Because our goal, after all, is not merely to defeat our enemies, but to represent the
best of humanity, the values and traditions that are America at our core.

Our struggle against terrorism is rooted in our strengths as a society, and one of
those strengths is resilience. Resilience has been a theme of this organization. How
does one nurture it? How does one create it where it is absent? Think about what
each of you has gone through. Before September 11, 2001, the people in this room
would have been strangers to one another. Now, you are a community—not of your
choosing, but because of the circumstance of your loss.

But that community has reached out to now 13,000 families. That community
has a website which, as Mary just told me, has millions and millions of hits. Because it is, of course, first and foremost, about our particular loss in New York, in
Washington, and in Pennsylvania. But resilience is sought after by people far from
New York who are wondering what they too can do to survive a tragedy, to channel
their grief, to be part of a new community.

I don't need to tell you what a difficult decade America has had or list for you
the challenges we face. But I will say this: America's strength and leadership in the
world is more important today than it has ever been. This country is called to greatness. We are charged to be a force for good. And we must summon that spirit, those
feelings we all had after 9/11.

As one man who lost his wife said, "The way I see it, we're already connected.
People don't see it. A fog that makes you forget we are all connected and knitted together instantly got lifted, and we need to get back to that." I know we can, because
that's who we are.

I look at all of you and those whom I've met and talked with this morning, and I cannot say I even can imagine the long nights—sleepless, tear-filled, sorrowful—that each of you has experienced. But I have also seen the strength and, yes, the resilience. And today, as I met the woman who brought her lawn chair with her so she could sit down in front of her son's name and tell me for the first time she felt close to him, or the family of a fire chief whom I had the privilege of knowing with now 15 grandchildren clustered around his name taking rubbings, or the child who came up to me and said, "I want to show you where my mother is," it was for me an important place to be—not because I'm a Secretary of State or I used to be a senator, but because I'm a mom, because I'm an American.

And what you did was so American. I am honored to represent our country all across the world. I don't know of any other place that has the history and the habits of volunteerism, of coming together, of deciding to go forward, the way we do here in this great country of ours. So let us work together to remind not only our country and the world but ourselves who we are, what we're capable of, what we can accomplish when we're at our best, how we face down terror and violence and choose life, choose the future. And let us not stop working together to make that future worthy of the sacrifice of all those whose names appear on the magnificent memorial we saw today.

Thank you all very much.

About Hillary Rodham Clinton

Hillary Rodham Clinton was raised in the Chicago suburb of Park Ridge. She attended Wellesley College and later Yale Law School, where she became interested in the intersection of children and the law and where she met her future husband, Bill Clinton. She moved to Arkansas and became a successful attorney, as well as an assistant professor at the University of Arkansas School of Law. As first lady of the state of Arkansas for twelve years beginning in 1979, Clinton launched a major campaign to reform Arkansas's education system. In 1992, Clinton became first lady of the United States when Bill Clinton was elected president. In this position Hillary Clinton continued to champion issues related to both children and families. With her 2000 election as senator for the state of New York, she made history, becoming the only first lady to run for and to win public office. During her time in the Senate, Clinton spearheaded efforts to provide greater access to affordable healthcare, and after September 11, 2001, she became a strong advocate for those who lost loved ones or suffered injuries as a result of the attacks. In 2008, Clinton was a leading candidate for the Democratic presidential nomination. Later that year, President Barack Obama nominated Clinton to the position of secretary of state, where she has set records as the most-traveled secretary of state in United States history.

Remarks at the Pentagon on the Tenth Anniversary of 9/11

Vice President Joe Biden

In this speech, delivered at the Pentagon on the tenth anniversary of the terrorist attacks of September 11, 2001, Vice President Joe Biden remembers not just the horror of the terrorist attacks, but the heroism they inspired in ordinary Americans. His message, inspired by the words of his mother, is that tragedy can inspire courage, that there can be a second life born of misfortune and that good can come of a bad situation. He holds that the events of 9/11 have shaped a generation of young Americans, making them warriors who understand sacrifice. For Biden, this 9/11 generation reveals a fundamental American instinct to rise up and face every challenge with courage.

Good morning. Mr. Secretary, it's I'm the one who is honored to be given the privilege to speak at such an important memorial ceremony.

Admiral Mullen, Speaker Boehner, members of our armed forces and above all, the family members gathered in front of me who suffered such a grievous loss here 10 years ago today. My wife, Jill, and I want you to know our heart goes out to you.

And those of you who survived that cowardly act, I say it again, I'm the one that's honored to be here with you. To the family members, I know what it's like to receive that call out of the blue, that the dearest thing in your life is gone. I know these memorials—and you've been through many—are bittersweet moments for you because as you sit here right now, unlike a month ago, everything has come back in stark relief. It's not a thought. It's precise. You remember that God-awful empty feeling you remember being sucked into your own chest, that feeling of hollowness. So I want you to know that I personally believe that the courage you're showing today is remarkable. It's hard to come back. You have that sense of overwhelming pride and love and devotion, but also that feeling of "oh, my God."

But I want you to know something else, your physical presence here today gives hope to thousands of Americans who under different circumstances are trying to come to grips with the losses that you had that they're going through. Because when they see—they see you here, you let them know that hope can grow from tragedy, and that there can be a second life.

My mom used to say, Joe, at everything terrible something good will come if you look hard enough for it. In the beginning there's no way to believe that. You're living proof to those people who are still scrambling and looking for that hope that it's possible.

So let me say that our thoughts—Jill's thoughts, mine, the whole nation's thoughts and prayers are with those who also were wounded in this attack last

Delivered September 11, 2011, at the Pentagon, Arlington County, Virginia, by Vice President Joe Biden.

night—wounded in an attack last night in Wardak Province, a stark and vivid reminder this war continues. The courage, determination and the sacrifices of our forces in Afghanistan and around the world is literally astounding. I'll have a little more to say about that in just a moment.

Ladies and gentlemen, milestones are especially—and especially those that are tragic—compel us to reflect and to remember, to honor and, with God's help, to heal because that's what this is ultimately about.

And so today, above all else, we recall 148 [sic] lives cut short on this site 10 years ago this morning—lives that touched every aspect of our national endeavor: a Marine who lost his leg, and nearly his life, in Vietnam but who used what he called a "second chance" to become a father of five; a three-year-old passenger aboard that fateful flight, who held her stuffed "lambie" each night, as her parents read her bedtime stories; the secretary who worked for American Airlines for 45 years, whose colleagues considered her a second mother, and who dressed as Mrs. Claus each Christmas; the Navy physicist, whose wife said after his death: "He was a wonderful dancer. I'll never be able to dance with anybody else. He was a perfect partner. And above all, he was a good, caring and loving man."

And so, so many others are remembered this morning with the moments of silence in small towns and bustling cities all across this country. But nowhere are the memories more immediate, more vivid, more compelling, more real than in New York City; Shanksville, Pennsylvania and right here in Northern Virginia at the Pentagon.

Although words cannot ease the pain of these losses—paying tribute by recalling not just the horror of that day but the heroism as well can hopefully give you some comfort and stiffen the resolve of this nation.

At 9:36 a.m., thousands of patriotic Americans were going about their daily business in the building behind me, in this great citadel of our national defense. And one minute later, 9:37 a.m., an unconscionable tragedy struck.

But what happened—what happened after that was far more remarkable than the damage inflicted in the building behind me. Those who worked in this building, many of you in front of me, and thousands more first responders across the region —firefighters from Arlington County, Fairfax County, Montgomery County, the District of Columbia and many others, they sprang to action, risking their lives so their friends, their colleagues and total strangers, people they had never met, might live.

From corporals to cafeteria workers, right up the chain of the command to the top brass, to Secretary Rumsfeld, who I pay special tribute today; I understand he is here. Secretary Rumsfeld himself did what he did as a young soldier, a young man, and did all his life—you and he and others streamed into that breach between the 4th and 5th corridors, where the devastation was the greatest, where death came in an instant, but also where there were survivors to be found.

Specialist Beau Doboszenski was a tour guide that morning, on the far side of the building—so far away, in fact, he never heard the plane hit. But he shortly felt the commotion. He could have gone home—no one would have blamed him. But he was also a trained EMT and came from a family of firefighters. So when people started streaming out of the building and screaming, he sprinted toward the crash site. For hours, he altered between treating his co-workers and dashing into the inferno with a team of six men.

Micky Fyock, a volunteer fire chief in Woodsboro, Maryland, 60 miles away, after working all day, when he heard that evening that the rescue workers at the Pentagon needed a fire truck—a small fire truck, small enough to fit through tight places, he knew he had a '54 Mack, which was the smallest one around. So fresh off an all-day shift, he barreled down the highway and battled the blaze all night with thousands of others.

And at dawn, exhausted and covered with soot—with soot, 14 hours on the job, he sat on a bench and confronted [sic] a man—a man who he said was wondering aloud, why am I still alive for had I not been at the dentist, I would have been in the office, my office, totally destroyed, with my colleagues gone. Why me?

It's a basic American instinct to respond to crises when help is needed, to confront [sic] the afflicted. An American instinct summoned by the collective strength of the American people that we see come to the fore in our darkest hours, an instinct that echoes through the ages—from Pearl Harbor, to Beirut; from Mogadishu to Ground Zero; Flight 93 to right here in the Pentagon.

Those in this building that day knew what they were witnesses. It was a declaration of war by stateless actors—bent on changing our way of life—who believed that these horrible acts of terror—these horrible acts of terror directed against innocents could buckle our knees, could bend our will, could begin to break us and break our resolve.

But they did not know us. Instead, that same American instinct that sent all of you into the breach between the 4th and 5th corridors, galvanized an entire new generation of patriots—the 9/11 Generation.

Many of them were just kids on that bright September morning. But like their grandparents on December 7, 1941, they courageously bore the burden that history had placed on their shoulders.

And as they came of age, they showed up—they showed up to fight for their country, and they're still showing up. Two million, eight hundred thousand of that 9/11 Generation moved to join our military since the attacks on 9/11, to finish the war begun here that day.

And they joined—they joined knowing that they were in all likelihood going to be deployed in harm's way—and in many cases deployed multiple, multiple times in Afghanistan and Iraq and other dangerous parts of the world.

Those of you, Admiral, who command this building turned this generation, this 9/11 Generation into the finest group of warriors the world has ever known.

Over a decade at war, they pioneered new tactics, mastered new languages, developed and employed advanced new technologies. They took on responsibilities once reserved only for those with considerably more seniority—responsibilities that extended beyond the base or the battlefield to the politics of Afghanistan, to the politics of Iraq, to the economies of those countries, and to the development tasks that ultimately will lay the groundwork for us to leave behind stable countries that will not threaten us.

> *The true legacy of 9/11 is that our spirit is mightier, the bonds that unite us are thicker, and the resolve is firmer than the million tons of limestone and concrete that make up that great edifice behind me.*

And along with the intelligence community and the law enforcement community, they relentlessly took the fight to al Qaeda and its affiliates. They were prepared to follow bin Laden to the hell's gate if necessary. And they got him.

My God do we owe those special ops folks and intelligence guys who got him, many of whom have subsequently lost their lives. But we will not stop—you will not stop—until al Qaeda is not only disrupted, but completely dismantled and ultimately destroyed.

And one more thing about this 9/11 generation of warriors—never before in our history has America asked so much, over such a sustained period, of an all-volunteer force. So I can say without fear of contradiction, or being accused of exaggeration, the 9/11 Generation ranks among the greatest our nation has ever produced. And it was born—it was born—it was born right here on 9/11. (Applause.)

And as the Admiral said, that generation has paid an incredible price—4,478 fallen angels in Iraq and 1,648 in Afghanistan, and more than 40,000 wounded in both countries, some who will require care and support the rest of their lives.

Having visited them multiple times like many of you, I am awed not only by their capability, but their sacrifice today and every day.

The terrorists who attacked the Pentagon, as Leon said, sought to weaken America by shattering this defining symbol of our military might and prowess. But they failed. And they also failed for another reason, not just physically failed. They failed because they continue to fundamentally misunderstand us, as they misunderstood us on that day. For the true source of American power does not lie within that building because as Americans, we draw our strength from the rich tapestry of our people—just looking at the people before me, looking at the families before me.

The true legacy of 9/11 is that our spirit is mightier, the bonds that unite us are thicker, and the resolve is firmer than the million tons of limestone and concrete that make up that great edifice behind me.

Al Qaeda and bin Laden never imagined that the 3,000 people who lost their lives that day would inspire 3 million to put on the uniform and harden the resolve of 300 million Americans. They never imagined the sleeping giant they were about to awaken.

They never imagined these things because they did not understand what enables us, what has always enabled us to withstand any test that comes our way. But you understood. You knew better than anyone because you knew every time this nation has been attacked—you particularly who wear the uniform—every time this nation is attacked, you knew it only emboldens us to stand up and to strike back.

But you family members, you also knew something else that a lot of us didn't know that day, that your loved ones, those who you lost, who we now call heroes, were already heroes. They were already heroes to you.

They were the father that tucked you in at night. They were the wife who knew your fears before even before you expressed them. They were the brother who lifted you up. They were the daughter who made you laugh, and the son who made you proud. I know. I know in my heart, so do all of the people on this stage know, that they are absolutely irreplaceable—absolutely irreplaceable.

As the Speaker heard me say yesterday in Shanksville, Pennsylvania, no memorial, no ceremony, no words will ever fill the void left in your hearts by their loss. My prayer for you is that, 10 years later, when you think of them—10 years later when you think of them that it brings a smile to your lips before it brings a tear to your eye.

My mom used to say that courage lies in every man's heart, and her expectation was that one day—one day it would be summoned. Well, here, on September 11, 2001, at exactly 9:37 a.m., it was summoned. It was summoned from the hearts of the thousands of people who worked here to save hundreds. It was summoned in the hearts of all those first responders who answered the call. For courage lies deepest in and beats the loudest in the heart of Americans. Don't forget it. We will not forget them.

May God bless you all. May God bless America. And most of all, may God protect our Troops.

About Vice President Joe Biden

Joseph Robinette Biden was born in 1942 in Pennsylvania, and moved with his family to Delaware at the age of ten. He graduated from the University of Delaware and Syracuse Law School before being elected to New Castle County Council in 1970. At age twenty-nine, he was elected to the Senate to represent the state of Delaware, becoming the country's sixth youngest senator in United States history. He served as senator for thirty-six years and as chair or ranking member of the Senate Judiciary Committee for seventeen years, recognized for his pivotal work on criminal justice issues, including the passage of the Violence Against Women Act. In 2008, Barack Obama selected Joe Biden as his vice presidential running mate and, early the next year, he became vice president of the United States.

My Personal Jihad

Defending Islam after 9/11

Maham Khan

In this speech, given at William Rainey Harper College in commemoration of the tenth anniversary of September 11, 2001, alumnus and former president of the Muslim Student Association on campus, Maham Khan reflects on the Muslim American experience since the 9/11 attacks. Acknowledging that many misconceptions about Islam still exist, Khan attempts to redefine the way Americans understand the term jihad. *Instead of something controversial or inflammatory, Khan holds that a jihad can be almost any personal struggle or crusade. In this light, she explains that the United States is involved in a constant jihad to protect the freedom and rights of its people.*

Good Afternoon, Asalamo-Walaikum: Peace be unto you.

When Harper asked me to speak a few months ago, my first thought was: do we really still need to talk about Islam on 9/11's anniversary? I thought, Americans get it; they know they can't blame an entire religion for the actions of a few mad men. And yet, the answer to my question became clear when I chose a title for my speech. I had wanted to call it 10 Years and Counting: My Jihad against Ignorance. But this title was met with concern by a few involved parties. They felt it was "insensitive," so they changed it. I understood where they were coming from, but that's also when I realized we still have a lot to talk about—and a lot to understand about Islam and about jihad.

Merriam-Webster.com defines jihad:

1. A holy war waged on behalf of Islam as a religious duty; also: a personal struggle in devotion to Islam especially involving spiritual discipline. 2. A crusade for a principle or belief

Perhaps I should have used the word *crusade* instead. Might have been less, well, insensitive.

But for the record, I wasn't trying to be insensitive or controversial—especially not today. I merely wanted to point out the full context of the word *jihad*. You see, for the last 10 years, I and millions of other Muslims have been fighting the actual jihad that Islam prescribes for the modern day we live in. It's the jihad of self-improvement through the actions I take to better my community. It's a jihad against misconceptions and hatred and injustice. It's jihad against the adulteration of my beautiful faith. Every time I stand up here to reiterate that Islam does not condone

---

Delivered September 10, 2011, at William Rainey Harper College, Palatine, Illinois, by Maham Khan. Reprinted with permission from Maham Khan.

murder, destruction or suicide—I am a jihadist. And I'm fighting with my heart, words and actions standing before you today. Just like Merriam-Webster says, it is my religious duty as a Muslim to defend my faith. And it's my duty to defend it, most importantly, against the perpetrators who attacked my faith—indeed, every faith—and my country on 9/11/2001.

It's a day none of us will ever forget.

Strangely, I remember almost everything leading up to the towers crashing. The day was absolutely beautiful, sunny with clear skies. I wore a red shirt and black pants. I had a bagel and cream cheese while driving because I was running late for my 9:20 public speaking class, right here at Harper. I ran up the stairs of Building L thinking of an excuse, because I knew my teacher would ask why I was late before marking me down a letter grade. But when I reached my classroom, everyone was crammed into the corner around the TV, fixated on the images we all wish we could forget. Then the hallways filled with confusion and fear. Campus security officers worked their way through the hallways informing us that there was a bomb threat. Then in an eerie, silent chaos we all rushed to go home to our families.

In the weeks following 9/11, once it became clear that the villains in this story had an identity defined solely by the same religion as mine, I knew my life was going to change—and not necessarily for the better. I had a feeling that now people, including myself, would want to know everything about Islam. I was right.

> *But despite this I am optimistic about the future, because I have so much faith in the American people. I love this country—because this country gives me the freedom to be who I am: a proud Muslim American. This country fights for my freedoms. This country is fighting a constant jihad to better the lives of its people.*

My friends and I brought the Muslim Student Association on campus back to life (which had been in hibernation for some time). Every Thursday we held an hour-long meeting and open discussion. Almost every week, dozens of non-Muslims showed up. They wanted to know what was the meaning of all this? What role did Islam play?

As we clarified Islam's stance, I realized how lucky we were to be in an environment that was conducive to learning and discussion. My time at Harper College was truly enlightening because I learned a lot about the nature of people in the wake of tragedy. I saw the power of compassion and cooperation rise above the destruction that happened on 9/11.

Even so, the last decade has been filled with incidents of "Islamaphobia," citywide Quran burnings, and misleading debates over the so-called Ground Zero Mosque. And when I hear and see these things, I think: they're winning. The bad guys are winning. Because this is exactly what they want to happen. They want Americans to be divided, fighting against each other and against their Muslim countrymen and -women, so that they can undermine our ideals of freedom and equality for all.

I am also hurt and disappointed with the conditions of the world around us. It's disappointing that while Facebook and Twitter have reminded us that the world is really very small, a great disconnect between the East and the West still remains. It hurts to see legally proven innocent Muslims—fathers and sons—come out of Guantanamo Bay after being tortured for years. And it hurts even more when people continue to die in the name of Islam or jihad. Ten years after 9/11, it's safe to say it's not easy being Muslim anywhere in the world today.

But despite this I am optimistic about the future, because I have so much faith in the American people. I love this country—because this country gives me the freedom to be who I am: a proud Muslim American. This country fights for my freedoms. This country is fighting a constant jihad to better the lives of its people.

Ten years from today, I hope and pray that on 9/11's 20th anniversary, we will look back and be relieved, celebrating a world without fear of terror. We will look back and be proud of how far we have come—how truly united we stand.

I believe that is the best way to honor all the lives that were lost on September 11th.

Thank you.

About Maham Khan

In 2001, Maham Khan was in her first year at William Rainey Harper College in Palatine, Illinois. In the aftermath of the terrorist attacks of September 11, 2001, Khan and other Muslim American students on campus rejuvenated the Muslim Student Association in an effort to educate fellow students about Islam. She served as president of this association for the remainder of her college years. Khan currently works in public radio as a production assistant for WBEZ 91.5 Chicago.

The Great American Spirit

Secretary of Defense Leon E. Panetta

In his speech presented at the 9/11 Tenth Anniversary Summit in Washington, DC, Secretary of Defense Leon E. Panetta shares his own memories of the 9/11 attacks and celebrates the strength of the American spirit he witnessed in the aftermath of the tragedy. Panetta holds that, as a nation, America is at its best when it responds to crisis. It is in these difficult times, he suggests, that the heart and soul of the American character is revealed. Thus, though we must honor and remember the victims of 9/11, we must also celebrate the great American spirit of endless determination and selflessness.

Thank you very much. Thank you for the kind introduction. Thank you for the opportunity to be able to speak to you this evening at this 9/11 10th anniversary summit. This is obviously a busy night, between 9/11 events, the president's speech and the opening of the NFL season.

I know that, you know, you've been fed, you're going to get your dessert. I really urge you to please continue to enjoy your meal. As an Italian, I'm used to speaking to people while they eat, so please continue to enjoy your meal.

This gathering includes a lot of friends and individuals that I've worked with and it includes the lives of people who have forever been impacted by the attack on 9/11. And it also includes those who played a very key role in demonstrating our nation's determination to recover, to respond and to make certain that the kind of violence, the kind of vicious attack that we experienced on 9/11 would never happen again.

In particular, I'd like to recognize my good friend Congressman Lee Hamilton and Governor Tom Kean and the others in attendance who were part of the 9/11 commission for the great work that they have done.

We also have with us 9/11 family members whose courage and determination to honor the victims of the attacks moved this country and showed the world the strength of the American character.

And finally, we have my Canadian counterpart, Minister of National Defense Peter MacKay, and representatives from the community of Gander, Newfoundland, a town, as all of us know, that provided comfort and welcome to over 6,000 passengers and crew members from diverted trans-Atlantic flights that were not allowed to enter the U.S. airspace. Canada is a true neighbor in every sense of the word, and particularly after that event.

So many individuals and organizations, I know, have played a role in putting together this event, including the Voices of September 11th and the Community and Regional Resilience Institute. But it gives me particular pleasure to see the Center for National Policy play a role here. I had the honor of serving as chair of the center from 2000 to 2002 and continued as the national advisory board chair until I re-entered the government in—whenever the hell it was. Seems like I've never left. Another organization with which I have long-standing ties that I know also played a role here is the Meridian Institute, and I want to thank them for their role in helping to build and develop this program as well.

As you know, today's summit focused on remembrance, renewal and resilience, and these are timeless themes in America and in American history. We have overcome wars, we've overcome disasters, we've overcome economic depressions, recessions, we've overcome crises of every kind, because of the fundamental American spirit that never, never gives up.

As the nation comes together this weekend to mark the 10th anniversary of the September 11th attacks, in commemorations large and small, we will remember the victims and their families.

But we will also celebrate the great American spirit that we have shown the world throughout history, from the beginnings of this country, from establishing this great nation, to our determined response to the worst terrorist attack in our history.

As we approach this 10th anniversary, all of us here tonight can recall that horrible moment when the tragedy struck. Let me share with you my own memories that are seared into my heart and into my mind. I was in Washington, here in this town. Although I wasn't in government at the time, I had come back to Washington to brief members of Congress at the Capitol on oceans issues. I was chairman of an oceans commission, and we were briefing them on some of the findings of our commission. A fellow member of mine on the commission leaned over to me and said that she had just received a message from her New York office that the trade towers had been attacked by terrorists. I shared that with the members of Congress at that moment.

All of them obviously shared the shock that we all felt from the news, and there was kind of a spontaneous decision that we should all leave the Capitol. And we did. The members left, and I got into a car and was driving away when I heard that another plane had gone into the Pentagon.

Like the rest of the country, I would learn later that it was likely that the terrorists onboard Flight 93 had intended to hit the Capitol building as well. But the heroic passengers onboard that fateful flight above Pennsylvania rose up and took out the terrorists, sacrificing their lives in order to preserve that great symbol of our democracy.

Like thousands of others, I was stuck here in Washington for a number of days. But finally I was able to rent a car and drive across the country to try to get back to California. It was a drive I will never forget, not only because I made it back in record time, but more importantly because of what I witnessed across this nation as I was driving back to California. Communities throughout the heartland of America had come together, were posting signs on storefronts, in front of motels: "God bless America." They were raising flags. They were gathering in churches. They were holding hands. You could sense that great spirit of America reacting to the tragedy that had happened.

And out of that terrible tragedy, I suddenly recalled the statement that Admiral Yamamoto made following the attack on Pearl Harbor, when he looked at his subordinates and said that "I fear we have awakened a sleeping giant." 9/11 awoke a sleeping giant.

And we will forever—forever—remember that defining moment of American history. Al-Qaida killed nearly 3,000 victims—victims who were innocent men, women and children who were going about their daily lives. They perished because of a hatred that was aimed squarely at the values that this nation stands for: liberty, tolerance, equality, fairness.

> *September 11th reminds all of us that this country is always at its best when it responds to crisis, because it is truly in the inherent spirit of the American people to pull together, to fight for our values, to protect what is dear to all of us.*

But out of that tragedy our nation drew tremendous inspiration, a resolve and determination to honor the victims, uphold our values and defend our country so that no such attack would ever happen again. We showed the world what the American character is all about, and we answered the enemy by acting justly and decisively in pursuing threats to our people, to our freedom and to our nation.

September 11th reminds all of us that this country is always at its best when it responds to crisis, because it is truly in the inherent spirit of the American people to pull together, to fight for our values, to protect what is dear to all of us. And in the immediate aftermath of 9/11, Americans were compelled to serve their fellow citizens and communities. Millions stepped forward to commit themselves to the hard work of keeping America safe. Thanks to the extraordinary efforts of the first responders, of law enforcement, the intelligence community, diplomats, men and women of our armed forces, our country has been kept free, safe and secure.

It's been a great honor to lead many of these dedicated individuals on the vital mission of protecting our country, first as director of the CIA and now as secretary of defense. The proudest experience of my life—40 years that I've spent here in Washington—the proudest experience of my life was working on the operation that finally brought bin Laden to justice. (Applause.) Thank you. Thank you.

Our military and intelligence officials spent years relentlessly trying to pursue al-Qaida's leadership. And even though most of the trails to bin Laden had run into dead ends, they continued, and continued and continued to pursue every possible lead.

We finally got a breakthrough last summer when they were able to identify and track a courier that had worked for bin Laden to the compound in Abbottabad. And after months of additional surveillance and painstaking work, we were never able to positively identify that bin Laden was in fact located in that compound, but we knew that we had the best evidence on his location since Tora Bora.

To be sure, there were huge risks that were involved in this operation. We were going 150 miles into Pakistan. What if the operation was discovered? What if a helicopter went down? What if there was a firefight on the scene? What if there was no bin Laden?

But for all of the risks, this was the one chance to get the worst terrorist in our history. I have to say that in the face of all those risks, the president of the United States made perhaps the toughest and most courageous decision that I've seen a president make, which is to proceed with that operation. And that faith in many ways was born out of the extraordinary displays of military skill and precision that we have seen throughout our nation's history—the skill of our intelligence officers, the skill of our servicemen that were involved in that operation.

And the end result was certainly the greatest achievement that we have been able to obtain in our war against al-Qaida. But having been in Washington on 9/11, and then having been in the operations room at the CIA when the bin Laden mission was completed, in many ways I felt I had gone full circle and so had the country. From a very tragic event, this country made a powerful and dramatic statement that we would spare no effort to protect our own and that no one attacks America and gets away with it.

Ten years after 9/11, we are a safer and stronger nation. We have shown the world our resilience, our nation's never-ending capacity to renew itself, to confront crisis and to confront challenges head-on. The terrorists badly misjudged us. They thought they could weaken America, and instead they strengthened America. Our enduring values, our enduring principles remain stronger than ever in the face of their hateful ideology.

Al-Qaida is facing unprecedented pressure. But make no mistake—please make no mistake: They remain a real threat. And the hard work of protecting America must go on. We must keep the pressure on. We must be vigilant. And we must keep up the fight.

Earlier this week I had the opportunity to visit the memorial at New York—at the World Trade Center in New York City. I can't tell you what a moving experience it was to see that extraordinary monument. But it was all the more special because I was accompanied by five service members who volunteered to serve this country in the aftermath of 9/11. And like millions of others, they chose to put their lives on the line in order to protect their fellow citizens.

These men and women represent the true strength of this nation. As secretary of defense, I see a lot of weapons of all kinds—planes, tanks, helicopters, ships, carriers, destroyers—weapons of all kinds, but the most important weapon we have is the men and women who are willing to put their lives on the line to serve this country. That is at the core strength of what this nation is all about.

The virtues of service, the virtues of sacrifice, of selflessness to a cause are greater than oneself. They are at the heart and soul of the United States of America. And as we honor the victims of 9/11, we must honor those who have taken on the burden of defending our nation—our troops, our military families and our veterans. They fight for the American dream, the dream that brought my immigrant parents to this country, the dream that my parents sought of making sure their children had a better life, the dream that drove our American forefathers, and it's the dream that all of us have to make sure that our children have a safer and better life in the future.

For all those reasons, may God bless all of those heroes, may God bless the values that we honor this evening, and may God bless the American spirit.

Thank you very much.

About Leon E. Panetta

Leon E. Panetta was born in 1938 in Monterey, California. He studied at the University of Santa Clara, where he received a bachelor's degree in political science before earning his law degree at the Santa Clara Law School. After serving in the United States Army from 1964 to 1966, Panetta was elected to the House of Representatives in 1977, where he represented the Sixteenth Congressional District of California for sixteen years. In 1994, President Bill Clinton appointed Panetta the White House chief of staff. From 2009 to 2011, Panetta served as director of the Central Intelligence Agency, during which time he oversaw the US military operation that led to the killing of Osama bin Laden. In 2011, Panetta was appointed the secretary of defense under President Obama. Panetta founded the Panetta Institute for Public Policy at California State University, Monterey Bay, with his wife in 1998; the two serve as codirectors.

Tenth Anniversary of 9/11

Senator Jeanne Shaheen

In her speech on the Senate floor just days before the tenth anniversary of September 11, 2001, New Hampshire Senator Jeanne Shaheen reflects on the legacy of the attacks and what that legacy reveals about the American spirit. While paying tribute to the memory of the victims lost, Shaheen claims that grief is not the only thing born of the 9/11 tragedy. For Shaheen, the story of 9/11 is not just about loss, but about how America responded as a nation in the face of incredible adversity. She holds that ultimately, 9/11 brought out the best in America, allowing its citizens to rise above politics and emerge united together as one. So when remembering 9/11, we must not merely hold on to the haunting image of the collapsing Trade Towers, but also the courage, resolve, and unity that 9/11 brought out in the American people.

Madam President, as you know so well as the Senator from New York, across the country this weekend Americans everywhere will gather to commemorate the 10th anniversary of the tragic events that took place on September 11, 2001. Families from every town, from every city and State will mark this day in their own solemn way and take a moment to remember and honor the nearly 3,000 victims of those senseless attacks. More than any episode in recent American history, the events of 9/11 were experienced on a very personal level all across this country.

No one was untouched by the tragedy of that day. All of us can remember exactly where we were when we heard the news. We remember those frantic hours as we tried to call loved ones. We remember the silence in our skies as our Nation's entire air system shut down. We remember mourning the loss of family, friends, and neighbors; and we remember the fear and uncertainty as we wondered if more attacks were coming.

We remember the sight we all watched on television, again and again—the sickening sight of the falling towers of the Trade Center. It is a vision that has been forever seared into every American's mind.

As Governor of New Hampshire at the time, I was actually in Washington for a National Governors Association event on early childhood education. I will never forget looking out of my hotel and seeing the smoke rising from the Pentagon.

The attacks of 9/11 forever changed us as a nation. Our entire notion of security was turned upside down. Our government changed, our policies changed, and our view of the world changed. For our children and grandchildren especially, this became one of the defining events of their generation and has left an indelible mark on their world view.

Delivered September 7, 2011, in Washington, DC, by Jeanne Shaheen.

As we gather this weekend, all of us in our own way will take a moment to recall those feelings of sadness and anger and to honor the memories of those we lost. But that loss is not the end of the story, and grief is not the true legacy of 9/11. We are not defined by what happens to us but by how we respond when we are faced with adversity. September 11 did not cripple us as a nation. Instead, it brought out the best in

> *We are not defined by what happens to us but by how we respond when we are faced with adversity. September 11 did not cripple us as a nation. Instead, it brought out the best in all of us.*

all of us. Our story is really how we responded in the face of this attack—with courage, resolve, and unity. In the aftermath of September 11, we showed the world the true meaning of the American spirit.

The story of America's response to 9/11 starts on that very day with accounts of heroism that we could never have imagined. We remember the firefighters and the other first responders climbing up the stairwells of the burning World Trade Center while others fled down, and how they made the ultimate sacrifice for their selflessness. We remember the courageous passengers on United Airlines Flight 93 who took away the terrorists' greatest weapon, fear, by fighting back even though it meant their lives. And who knows how many lives they saved when they stopped that attack.

In the days that followed, all Americans stepped forward in any way they could. Red Cross centers were overwhelmed with volunteer blood donors. Millions of us donated money and offered up prayers. In New Hampshire in the days following the attack I remember joining a crowd of hundreds for a prayer service at St. Paul's Church in Concord. We came together to honor the victims and to comfort each other. The response was incredible. The crowd spilled out into the streets with many waving American flags, holding candles, and singing "God Bless America."

In New Hampshire, our State government and our employees refused to buckle under the terrorist threat. We kept the State working on September 11.

I will not forget the more than 100 fire departments across New Hampshire that called our State fire marshal's office to offer their services for assistance in New York or the countless physicians, rescue workers, and volunteers who made themselves available to help at a moment's notice.

Of course, we cannot tell America's story without telling the story of the men and women in our military who have spent the last decade trying to make sure an attack like this never happens again. Since September 11, more than 5 million men and women have voluntarily joined the Armed Forces to protect America and defend her freedom abroad. More than 6,200 Americans, including 37 troops from New Hampshire, have given the ultimate sacrifice in our Nation's defense. Over 45,000 more have been wounded or injured and returned home with lasting scars. Millions of troops and their families have sustained the toughest, most debilitating tempo of deployments in our Nation's history, often being deployed into war five or six times, enduring constant mental and physical strains in service to our country.

The resolve our troops have demonstrated since 9/11 has yielded a string of successes on an extremely complex battlefield. Our men and women in uniform have done everything that has been asked of them. Osama bin Laden has been brought to justice. Countless other high-level terrorist operatives, including the mastermind of the 9/11 attacks, have been killed or captured, and the organization's bases in Afghanistan and Pakistan remain under constant pressure. Al-Qaida and its extremist affiliates' deadly ideology is being questioned around the globe, and the remnants of al-Qaida's diminishing leadership are disorganized and struggling to reestablish themselves in the face of an aggressive U.S. offensive.

As our current Secretary of Defense, Leon Panetta, has remarked, we are "within reach of strategically defeating al-Qaida."[c] Although we can't be complacent and we must remain steadfast in our pursuit, our military should be honored for the gains our Nation has made against the terrorists who attacked us on September 11.

In New Hampshire our Air National Guard deployed almost immediately after the attacks, and every day since September 11, 2011, they have been providing persistent air refueling coverage for homeland defense and for our command issues in Iraq and Afghanistan.

I will forever remember walking through the New Hampshire airport with the New Hampshire National Guard when flights resumed after 9/11. As we walked through, people everywhere stopped what they were doing to applaud the National Guard for their efforts to keep the people of New Hampshire safe.

In the decade since the attacks, Americans have found new appreciation for the service these citizen soldiers provide, and Americans outside the military have learned they have a role to play too. With the heroes of United Flight 93 as their inspiration, everyday Americans have stopped a number of terrorist plots from succeeding. Passengers and flight personnel stopped the December 2001 bomber, the attempt by shoe bomber Richard Reid, and they stopped the Christmas Day 2009 attempt onboard the Northwest Airlines flight. The attempted Times Square bombing last year, as you remember, was in part averted by an alert New York City street vendor.

Perhaps most importantly, as we remember America's 9/11 story this weekend, we should all reflect often the unity we demonstrated in the face of this terrible attack. On September 11 we were not Republicans or Democrats, Black or White, rich or poor. We were all Americans. The attack focused our attention on our common bonds and on the American ideals we all hold dear. We were determined to prove, despite our differences, that the United States of America would persevere and endure. While we have not always maintained that sense of unity in the years since, our memory of it has inspired us and continually reminded us of what is possible when we reach for the best within ourselves.

When the history books are written and America's 9/11 story is told to the generations to follow, I hope it will tell of how we came together to remind the entire world of what this country stands for and who we are as a people; how after our darkest day we rose up with new determination; how instead of turning inward, we chose to confront the evil that had visited our shores and to fight on; and how we continued to be the beacon of hope, liberty, and opportunity that we have always been to the world.

About Jeanne Shaheen

Born in 1947 in Saint Charles, Missouri, Jeanne Shaheen, née Bowers, earned a bachelor's degree in English from Shippensburg University of Pennsylvania and a master's degree from the University of Mississippi. She taught at schools in Mississippi and then in New Hampshire, where she also owned a small business. She served in the New Hampshire State Senate from 1990 to 1996, and was then governor of New Hampshire from 1997 to 2003. She was elected to the US Senate representing New Hampshire in 2009.

4
Education Today

(Alexis C. Glenn/UPI/Landov)

Secretary of Education Arne Duncan speaks at the SHEEO Higher Education Policy Conference, in Chicago, about ways to address America's fall in international ranking for college graduates to 16th, calling for bipartisan efforts by states and the federal government to increase college enrollment.

Res Non Verba—Deeds, Not Words

US Deputy Secretary of Education Tony Miller

Speaking at the commencement of Fayetteville State University in North Carolina, US Deputy Secretary of Education Tony Miller describes the school as a great example of the success of historically black colleges and universities (HBCUs). Citing his boss Arne Duncan's belief that education is the civil rights issue of our time, Miller urges the new graduates to spread the benefits of a good education to others, if not by pursuing a teaching career, then by tutoring and working to improve the education system.

Thank you, Jermaine—and my thanks to the Student Government Association and to all of the class of 2011 for having me here today.

First things first—let me just say how disappointed Secretary Duncan was that he couldn't make the trip today. But he asked me to convey his praise and pride for the hard work that brought you to this graduation day and earning your degree.

To the esteemed 18 representatives from Fayetteville State's five partner universities in China here today, I am glad you are joining this celebration. Having visited with my counterparts in China, Brazil, India, Australia, and New Zealand, I can personally attest to the commitment countries across the globe are placing on education.

So this is a day to celebrate. In fact, I hear there hasn't been a celebration on campus like this since Fayetteville State beat Winston Salem State in the CIAA tournament!

The truth is I'm delighted to have the opportunity to speak here. I myself am a product of HBCUs—my parents met at Virginia State University and got married there my dad's senior year.

And yes, I saw that *before* Fayetteville State knocked Winston Salem out of the CIAA tournament, the Broncos whupped Virginia State in the first round. . . .

I look forward to speaking at commencements for a reason: They provide an opportunity to do something that we do too little of in the field of education—and that is to celebrate success.

Congratulations to each and every one of you on this moment of passage and great accomplishment. Can every graduate who is the first in their family to graduate from college put their hands up? How about a round of applause for their great achievement?

I want to extend my congratulations to your parents, friends, spouses, and children, and the faculty and staff who not only share in your success but helped bring you to this day. Can we have a round of applause for them, too?

Delivered May 7, 2011, at the Fayetteville State University commencement.

As I thought about what to say today, my mind flashed back to my own graduation. Looking back, two things stand out. First of all, I can't remember a word of what our distinguished commencement speaker said . . . And second, if you had told me on graduation day that I would live in London and Tokyo, and learn Japanese, or that I would end up as the Deputy Secretary of Education, I would have thought you were crazy.

Nothing, absolutely nothing, could have been further from my imagination. But Class of 2011, let me tell you. I had a far more exciting plan when I was in college: I was going to be an industrial engineer.

It didn't take me long to figure out that I didn't really want to be an engineer. I preferred working in technology on the marketing side of the business. So I went to work after graduation at GM-Hughes in their automotive technology branch. I hoped, one day, to be the CEO of GM-Hughes.

After six years I realized I could get to the CEO suite faster by working *with* CEOs, instead of working my way *up* the corporate ladder. I went back to school, got an MBA, and went to work as a management consultant. But that wasn't my final path either. I wanted to run something—or even better, own a company. And so I shifted into being a partner at a private equity firm.

Looking back on graduation day now, I take away a couple of lessons. I tell the story of my career, not because it is unique but rather because the lessons I learned are in many respects universal in the information age.

Most of you will explore multiple jobs and careers after you graduate. And the course of your life is almost sure to take a few unexpected twists and turns—even if you don't end up learning Japanese.

In the global economy, the days of the Organization Man or Organization Woman are over. You will no longer get your degree and then go on to work for just one employer or even in one career.

In the 21st century, it is not just knowledge and subject mastery that are going to count, as important as they are. Your ability to adapt, to be creative, and pursue your passion are, in large measure, going to determine how you fare in the job market and in life.

Employers today are looking not just for strong academic skills but for the ability to analyze and solve problems, write succinctly, and communicate. They are looking for employees who work well in teams and know how to surround themselves with talented colleagues.

All of those traits of critical thinking, entrepreneurship, cross-cultural competence, and team-building are hallmarks of a Fayetteville State education and the re-imagined HBCUs of the 21st century.

In his installation speech as Chancellor, Dr. Anderson's theme was "Future is Our Focus." Pair that with Fayetteville State's official motto, Res Non Verba—which means "Deeds, Not Words"—and you have a potent combination. As you graduate, you will be thinking about the future. And ultimately it is your deeds, not your words, that matter most.

HBCUs were originally created in response to Jim Crow laws to educate African American students shut out of higher education. Virtually all HBCUs, including

Fayetteville State, started out as schools that trained African American teachers. My mother got her degree in education and went on to teach high school.

Contrast that history with Fayetteville State today and the education you acquired here as students. What was once provincial has become panoramic. What was once girdled has become global.

No HBCU in the nation has a footprint in China like Fayetteville State. You have strong dual-degree exchange agreements with five universities in China—as well as with universities in South Africa, Morocco, Poland, Grenada, and France.

Next fall, FSU education students will be taking a course in educational psychology and measurement taught concurrently by video to students at Baotow Teachers College in Inner Mongolia, China. And students from around the world come to see and use FSU's Electron Microprobe—a rare, state-of-the-art microscope.

Your many courses for military members and non-traditional students from Fort Bragg and Pope Air Force Base include the only Bachelor's program in the UNC system in Intelligence Studies, as well as a unique on-base master's degree in social work for active-duty personnel.

FSU's School of Business and Economics is the only HBCU program in the country ranked in the top 200 business schools—and you edged out mighty Wake Forest in the rankings.

As you know, the business school here places a strong emphasis on entrepreneurship. Going head to head with students from 50 other business schools, FSU business students won the top honors at the Venture Challenge Entrepreneurial Conference four of the last six years. And I want to wish good luck to the student team that recently won the regional Students in Free Enterprise Competition. They are headed in a few days to the finals in Minneapolis.

Finally, your teacher preparation program is among the strongest in the state. Nearly 160 members of the class of 2011 are graduating with a degree in education. A large, rigorous study of UNC teacher preparation programs last year found that FSU education graduates were significantly more effective at boosting student achievement in high school science and English than teachers from other institutions.

The Cross Creek Early College High School at FSU is a beautiful on-campus example of educational innovation that blends high school and college and provides an accelerated path to a degree. I believe the 2009 valedictorian of Cross Creek Early College High School is graduating today—only two years after entering FSU.

Now, in a way all of this begs the question on many graduates' minds. Yes, you have an education that helped prepare you to compete in a global economy. You are building those skills of creativity, entrepreneurship, and teamwork that can help you succeed. But the question remains: What are you going to do with a 21st century education now that you have it?

As you pursue your passions, your careers, and build a family in the years ahead, I would like to add one more path to follow.

I hope that every graduate comes to feel an obligation to be involved in some way in transforming education so that the students behind you go to college and earn

> *I hope that every graduate comes to feel an obligation to be involved in some way in transforming education so that the students behind you go to college and earn their degrees too. Take your education and pay it forward. Res Non Verba. Deeds, not words.*

their degrees too. Take your education and pay it forward. Res Non Verba. Deeds, not words.

In the knowledge economy, education, more than ever, is the great equalizer. It is the one force today that can consistently overcome differences in background, culture, and privilege.

But if education is the new game-changer that drives economic growth and combats poverty, we also know that far too many children of color are dropping out of high school and failing to finish college.

Our children, our communities, our country cannot win the race for the future if we let children and youth fall behind at the starting line. That is why Secretary Duncan says that education is the civil rights issue of our generation.

To all the graduates here who are about to embark on careers as teachers, I can't thank you enough. Great teachers are our nation's unsung heroes—and we know that minority students have too few teachers of color.

On the way here, I read up on one of FSU's great teachers, Carole Boston Weatherford. She is an extraordinarily accomplished poet and children's novelist. She has been a best-selling author, and has won both the Caldecott and the North Carolina Award for literature.

But as impressive as her awards and accomplishments were, two things jumped out at me about her story. When she graduated from college, Professor Weatherford wanted to go into public relations. And when she started submitting her poems and short stories for publication, she got a lot more rejection letters than acceptance letters. She changed her career goal. But she never gave up pursuing her passion.

I loved what one of Professor Weatherford's students, senior Mary Ann Hull, told the *Fayetteville Observer* about her professor. Mary Ann Hull said Professor Weatherford's example inspired her to think that she also could write a memoir.

"It's almost like a passion or a vision," Mary Ann said. "[Professor Weatherford gave birth] to something in me. She may never know this, but she did that for me."

Well, Mary Ann, I think your secret is out. Professor Weatherford has heard you. But think of how a great teacher can change the course of a student's life.

Now, I recognize that most of the graduates today are not planning to be teachers. But you can still assist the cause of elevating and transforming education in America. Tutor, coach, join the PTA, run for the school board. Help with fundraising for special initiatives. Put your managerial and financial training to work for a school board, as I had the opportunity to do in Los Angeles.

You have so many great examples of FSU graduates who have elevated education. Ask Carl Person, a proud son of Fayetteville State who worked for 20 years in the U.S. Department of Education. He ultimately administered 15 higher education programs with a billion dollar budget. Today he is NASA's program manager for HBCUs. He helps ensure the participation of underrepresented and underserved populations in NASA's programs.

Ask Jessica Henderson Daniel about giving back. She is now an award-winning professor at Harvard Medical School and a renowned mentor and advocate for women entering the psychology profession.

Ask Superintendent Annette Cluff. She and her husband didn't like the schools available to her preschooler in Houston. So they took $10,000 of their savings and opened their own school. They had 10 students, no business plan—and almost no bankers willing to invest in their school.

Twenty-five years later, Annette Cluff is the superintendent of a publicly-funded charter school district with not one but three campuses and 1,700 students. Last year, one of her schools won the U.S. Department of Education's prestigious Blue Ribbon Award for being one of the highest-performing schools in Texas. Ninety-eight percent of her students qualify for free and reduce-priced lunch.

Do you know what Annette Cluff said when she found out her school had won a Blue Ribbon award? She said, "We will not rest on our laurels. We will continue to provide a quality education at all three of our campuses."

Last, but not least, ask FSU grad Michele Jones. She originally joined the Army because she liked the uniforms. No one else she knew was enlisting. She wanted to be different.

Guess what? Michele Jones turned out to be a trailblazer. She became the highest-ranking African-American female enlistee in any branch of the U.S. military, and the first woman to be a Command Sergeant Major in the U.S. Army Reserve.

Today, she works for First Lady Michelle Obama's Military Families Initiative and the President's Veteran's Employment Initiative. *Ebony* magazine has named her one of the 35 most remarkable women in the world.

When Michele Jones gives a speech, she often points out that "no one gets mentioned in history or has made history because they did something just for themselves. The people who have made the biggest impact on our world did it for everyone else."

So pursue your passions—not just for yourself but for the good of everyone else. Include, not exclude—and your lives will be richer for it.

I congratulate every one of you on your wonderful accomplishment today. Class of 2011, you show deeds, not words.

Today, I hope you celebrate your journey here. Tomorrow—and in the years ahead—I hope you continue that journey as lifelong learners.

Everyone here today is so proud of each and every one of you. We look forward eagerly to the next stage of your journey. Congratulations! And good luck.

About Tony Miller

Serving as the deputy secretary of education since 2009, Anthony "Tony" Miller earned a bachelor's degree from Purdue University and an MBA from the Stanford Graduate

School of Business. He was executive vice president of LRN Corporation, a company that provides consultations and legal services to businesses worldwide, from 2003 to 2006. From 2007 to 2009, he worked as an operating partner for the investment firm Silver Lake Partners. Prior to joining LRN, he worked for ten years as a partner at the management consulting firm McKinsey and Company, and from 1997 until 2000, he served in the Los Angeles Unified School District.

Education Is Essential to a Better Life

Secretary of Defense Leon E. Panetta

Speaking to the Military Child Education Coalition, a Texas-based organization that works to ensure the best education possible for children of servicemen and -women, Secretary of Defense Leon E. Panetta describes how the repeated deployments of military parents to the Middle East takes a toll on their children's education. He stresses the importance of education in society, and especially its importance to the military, linking the quality of a nation's education to the quality of its military.

It is a distinct privilege for me to be able to come down to Texas and to be among so many who share a dedication to helping our military children have a better future, and that's what it's all about.

I feel a special relationship to this group, not just because I'm Secretary of Defense, but because I spent two years in the Army with my family and with my kids and I had the opportunity to see the great work that was done as just a trooper on the lines seeing exactly the services that were provided. And also, I had a sister-in-law who taught at one of the schools that I was at. So I've got a good sense of the dedication that's involved by all of you to try to make sure that our military kids get the best education possible.

I am pleased to be joined by the Chairman of the Joint Chiefs who also will be here, as well as a number of our Service Chiefs and I think that tells you a lot.

Their presence underscores the importance of education to military families and to the ability of our armed forces. And it does relate to this and we shouldn't lose sight of it. What you do relates to our ability to carry out the mission of defending the country.

We are all here—the Chiefs, those involved in military leadership—to say thank you. Thank you on behalf of the Department of Defense. I deeply appreciate all of the work that so many here and around the country are doing to help our military families.

In a democracy, we are dependent on good education. Education is the key to self-government, it's the key to opportunity, it's the key to equality, it's the key to freedom, it's the key to a better life.

As you know, I am the son of Italian immigrants who came to this country like millions of others seeking the opportunity that this country has to offer. They came with little money, few language abilities, few skills.

My son—I've got three sons—my youngest son looked up the manifest for when my parents came through Ellis Island. And my parents are listed and my father's occupation was listed as "peasant." So he had to come to this country to work hard and to be a part of what America has to offer.

I used to ask my father "Why would you do that? Why would you travel all that distance, not knowing where the hell you were going, not having any idea, why would you do that?" And yes, they came from a poor area in Italy. But they also had the comfort of family. Why would you pick up and suddenly leave all of that to travel thousands of miles to come to a strange country? And my father said the reason was that my mother and he thought that they could give their children a better life.

And that's the American dream—that's what all of us want for our children and it's hopefully what they will want for their children because that is the fundamental American dream, giving our kids a better life. It is what we want for our children and for this country.

And helping to give future generations a better quality of life is what goes to the very heart of our military, and what everybody here is doing. That is because giving our children a quality education is essential to giving them a better life.

I've long believed that this country has an obligation to make education a top national priority. I would not be here as Secretary of Defense were it not for the opportunities that were given to me by education. I have a lot to be thankful for—thankful to my parents who basically kicked my ass and said, "You better get a good education," thankful to the nuns that taught me in Catholic grammar school who also incidentally kicked my ass, thankful to a lot of inspiring teachers at the public high

In the military, about 44 percent of all service members are parents. The quality of education available to military children affects our overall readiness, it affects our retention, it affects the very morale of our force.

school that I went to in Monterey, thankful to the Jesuits who taught me at the University of Santa Clara and who taught me that one of the fundamental purposes of education is to help our fellow human beings.

Over the course of my career, because of what education gave to me, I had the opportunity to be able to give back and to help strengthen the national commitment to education. I served as Director of the Office for Civil Rights at the old Department of Health, Education and Welfare, had the opportunity to work on efforts to promote equal education for all, served in Congress and as Budget Chair, worked on education budgets, did that as Director of the Office of Management and Budget, and ultimately as White House Chief of Staff to President Clinton.

After I left government and went back home, my wife and I decided to establish an institute for public policy at California State University at Monterey Bay. It is an institute—and my wife continues to run that institute—dedicated to attracting the best young men and women to lives of public service, and to try to inspire them how important it is to give something back to this country, and to try to give them the tools and the knowledge they need in order to succeed in their careers.

Now, as Secretary of Defense, I am determined to do everything possible to give our military children the tools they need to succeed in the future.

Educating military children is not only important to *their* future, and it is important to their future. But it's also critically important to the future of *our* military and, indeed, to the future of *our* nation.

In the military, about 44 percent of all service members are parents. The quality of education available to military children affects our overall readiness, it affects our retention, it affects the very morale of our force.

Service members consistently rate educational opportunities for their children as one of the most important factors in their career decisions and in deciding whether or not they stay in the military.

In equipping our military children with the best education, the best knowledge, the best skills that they need for the future, the Department is investing in its own future. Many of these young men and women will eventually follow in the tracks of their parents and will join the military themselves. Education is also a national security priority, and for that reason we support efforts by the National Math and Science Initiative to build technical proficiency, and support expanding the instruction of critical foreign languages.

I have often said that when it comes to education there are four R's, not just three—Reading, Writing, Arithmetic, and Reality—the reality of the world, the global world that we live in, in which you damn well ought to have the language capability to understand that world, to understand the cultures we deal with, to understand where they're coming from. Frankly, one of the best things in dealing with the threats we confront is to understand who we're dealing with. And the ability to have language skills is truly important to that effort.

These efforts give young people a leg up in a complex and globalized world, and help develop a cadre of experts—such as engineers and linguists—that will in turn strengthen our force.

The bottom line is that our military is better able to defend the country when we address the long-term educational needs of those who serve and their children.

There are about 1.5 million school-aged military children, and more than 80 percent of them attend public schools in every state. These military-connected students learn a great deal from their parents' work, their parents' ethic, their parents' dedication to duty. Many of them travel the world at a young age, gain a deep appreciation for what public service is all about, and bring all of these traits and all of this wonderful, unique perspective to the classroom.

For these reasons, military children represent an enormous resource, enormous asset for educational communities.

They know better than most that their mom or dad—or both—serve so that the children in this country can have a better life, a more secure life. That is a tremendously powerful and positive message, but it also does not erase the hardships that these young people often must confront.

The past decade of war has placed a heavy burden on those who have served and it has placed a heavy burden on the children as well. Since 2001, more than one million children have had to deal with the emotional stress and the extra responsibilies of having a parent deployed, time and time again, to Iraq, to Afghanistan.

By the time military children finish high school, they will have moved an average of six to nine times, and twice during high school.

Each move, as we all know, means a transition to new friends, to a new school system, and potentially inconsistent academic opportunities and standards. This can pose particular challenges for the estimated 195,000 military children with special needs, as the quality and availability of service varies from school district to school district. It raises even greater challenges for these kids.

And of course, there are those students who have to endure the heartache of a Mom or Dad who never returns from the battlefield, or who returns alive to them but sometimes changed forever by the horror of war.

The toughest part of my job is to write notes to the families that have lost a loved one in battle—more importantly, to write a note to their children. It's tough to find the right words. The only thing I can say is that their loved one loved them, loved life, loved this nation, and gave their life for all they loved. And that makes them a hero forever in this country.

These sacrifices, large and small, take a toll on military children over time.

This hit home for one special operations soldier when he was at home celebrating his daughter's 18th birthday. He asked his daughter, innocently enough, when was the last time he was home for her birthday. She said, "Dad, when I was 10."

Our military families have to deal with many tough moments like that. They have to sacrifice a great deal for this country, and thank God that they're willing to do that. We have the best fighting men and women in the world. But one thing that military parents should never have to sacrifice is the education of their children.

This is why we all need to do more together to ensure that we meet the learning needs of our military families.

The vast majority of our service members rely on local public school systems to meet their children's educational needs, and that means meeting those needs has to be a team effort.

Therefore, the Department continues to work collaboratively with the Department of Education, with states, with local school districts, and with organizations like the Military Child Education Coalition in order to ensure military-connected children receive an outstanding education.

But we cannot deliver on our commitments to these children without the active support, cooperation, and partnership of all stakeholders. I am deeply gratified by the significant progress that has been made over the past several years in deepening the cooperation and helping all military students receive the best possible education. It takes teachers, it takes counselors, it takes parents, it takes community leaders, all of them working together to make this happen.

For example, the Pentagon, together with federal, state, and local officials and administrators, and military family organizations, has developed an Interstate Compact on Educational Opportunity for Military Children.

That compact is designed to alleviate many of the school transition problems that are caused when a military family has to move from place to place, from base to base. It makes sure that transferring students are not disrupted by inconsistent policies in the areas of eligibility, enrollment, placement, and graduation.

That includes everything from immunization records to special education services, to extracurricular participation and course waivers.

Four years ago, 10 states had signed that compact. But as of this month, 43 states have done so, including most of the states with large numbers of military residents. That makes a great difference. I'd like to commend the State governors who signed on to the compact. Together, we must continue to push all states to adopt it, and we must make sure that states and local school systems are fully implementing the provisions.

The Department has also expanded its partnership with local school districts, in an effort to provide stronger support to schools on or near military installations.

The Department of Defense Education Activity Partnership Grant Program supports outreach activities and provides grants that improve academic programs in military-connected school districts. So far, this program has awarded more than 140 three-year grants worth roughly $180 million.

These grants are providing an important infusion of resources to over nine hundred public schools that are serving 400,000 children from military families. This will enhance student learning opportunities, it will provide social and emotional support, and it will provide professional development for educators at military-connected public schools.

We are working to strengthen and to modernize the Department of Defense's own school system, which serves about 86,000 students worldwide.

My goal is to ensure that these schools remain a strong partner in sharing expertise and resources with local school systems around the country.

The Department is also actively working, in partnership with Congress and with local school districts, to improve the facilities of the 161 public schools on military installations. Through the "Public Schools on Military Installations" program, the Department is funding the maintenance, repair and revitalization of public school facilities on bases, while local education agencies match a share of that funding.

To date, Congress has appropriated a total of $500 million with the aim of helping to address the most urgent deficiencies. It's been my experience that if a school is not a proper facility, doesn't have the proper atmosphere, doesn't have the proper supplies and the proper equipment to do a good job, it makes it a hell of a lot tougher to provide a decent education. Today, I am pleased to announce that a total of nearly $60 million in grants have been awarded for 3 schools across the country, including an elementary school at Fort Bliss here in Texas, as well as two schools at Joint Base Lewis-McChord in Washington state to improve their facilities.

We will award additional grants this summer as part of our continuing effort to address capacity or facility condition deficiencies. We're going to do that at an estimated 21 public schools located on military bases.

I want you to know that the Department of Defense has listened. It's not always easy to get that big bureaucracy to listen but we have listened—listened to school districts, listened to organizations, listened to parents—and we will continue to listen to you. We will continue to fight to give our military children the very best educational opportunities.

This is and it must remain a team effort, and I am deeply appreciative to the Military Child Education Coalition, and all of you, for being such important members of this team.

We truly are one family in the military community. We have to be a family and we've got to hold each other's hands because it is extremely important that as a family we take care of our family members. Our men and women fight and sacrifice and die so that their children can have a better life and a better future. And I want to be sure that all of us will fight as well to deliver on that promise for them, the promise for their children, and for this country.

There's a story I often tell that makes the point of the rabbi and the priest who decided they would get to know each other so that they could understand each other's religions. They would go to events together in order to be able to use that opportunity to talk about their religions. So one night they went to a boxing match and just before the bell rang, one of the boxers made the sign of the cross and the rabbi nudged the priest and said, "What does that mean?" The priest said, "It doesn't mean a damn thing if he can't fight." Now ladies and gentlemen, we bless ourselves with the hope that everything is going to be fine in this country. But very frankly, it doesn't mean a damn thing unless we're willing to fight for it.

You, by virtue of your presence here, have made very clear that you are willing to fight—fight to improve the education of our children, fight to help our military families and give them the support they need, fight to make sure our children have that better life, and I guess most importantly fight to make sure that we always protect and strengthen a government by and for the people.

Thank you very much and God bless all of you.

About Leon E. Panetta

Leon Panetta has served as the US secretary of defense since 2011. Born in 1938 in Monterey, California, Panetta earned a bachelor's degree in political science at Santa Clara University and a law degree from the university's law school. After serving in the Army, he entered politics and served as the director of the Office for Civil Rights and as special assistant to the secretary of the Department of Health, Education and Welfare. Beginning in 1976, he served nine terms in Congress, holding several committee chairmanships. Bill Clinton appointed him his chief of staff in 1994, a position he held for three years. In 2009, Barack Obama made him director of the Central Intelligence Agency, where he served for two years until moving to the secretary of defense post.

Remarks of US Secretary of Education Arne Duncan to the State Higher Education Executive Officers' Higher Education Policy Conference

US Secretary of Education Arne Duncan

At a Chicago conference of the State Higher Education Executive Officers, US Secretary of Education Arne Duncan bemoans the country's rank as sixteenth in the world in terms of college attainment rates, and describes improving that status as a vital national mission. After calling on all stakeholders—students, schools, and states—to improve their performance, he presents dispiriting data about state cuts to education funding. He touches on the problem of enormous student loan debt, and cites the Obama administration's efforts toward transparency in this area. He touts the administration's support of higher education, highlighting innovations by some states, finally asserting that he is optimistic about the possibility of the United States reaching number one in college attainment by 2020.

Thanks very much, Rahm, for that generous introduction.

I'm not sure what I've done to deserve such a glowing introduction. But I have a hunch that Rahm will let me know in a few minutes. He said something about wanting to have, quote, "a frank exchange of views."

All kidding aside, it's an honor to have Rahm here. For more than a decade, he has helped lead and pioneer federal, state, and local efforts to boost college access and completion.

And I'm grateful to have the chance once again to speak with the state higher education executive officers. You've taken on a terrific array of cutting-edge topics at this conference. And your steadfast commitment to strengthening America's education system has been exemplary.

As I've said on many occasions, the best ideas for reform in education don't originate in Washington. They come from state and local government. And your leadership has been vital to challenging the educational status quo when it fails to put the interests of students first.

I am going to keep my remarks relatively short to allow time for discussion. I want to talk today about a couple of subjects.

Let me start by providing a preliminary assessment of state progress toward the bipartisan goal of regaining America's place as the nation with the highest college

Delivered Aug. 9, 2012, by US Secretary of Education Arne Duncan to the State Higher Education Executive Officers' Higher Education Policy Conference in Chicago, Illinois.

attainment rate in the world by 2020. Being 16th in the world is simply unacceptable. We are paying an economic price for that low international ranking today.

And then, I want to highlight some troubling trends that are impeding progress toward the 2020 goal.

The common theme or takeaway messages here are really two-fold. Boosting college access and completion is vital to the future economic prosperity and civic vibrancy of your home states. That is why accelerating college attainment is not just a policy and institutional concern for academia; it is really an urgent national mission.

And second, I can't stress enough that this is a national mission with shared responsibility for all stakeholders. As President Obama has said, "There is no better economic policy than one that produces more graduates . . . [And] that's why reforming education is the responsibility of every American—every parent, every teacher, every business leader, every public official, and every student."

The theme of shared responsibility that the President articulated is very much in keeping with SHEEO's recent Open Letter to the President.

Your Open Letter states that "Neither the states, nor the federal government, nor students and their families can reasonably be expected to bear the full burden of maintaining [college access]. All of us will need to make hard choices about priorities among the activities consuming scarce resources within and beyond education."

I couldn't agree more. Students need to do their part by staying on track, by applying for federal, state and campus aid, by taking out loans they can afford, and by striving to earn their degrees and certificates on time.

Colleges must do more to increase access, tighten their belts, employ technology more creatively, and boost completion rates.

And yes, states must do more to prioritize higher education funding. States can also do more to constrain growth in what families pay for college, and incentivize innovation, encourage productivity, and accelerate completion.

I know these tough choices are very much in the forefront of not only your minds today but of almost every Governor in the country.

I have yet to meet a Governor who does not wish to be remembered as the education governor. And I have yet to meet a Governor who did not want America to be first in educational attainment.

State leaders like you understand better than anyone that education is the engine of economic growth and the great equalizer in today's knowledge-based, global economy.

So today we're providing each of you with a snapshot of how your State is doing in meeting the goal of making America number one again in college attainment. And that analysis suggests that our country, and many of your States, face some serious challenges to meeting the 2020 goal.

The data that we are providing today show the current trend in educational attainment in your home state and the increase in educational attainment needed to meet the President's 2020 goal.

The charts for your states also show trends in state funding per full-time student between fiscal 2008 and 2011, recent changes in the average net price at leading public universities, and changes in the median household income.

There is a lot of important data to absorb in this preliminary analysis. I won't go into it all in detail. But I will point out a couple of findings that stand out.

First, the Great Recession clearly hampered most states' efforts to take big steps toward reaching the 2020 goal. Most states will need to substantially accelerate their production of undergraduate degrees during this decade if America is going to have the best-educated, most competitive workforce in the world by 2020.

It's true that the number of people with college degrees is rising. It's just not rising fast enough.

Since the President first announced the 2020 goal in 2009, the nation has made progress in boosting attainment. Over 43 percent of our 25- to 34-year olds have an associate's degree or higher.

That's an increase of two percentage points since 2009. It means an additional 1.3 million adults now have college degrees in America than at the start of the Obama administration.

> *Boosting college access and completion is vital to the future economic prosperity and civic vibrancy of your home states. That is why accelerating college attainment is not just a policy and institutional concern for academia; it is really an urgent national mission.*

That's a good thing, and that's progress—but it's not nearly fast enough. We need that kind of growth each year to meet the 2020 goal.

While money is never the only answer, it's hard to boost completion when so many states are contributing fewer resources to higher education. Even in states that boosted total higher education funding from 2008 to 2011, only a handful increased their funding per student.

SHEEO's data shows that 26 states—just over half—increased their total higher education funding from fiscal 2008 to 2011. But for 2012, 82 percent of states decreased higher education funding. At a time of rising enrollment, reducing funds or just holding the line on funding will cause a downward spiral that will be hard to turn around. Of those states that did not cut funding, SHEEO reported that just four states increased their funding per student between 2008 and 2011.

Some states saw funding decrease by as much as 20 percent per student—even when adding overall funding.

That is not the way to invest in the future—or to dramatically accelerate attainment. Disinvestment is not the strategy other countries are employing—quite the opposite.

As your Open Letter to the president points out, "State support in constant dollars per student was lower in 2011 than it has been in more than 25 years."

The result, as your letter says, is that "financing in higher education is in disarray, since state governments . . . have not funded enrollment growth in public higher education."

Now, it's no secret that states face a brutal budget climate today. It's tremendously tough out there—and I don't for a second minimize those real challenges.

We know this is also a question of priorities—of where state leaders choose to invest. One northeastern state, for example, ran a budget surplus of a billion dollars but still cut higher education funding by more than $20 million. That is not the way to make higher education a priority investment.

It will come as no surprise that public universities and colleges are raising tuition and net price to compensate for state funding cutbacks.

When that happens—at the same time that median household income is stagnant or declining—the middle class gets squeezed. And it gets squeezed hard.

Every capable, hard-working, and responsible student must be able to afford to go to college. That's not a Democratic dream or a Republican one. It's the American Dream.

In America, we don't believe higher education should be a luxury reserved for those who can afford it. "In America," as President Obama says, "no one should go broke because they chose to go to college."

But when you start to ask the average household to spend 25 percent, 30 percent, even 40 percent of their income for college, you start pricing college out of reach for the middle class.

That's not good for the economic vitality of your state, or the country as a whole. And it's going to put hard-working families and students that are doing the right thing at a big disadvantage in a knowledge-based economy.

The long and short of it is that state funding cuts in higher education and tuition increases are jeopardizing our ability to reach the 2020 goal.

But these state-by-state charts and tables suggest one last message as well. Boosting attainment is not just about funding, as vital as it to accelerating college completion. It is also about making smarter use of state dollars.

There is considerable variation among states in making progress toward the 2020 goal. Several states are doing a better job of meeting their 2020 goals, even in a tough economy.

Montana, for example, had one of the biggest increases in college attainment of any State last year. Montana used to lag the nation in attainment. Now, it's above the average.

If it can continue its growth, Montana will comfortably meet its share of the 2020 goal. But it's troubling to see that per-student funding levels are requiring families to pay more to attend state universities in Montana, too.

The picture is similar in other states. Colorado had attainment gains three times the national average. But low investment in higher education, and high prices compared to family income there, could make it harder for students in the future to access and complete college.

At the same time, states that are currently leading the country in college attainment cannot become complacent.

Massachusetts has the highest college attainment rate of any state. But its attainment rate was essentially unchanged from 2009 to 2010. With more than half of its young adults already holding a college degree, Massachusetts does not have as far to go as other States to meet the 2020 goal. But it still has to elevate its attainment rate if our nation is going to meet the 2020 goal.

At the federal level, the administration has undertaken a number of transformational reforms to pursue the 2020 goal.

During the last four years, the federal government has funded the biggest increase in college aid since the days of the GI bill. That investment, made without going back to taxpayers for a nickel, is one of the accomplishments I am most proud of. The number of college students using Pell grants to help them pay for college has increased by more than 50 percent.

In 2008, six million students with Pell grants were enrolled in our nation's colleges and universities. Today, more than 9.6 million students rely on Pell grants to attend college. And just as encouraging, applications from low-income students with family incomes below $10,000 a year, are increasing twice as fast as the overall growth rate in applications.

The best way to break cycles of poverty is to increase access to college.

As you know, from day one, the Administration has also given community colleges unprecedented attention and support. For far too long, community colleges were something of a neglected jewel of America's higher education system.

Our wonderful undersecretary and my partner, Martha Kanter, is the first community college leader to serve as undersecretary. Jill Biden is the first Second Lady in the White House to be a community college professor. Even as Second Lady, she continues to teach English at Northern Virginia Community College.

Together with the US Department of Labor, our department has launched a two billion dollar, competitive fund to help community colleges accelerate completion and develop programs tied to workforce needs.

The Trade Adjustment Assistance community college training initiative seeks to improve student retention and achievement rates. It aims to reduce time to completion. And it dramatically expands online and technology-enabled learning for high-wage, high-skill industries.

I'm proud of that record. But the fact is that the federal government still has a lot more to do, too, to support the 2020 goal. That is why we are looking to do more to incentivize college completion, innovation, and boost quality and productivity in postsecondary education.

Earlier this year, President Obama proposed an unprecedented one billion dollar Race to the Top competition to promote college affordability and completion. This Race to the Top fund would incentivize statewide efforts to improve quality and productivity, while supporting state efforts to keep higher education affordable.

To meet the 2020 goal, colleges and universities must make it easier for parents and students to finance their college education and understand their financial obligations. And meeting that challenge requires greater transparency.

As you know, the Administration has undertaken a series of initiatives to increase transparency and reduce student debt.

I won't review all those initiatives here. But I will say that I've talked with far too many students who have told me that the first time they understood how much student loan debt they had was after the first bill arrived. That is crazy and costly—and totally avoidable.

There are more than 7,000 institutions of higher education in America. Each one has its own financial aid award letter. Some award letters are good. Others are confusing—or even misleading.

But there is absolutely no reason that financial aid award letters should be mysterious. And there is absolutely no reason that prospective students should forego college because they mistakenly think they can't afford it.

That's why our Department has proposed a new easy-to-use Shopping Sheet or model financial aid award letter that would standardize information for parents and students in an easy-to-use form.

I've written every college president in America and encouraged them to adopt the college shopping sheet. Many already have, and I thank them for their leadership. I want to stress that adopting this form is entirely voluntary. But this new, standardized award letter is a tool that institutions can use to hold themselves to a higher standard of transparency—at little or no additional cost.

These initiatives to increase transparency, boost productivity, and encourage innovation and technology-based learning are all especially important because major expansions of federal aid won't continue indefinitely.

Too many folks in Congress think of education as an expense, not as an investment.

I'm also deeply concerned about the potential for sequestration to jeopardize our nation's ability to develop the best educated, skilled workforce in the world by 2020.

If Congress imposes sequestration at the start of 2013, our Department would need to slash spending on contracts to support the processing and origination of student loans. That could cause delays that will hurt students as they make decisions about college. And it could reduce services for borrowers seeking to repay their loans.

Work Study programs would be slashed. So would TRIO—and many other grant programs.

Imposing automatic budget cuts is absolutely the wrong way to make tough budget choices. We're playing "chicken" with the lives of American students.

For all of these reasons, the imperative to develop the best-educated workforce in the world is in jeopardy today. And just as the federal government has to do more to reach the 2020 goal, states and institutions of higher education will need to meet us halfway in doing more to keep college costs down and boost completion.

Despite today's tough budget crunch, I am actually optimistic that states and institutions can take important steps toward meeting the 2020 goal.

I am optimistic because, away from the dysfunction in Washington, states themselves are leading the way in thinking creatively about new ways to promote college completion and affordability.

There are so many statewide examples of new and innovative initiatives now taking hold all across the country.

Missouri has announced a plan to offer $10 million in Innovation Campus Grants to public colleges and universities to develop accelerated, three-year tracks for some undergraduate degrees.

New Jersey has passed legislation that established "credit for prior learning" centers that will certify different types of prior learning as college-credit-worthy, like stable apprenticeship programs or military experience.

In Wisconsin, the University of Wisconsin system is also providing college credit for prior learning experience in the hopes of enrolling more non-traditional adult students.

And in Washington, the State Board for Community and Technical Colleges is in the vanguard of the open educational resources movement.

It launched the Open Course Library late last year. It's a collection of high-quality educational materials for 42 of the state's courses with the highest enrollment. It includes textbooks, syllabi, readings, and assessments—and it costs thirty dollars or less per student. The course materials are available for free online, anywhere in the world.

Other states are taking on the challenges of boosting college and career readiness by reforming and reducing the need for remedial instruction. New legislation in Florida established common placement testing for public postsecondary education. It requires that 12th grade students complete appropriate remedial instruction before graduating from high school.

Virginia's community college system, meanwhile, is redesigning remedial education at all of its 23 colleges. Their goal? To increase the number of community college students who complete a degree by 50 percent. In fact, they are already halfway towards hitting their goal.

Other states, including my home state of Illinois, Arkansas and Michigan, have all instituted performance-based funding schemes that tie funding, in part, to common sense metrics like graduation rates, course completion, and constraining the growth in tuition at public institutions.

These are just some of the examples of states that refuse to throw up their hands in the face of budgets cuts in state funding for higher education.

We know states are being penny-wise and pound-foolish when they cut state funding for higher education. States that continue to disinvest in higher education are not going to reach their 2020 goals, and will have a harder time attracting and retaining industry in their states.

But I am inspired by so many state leaders, who are responding to funding cutbacks by making smarter use of scarce dollars.

As I said at the start of my remarks, the goal of having the best-educated workforce in the world is a shared goal. And it must be a shared responsibility.

Working together, with your commitment and your hard work, I believe we can reach that ambitious goal by the end of the decade. The need to dramatically elevate college attainment is an urgent one—for our students, our families, our communities, and our nation.

Thank you all for your leadership and creativity in these difficult economic times. Please challenge me and my team to be the best partners possible. We strive, together, to lead the country where we need to go.

And now I would love to hear your thoughts about what can be done to regain America's place as the best-educated workforce in the world by 2020.

Thank you.

About Arne Duncan

Born in Chicago on November 6, 1964, Arne Duncan graduated magna cum laude from Harvard University in 1987, having majored in sociology. From 1987 to 1991, Duncan played professional basketball in Australia. In 1992, he became director of the Ariel Education Initiative, a mentorship program for children enrolled in one of Chicago's worst-performing elementary schools. He worked there until 1999, when he became deputy chief of staff for former Chicago Public Schools CEO Paul Vallas. Chicago Mayor Richard M. Daley appointed him CEO of the Chicago Public Schools in 2001. He served in that position until President Barack Obama named him secretary of education in 2009.

Here's to Another Outstanding Twenty-Five Years

Joanne Weiss, chief of staff to
US Secretary of Education Arne Duncan

Speaking at the twenty-fifth anniversary celebration for the National Board for Professional Teaching Standards, Joanne Weiss, chief of staff to US Secretary of Education Arne Duncan, pays tribute to the organization, lauding its success in professionalizing the teaching field. She calls on nationally certified teachers to take on roles of increasing responsibility, and makes a plea for them to bring their expertise to the nation's underperforming schools.

It's an honor to be here, and to be sandwiched between education luminaries like Secretary Riley, Michele Cahill, Governor Wise, and Governor Hunt.

In light of our list of distinguished speakers, I'm going to keep my comments brief. The Secretary is sorry he couldn't be here, but he asked me to make two points. First, he wanted me to give a big shout-out to the National Board for its tremendous accomplishments over the last quarter century. And second, he asked that I talk about some of the challenges—and very real opportunities—that lie ahead.

It is easy to forget now, but when the National Board started 25 years ago, it faced a lot of skeptics. Many educators and analysts thought the board had embarked on "mission impossible."

Your goal of creating professional standards for what teachers should know and be able to do was treated as a well-meaning fantasy. Educators and experts alike questioned whether the Board could really come up with valid ways to measure teacher quality and reliably distinguish excellent educators.

Today, it's clear that the National Board proved the skeptics wrong. You succeeded in creating, testing, and implementing rigorous assessments of teaching practice in 16 content areas that span 25 certificates. And you are committed to keeping your certifications current—as demonstrated by your newly updated mathematics and reading language arts standards, aligned with the Common Core. You are truly demonstrating a rigorous approach across a wide-ranging set of content.

You also pioneered the use of videotaped classroom work and portfolios for evaluating teacher practice and student learning—two practices finally gaining real currency nationwide.

And the National Board's high-quality, multiyear professional development is credited by teachers with helping them to powerfully reflect on, and improve, their

Delivered June 12, 2012, by Joanne Weiss, chief of staff to US Secretary of Education Arne Duncan, at the twenty-fifth anniversary celebration for the National Board for Professional Teaching Standards.

craft. Many call it the most powerful professional development they ever experienced.

Not coincidentally, the number of board-certified teachers has soared—from just 177 teachers in 1994 to more than 97,000 today. In North Carolina, Jim Hunt's home state, nearly one in five teachers is National Board certified.

We both seek to build a true profession for teachers—one anchored in demonstrated expertise and offering the career opportunities, autonomy, collaboration, compensation, and status that accrues to comparable professions.

I have to point out, too, how much the Obama Administration has learned from your work. Our new RESPECT program has the same essential mission the National Board has had for the last quarter century. We both seek to build a true profession for teachers—one anchored in demonstrated expertise and offering the career opportunities, autonomy, collaboration, compensation, and status that accrues to comparable professions.

And we need you—all 97,000 of the National Board certified teachers—to continue to lead the way.

We need you promoting career pathways that provide opportunities for increasingly responsible roles, whether teachers choose to stay in the classroom, become instructional leaders, or move into administration.

And we need your help rethinking teacher compensation so it's more aligned with teachers' effectiveness and levels of responsibility, so that it's high enough to attract and retain a highly skilled workforce, and so it's consistent with the societal regard accorded to comparable professions.

We need you to stay out in front, calling for distributed leadership and shared responsibility for schools where coalitions of principals and teacher leaders create cultures of continuous learning.

We need all of this—and then a little bit more.

We would like to see the National Board make student learning a core component that is systematically evaluated in each of the 25 certificate areas, building a robust link between Board certification and classroom effectiveness. I cannot overemphasize the importance of linking your invaluable thinking about practice with evidence, taken from multiple sources, of student academic growth.

And we'd like to see the National Board continue to expand its ranks in school leadership positions, especially in the nation's highest need schools. Today, more than half—55%—of NBCTs teach in Title I–eligible, high-need schools. That's terrific—but it's not enough. Your voice can help make our neediest schools the most prestigious places to work in education, the capstone of great teachers' careers.

As you all know, when Secretary Duncan was CEO of the Chicago Public Schools, he pushed for a dramatic expansion of National Board certified teachers. During his seven-year tenure, the number of NBCTs in Chicago's Public Schools went from 11 teachers to more than 1,200.

Even more encouraging, today, nearly 90% of Chicago teachers who became NBCTs are still teaching in CPS.

Chicago is a great example of extending the reach of NBCTs. But the country needs an accomplished teacher in every classroom. Instead of just 3 percent of teachers being NBCTs, we want every student to have effective teachers. That should be the norm, not the exception.

In other professions like medicine, accounting, engineering, and architecture, board certification is expected. About 90% of physicians are board-certified—and most of us would never consider going to one who wasn't.

As Ron Thorpe has said, NBCTs should not seek to become the MENSA of the teaching force. You should set the standard to which all members of the profession aspire. You have the Secretary's full support in scaling toward this goal.

Let me just close by saying a word about Ron Thorpe. I had the great pleasure to work with Ron in organizing the first two International Summits on the Teaching Profession. Ron is an outstanding teacher himself, and a scholar in the field. But on top of that, Ron is a smart, creative, deeply caring, can-do person.

It's no secret that in this era of tight budgets, earmarks are drawing to an end. That's hard for nonprofits like the National Board. And it's hard on education in general.

But in Ron, you have found an innovative fundraiser and, most importantly, a visionary leader. You couldn't have picked a better person to lead the organization into its next quarter-century.

So congratulations to Ron—and here's to another outstanding 25 years for the National Board for Professional Teaching Standards.

About Joanne Weiss

Joanne Weiss is chief of staff to Secretary Arne Duncan at the US Department of Education. She holds a degree in biochemistry from Princeton University. She began her career as vice president of education research and development at Wicat Systems, where she was responsible for the development of multimedia curriculum and assessment products for K–12 schools. She then served as chief executive officer of Claria Corporation. She went on to become executive vice president of business operations at the K–12 educational technology company Wasatch Education Systems. She was cofounder and chief executive officer of products and technologies at Academic Systems, a company that helps underprepared college students improve their mathematics and writing skills. Following that, she was partner and chief operating officer at NewSchools Venture Fund, a venture philanthropy firm working to transform public education. She joined the Department of Education in 2009 as senior adviser to the secretary and director of the Race to the Top program.

Investing in America's Future

A Blueprint for Transforming Career and Technical Education

Assistant Secretary of Education Brenda Dann-Messier

Discussing the Obama administration's Blueprint for Transforming Career and Technical Education, Assistant Secretary of Education Brenda Dann-Messier asserts that the Carl D. Perkins Career and Technical Education Act of 2006 should be renewed and refined. She explains how career and technical education programs should better serve job-market needs, should be collaborative among institutions, and should place a premium on innovation.

Thank you, Arne—for being here today to highlight this critically important initiative for our nation's economic prosperity.

I am pleased to be here at Des Moines Area Community College to discuss the Administration's Blueprint for Transforming Career and Technical Education. The exemplary work that DMACC has done is simply remarkable—and it's true, as the Secretary stated, that the work going on here is indicative of the leadership Iowa has shown on this issue.

I am grateful to have the opportunity to engage with you all in today's town hall—and I hope that all of you leave here with the understanding that the President believes that education is a cornerstone of building an American economy that will last.

As the Secretary stated, our blueprint for the reauthorization of Perkins is designed to transform CTE and usher in a new era of rigorous, relevant, and results-driven CTE shaped by four core principles. Our four core principles are focused on effective alignment; building strong collaborations; establishing meaningful accountability; and placing a greater emphasis on innovation.

The Carl D. Perkins Career and Technical Education Act of 2006 introduced important changes in federal support for CTE. These changes helped to improve the learning experiences of students. But they did not go far enough to systemically create better outcomes for students and employers competing in a 21st century global economy.

We need to reauthorize and transform the Perkins Act. Here is what we are proposing.

Our first principle of reform seeks to ensure better alignment between CTE and labor market needs to equip students with the skills they need for in-demand jobs within high-growth industry sectors. Our proposed reforms will provide States

Delivered Apr. 19, 2012, at the Des Moines Area Community College Town Hall, by Assistant Secretary of Education Brenda Dann-Messier.

with clearer guidance on establishing high-quality programs, and empower States to work with their workforce and economic development agencies to identify the occupations and sectors on which CTE programs should focus.

Our second principle of reform emphasizes the importance of building and maintaining strong collaborations among secondary and postsecondary institutions, employers, and industry partners to improve the quality of CTE programs. All CTE programs under Perkins would be funded by consortia to ensure collaboration among secondary and postsecondary institutions and their partners. In addition, we propose that States use a private sector matching contribution to strengthen the participation of employers, industry, and labor partners in program design and implementation.

Our third principle of reform is establishing more meaningful accountability for improving academic outcomes and building technical and employability skills in CTE programs. We want to provide states increased autonomy to select and fund high-quality programs that are responsive to regional labor-market needs. And we are proposing within-state competitions.

Our federal investment in CTE must be dramatically reshaped to fulfill its potential to prepare all students, regardless of their background or circumstances, for further education and cutting-edge careers.

Our proposal includes several provisions to ensure that competition will have no adverse impact on access for students, including those who live in rural communities, because all students, regardless of their background, should have access to and be able to participate in and complete high-quality CTE programs.

Also, we are proposing that States establish common definitions and clear metrics for performance to create high-quality data systems that enable meaningful comparisons and identification of equity gaps.

In addition, our accountability reforms include ways to reward local recipients that exceed their performance targets. These reforms are aimed at improving student outcomes and incentivizing the closure of equity gaps in CTE programs.

Lastly, our fourth principle for reform places more emphasis on innovation, by promoting systemic reforms in state policies and practices that will support the implementation of effective CTE practices at the local level.

In line with this effort, we are proposing a competitive CTE Innovation and Transformation Fund—administered by the US Department of Education—to incentivize innovation at the local level and support system reform at the State level. The Fund would comprise up to 10 percent of the total Perkins funding.

As we usher in a new era of rigorous, relevant, and results-driven CTE, we must continue to support the expansion of programs with a record of success. This is why President Obama's FY13 budget proposal for a new $1 billion competitive fund to increase the number of high-quality career academies will be crucial to our overall vision of expanding effective CTE programs across the country. The proposal would dramatically expand the number of career academies by 3,000 nationwide and provide services to an additional half a million students—a 50 percent increase.

This administration believes that career and technical education is central to rebuilding our economy and securing a brighter future for our nation. Our federal investment in CTE must be dramatically reshaped to fulfill its potential to prepare all students, regardless of their background or circumstances, for further education and cutting-edge careers.

I am so pleased to have Secretary Duncan's advocacy and leadership for CTE reform—and I thank him once again for taking the time to spotlight this vitally important initiative.

We look forward to working with all of the students, teachers, administrators, and parents as we work to transform this critical investment in America's future. I hope we'll have your support as we work to roll out these priorities. And I thank you all in advance for rising to meet this challenge.

We are proposing a competitive CTE Innovation and Transformation Fund—administered by the US Department of Education—to incentivize innovation at the local level and support system reform at the State level.

About Brenda Dann-Messier

Born in West Orange, New Jersey, Brenda Dann-Messier earned her bachelor's in history and secondary education, as well as a master's degree in instructional technology with a certificate in adult basic education, at Rhode Island College. She received her EdD in educational leadership from Johnson and Wales University. From 1993 to 1996, Dann-Messier worked for the Clinton administration under Secretary of Education Richard Riley, serving as the secretary's regional representative for Region I, which includes Connecticut, Maine, Massachusetts, New Hampshire, Rhode Island, and Vermont. She then served for a decade as president of the Dorcas Place Adult and Family Learning Center, a community-based adult education agency based in Providence, Rhode Island. She has served as assistant secretary of education since 2009.

5

Occupy Wall Street

(The Washington Post/Getty Images)

Occupy protestors from around the country—including Sean Stewart, from West Haven, CT (center)—gather on the West Lawn of the US Capitol, January 17, 2012.

Who Rules? By What Authority?

Virginia Rasmussen

In her address, Virginia Rasmussen analyzes some of the legal precedents for the US Supreme Court's Citizens United decision that, for many Americans, has become a sign of the degeneration of democracy. She calls for the Occupy Wall Street movement to question not only recent court decisions but the very founding documents and ideas— myths, as she calls them—on which the United States is founded.

It's thrilling to be present in times of awakening, and so it's thrilling to be here.

Emma Goldman said that "no great idea in its beginning can ever be within the law. How can it be within the law? The law is stationary. The law is fixed. The law is a chariot wheel which binds us all regardless of conditions or place or time."

The *Citizens United* Supreme Court decision helped many people learn about the law of our place and time, including that under law, corporations are people too. "Well, that doesn't sound right," they said. Suddenly my "abolish corporate personhood" bumper sticker got a little respect rather than the confusion and disregard of its first ten years stuck to my car.

And that court decision was a two-fer. People also learned the money is legally equal to speech. And that all persons, natural or artificial, are free to speak as much as they can afford in our electoral process. So says the First Amendment.

Note: There are a lot of Supreme Court decisions at work here. Four monumental empowerments of the propertied few. The 2010 decision declaring that corporations can spend what they will in elections is the consequence of a 1976 decision declaring money equal to speech and an 1886 decision declaring corporations persons under law with First, Fourth, Fifth and Fourteenth Amendment protections. And a decision way back in 1819 declaring that corporations will not be the public creations we intended, subject to our instruction, but private entities, essentially beyond the people's authority.

And these four decisions set precedent for countless low and high court decisions throughout our history that handed right after right to the corporate class and their vehicle for accumulating wealth and power: the business corporation

That's how the corporation became the governing tool of the one percent. A tool awash in constitutional, legal and cultural powers to define every aspect of our lives: a health care system that serves the few and sickens the many; an education system that keeps the majority down and democratically impaired; an agricultural system that poisons field and food; a financial system riddled with stunning hocus-pocus that relentlessly transfers wealth from poorer to richer; and an energy agenda that uproots the land and fouls the waters to extract every last lump of coal, drop of oil and bubble of gas for a corporate economy of endless "more"—endless more production and consumption, demanding endless more energy

Will we be poisoned by 200 parts per million or 150 parts per million? Will the smokestack be 90 feet high or 75 feet high? Will the fracking pad be a mile from the elementary school or three quarters?

The corporate class has engaged in massive usurpations, insatiable takings, of our sovereign right to define our lives, communities, work, economies and future in a sustainable relationship with one another and the Earth. In light of this history, it's a celebration to see the Occupy movement shifting its focus from issues of corruption, greed and inequality, real as these are, to the underlying problem of power, of authority to govern.

Who rules? Who gets to set the agenda and then write the laws that turn that agenda into reality? Who brought us this mess? Such questions can drive this movement to a place of deep understanding, to arguments and actions that can bring sustainable change toward self- and mutual governance. We the people currently have no remedy for our grievances within the law our courts administer, nor have we remedy through regulatory law and its myriad agencies, a kind of law devised by corporate managers to keep us at a distance, exhausted and channeled into issues of little consequence.

Will we be poisoned by 200 parts per million or 150 parts per million? Will the smokestack be 90 feet high or 75 feet high? Will the fracking pad be a mile from the elementary school or three quarters? Nowhere in this picture do we the people have a right to say "No," to define our own reality.

"Ah, but you have all those rights of dissent," we're told. "You can march and demonstrate and rally in public squares." But the 99 percent are increasingly aware the only right that really matters is not the right of dissent but the right to decide. This work is about us. It's we who have to change. It's we who have to understand the challenge of doing real democracy and of tearing down the impenetrable legal barriers that the few have put in our way. Through teach-ins, occupying strategies, democratic skills and process, by community organizing, we can challenge the corporate state and the mythologies on which it rests.

What myths, you ask? How about our venerated U.S. Constitution? Yes, it has some fine content, and we'll keep those parts. But it remains a minority-rule document, written by the well-knickered Federalists—the propertied few who feared the majority, who feared democracy. This founding document should have been revisited many times since 1787. Thomas Jefferson advised we re-write it in every generation.

And can we shed a second myth? The much-too-sanctified rule of law. Let's all interrupt the silly claim that this is a nation of laws, not of men. Who, pray tell, writes law? These times of ferment have brought us three organizations or projects to the fore that I urge you to explore if you have not already done so.

The first is Move to Amend Coalition, working to unequivocally stating that Constitutional rights belong to human beings, not to artificial legal entities. Check out their website at movetoamend.org.

The Program on Corporations, Law and Democracy (POCLAD) has been researching, writing and engaging others around contesting the authority of corporations to govern. They've prepared a democracy insurgency packet of articles and materials relevant to history, analysis and democratic process vital to doing this work. You can find them at poclad.org.

And lastly, Richard Grossman, POCLAD cofounder and rigorous critic of ineffective activist strategies, who died this past November, suggests we begin to criminalize corporations, to criminalize the corporate leaders who direct them and criminalize activity especially related to the hydro-fracking corporations. For a copy of that law and more understanding of that work, see frackbustersny.org.

So here's to Occupiers and people everywhere engaging this critical struggle to roll the chariot wheel beyond the tyranny of a propertied minority and toward real democracy!

About Virginia Rasmussen

Virginia Rasmussen is a principal with the collective organization Program on Corporations, Law and Democracy (POCLAD) and is currently active in the movement to criminalize hydraulic fracturing in New York State (FrackBustersNY). Rasmussen was cofounder of the Women's International League for Peace and Freedom (WILPF) campaign. She was formerly director of the environmental studies program at Alfred University, in Alfred, New York, and served as deputy mayor of Alfred. She has also served as the education director at the New Alchemy Institute on Cape Cod and the director of the Cape Cod Campaign for Civil Rights. She has a PhD in inorganic chemistry from Syracuse University and has taught in the United States, Zambia, and Turkey.

Don't Stop until You Have Restored Democracy

Lawrence Lessig

In this address, Lawrence Lessig argues that while individuals often act in the interests of the common good, corporations are established in order to generate revenue and have no interest in doing what is good or right. Lessig argues that corporations should then not enjoy the same rights accorded individuals in the political process. He argues that broader changes are required in order to restore America to a form of democracy its founders would recognize.

The people who started this country were called Republicans. I don't mean George Bush Republicans, I don't mean Rick Perry Republicans, I don't mean Rick Santorum Republicans. These were classical Republicans. What they thought was that representatives and citizens should think about the common good. Fucking naïve, they were, but that's what they thought. They should think about the common good. They should think and act as citizens thinking about the common good.

And sometimes, individuals do that. Not often, but sometimes. Sometimes individuals volunteer to go fight fascism in a war. Love of country, to go fight in a war and fight fascism. They do that because they think about the common good. Sometimes they race up a tower on fire, not because they're thinking about themselves, but because they're thinking about the public good. Sometimes they sleep in Zuccotti Park because they're thinking about the public good, not about themselves. Sometimes individuals, persons, think about the common good and not themselves.

Now—corporations can't do that. By law, corporations can't do that. Corporations are formed, and their charter says, they are there to make money for themselves. That's their job. That's what they're hired for and that's what their presidents are fired for if they don't do. They don't think about the common good. They think about themselves.

This fundamental, obvious fact, the Supreme Court forgot when they said, "Corporations are just like us! They get to spend their money in political elections just like us. They are persons just like us." They are not. They are one more fucking greedy influence in the system that's not thinking about the common good! They're thinking about themselves!

Now, it's obviously right that two years after this decision, we've gotta find a way to reverse this decision, to get us back to a place where we don't think that

Delivered January 20, 2012, in Foley Square, New York City, at an Occupy Wall Street demonstration on the eve of the second anniversary of the US Supreme Court decision *Citizens United v. Federal Election Commission*. Copyright © 2012 by Lawrence Lessig. Reprinted with permission. All rights reserved.

> *Sometimes [people] race up a tower on fire, not because they're thinking about themselves, but because they're thinking about the public good. Sometimes they sleep in Zuccotti Park because they're thinking about the public good, not about themselves.*

corporations are just like us. They're not. We gotta do that. But here's the hard fact. On January 20, 2010, the day before *Citizens United* was decided, this democracy was already broken, and we will not get to a democracy merely by reversing *Citizens United* and declaring corporations are not persons. That is not enough. This movement cannot stop with fixing the mistakes of the Supreme Court. That is not enough. This movement will achieve nothing if we don't achieve publicly funded elections. That is the only way we begin to reallocate the power that democracy springs from.

We talk about the one percent. Point-two-six percent of Americans give $200 in a Congressional election. Point-zero-five percent give the maximum amount. Point-zero-one percent give $10,000 or more in a cycle. We're not the one percent. We're not the 99 percent. You are the 99.99% who don't have the influence that the .01% has, and until we change that, we don't change anything.

So I have enormous respect for what you've done. But don't stop with this symbol of corporations aren't persons. Don't' stop until you're restored this democracy to a democracy that the classical Republicans could respect—a democracy where we think not about ourselves, but [about] what is in the common good.

About Lawrence Lessig

Born June 3, 1961, in Rapid City, South Dakota, Lawrence Lessig earned bachelor's degrees in economics and management from the University of Pennsylvania in 1983. He completed his master's degree at Trinity College in Cambridge, England, before entering Yale Law School and earning a JD in 1989. From 1990 to 1991, Lessig served as a law clerk for Justice Antonin Scalia. He began work as an assistant professor of law at the University of Chicago Law School in 1991, becoming a full professor in 1995. Lessig began teaching at Harvard Law School in 1997. In 2002, he moved to Stanford Law School, where he taught courses in constitutional law and codirected the Center for Internet and Society. In 2009, he returned to Harvard University where he directs the Edmond J. Safra Foundation Center for Ethics.

"We the People"

Judith Butler

Rebutting the criticisms commonly made of the Occupy Wall Street Movement—that it has no demands or that its demands are unrealistic—Judith Butler offers an endorsement of the movement and offers a list of demands, as well as an argument that coming together as physical bodies is essential.

Hello everybody. I'm Judith Butler. I have come here to lend my support and offer my solidarity for this unprecedented display of popular and democratic will. People have asked, so what are the demands that all these people are making? Either they say there are no demands and that leaves your critics confused, or they say that demands for social equality, that demands for economic justice, are impossible demands, and impossible demands are just not practical.

> *If hope is an impossible demand, then we demand the impossible. If the right to shelter, food, and employment are impossible demands, then we demand the impossible. If it is impossible to demand that those who profit from the recession redistribute their wealth and cease their greed, then yes, we demand the impossible.*

But we disagree! If hope is an impossible demand, then we demand the impossible. If the right to shelter, food, and employment are impossible demands, then we demand the impossible. If it is impossible to demand that those who profit from the recession redistribute their wealth and cease their greed, then yes, we demand the impossible.

Of course, the list of our demands is long. These are demands for which there can be no arbitration. We object to the monopolization of wealth. We object to making working populations disposable. We object to the privatization of education. We believe that education must be a public good and a public value. We oppose the expanding numbers of the poor. We rage against the banks that push people from their homes, and the lack of health care for unfathomable numbers. We object to economic racism and call for its end.

It matters that as bodies we arrive together in public. As bodies we suffer, we require food and shelter, and as bodies we require one another in dependency and desire. So this is a politics of the public body, the requirements of the body, its

Delievered October 2011, in Washington Square Park, New York City, at a gathering of Occupy Wall Street protesters. Copyright © 2011 by Judith Butler. Reprinted with permission. All rights reserved.

movement and its voice. We would not be here if electoral politics were representing the will of the people. We sit and stand and move as the popular will, the one that electoral politics has forgotten and abandoned. But we are here, time and again, persisting, imagining the phrase, "we the people." Thank you.

About Judith Butler

Judith Butler was born February 24, 1956, in Cleveland, Ohio. She studied at Bennington College in Vermont, before transferring to Yale University, where she earned a BA in 1978 and a PhD in 1984. She taught at Wesleyan University and Johns Hopkins University, before becoming professor of rhetoric and comparative literature at the University of California, Berkeley, in 1993. She is the author of numerous books, including Gender Trouble: Feminism and the Subversion of Identity *(1990),* Bodies That Matter: On the Discursive Limits of "Sex" *(1993), and* Hegemony, Contingency, Universality, *with Ernesto Laclau and Slavoj Zizek, (2000). Butler has served as a professor at the European Graduate School, in Leuk-Stadt, Switzerland, since 2006, and as a visiting professor at Columbia University since 2012.*

The Occupy Movement

We'd Better Pay Attention

Bobby Rush

Comparing Occupy Wall Street protests to the Boston Tea Party, the women's suffrage movement, the fight for abolition, and other great examples of American civil disobedience, Representative Bobby Rush voices his support for the Occupy movement. Criticizing police brutality against Occupy protestors the previous night in Oakland, California, Rush points out that the demonstrators' frustration with a society that values wealth above all else is more than understandable and long overdue.

Mr. Speaker, I would like to express my outrage and my disappointment at the Oakland, California, Police Department, which reacted with brutality to those peacefully protesting. Mr. Speaker, I want to remind our Nation's law enforcement authorities all across the land that civil disobedience is as American as apple pie. It is the act through which our great Nation was conceived. It required great courage to do what they did at the Boston Tea Party. It required great courage for the great American, Henry David Thoreau, to refuse to go to war against Mexico in 1849, an act that gave birth to the anti-war movement that continues today.

The equalities that we as Americans enjoy today are the result of those great, courageous Americans that fought for our liberties, Mr. Speaker. The women's suffrage movement went from 1848 to 1920. Generations of courageous women marched, they fasted, and they were arrested. Finally, in 1920, the 19th Amendment gave women the right to vote. It took more than seven decades of civil disobedience to achieve the change that they sought.

Let's not forget, Mr. Speaker, that the abolition of slavery, the labor movement and the eradication of child labor, the civil rights movement, and the environmental movement all used civil disobedience as a powerful and peaceful weapon to change laws and to protect all of our liberties.

Members of the Occupy Movement now emerge as yet another generation of courageous Americans voicing a general frustration that many citizens feel: It was a money-driven elite that mismanaged the American economy. They are challenging us, this Congress, our government, to reform not only Wall Street but reform a culture of selfishness and greed that has distorted who we are and made the American Dream appear unattainable. We are losing ground as a result of these individuals, this grotesque, American, greedy and avaricious elite.

The Occupy Movement, Mr. Speaker, embodies a sense of growing disillusionment with the direction of our country. I, for one, understand that feeling. With deadlock a daily occurrence in this very House, it is hard for the American people not to feel a sense of utter frustration. They see their elected representatives unable to govern at this crucial time.

Mr. Speaker, a betrayal of American values occurred last night in Oakland, California, when police fired tear gas on those peaceful demonstrators. It occurred in New York City when police maced and beat protesters. Government violence against our own people? Is this not the very thing that we condemn in other places all around the world? How dare we denounce an action when committed abroad but yet remain silent when it happens in our own, very own—our own backyards.

I, for one, cannot remain silent. History teaches us that a violent response to civil disobedience never, ever works. It makes people angrier and turns public opinion against law enforcement, against the police. It is counterproductive, and it never achieves the goals of those who are trying to impose order.

Getting arrested is a fundamental part of civil disobedience. The Occupy Movement demonstrators expected to be arrested. Civil disobedience participants all expect to be arrested, but they should also expect that the police will conduct themselves with professional understanding and a sensitivity of the power that they possess and of the government they represent. They carry weapons. They have the power to maim, to kill, to wound, and to arrest.

With that great power comes an even greater responsibility. That greater responsibility includes the freedoms that were promised to all American citizens in that great document, the preamble to the Constitution and the Bill of Rights, which is the freedom from "unreasonable searches and seizures" as promised in the Fourth Amendment of the Constitution; the freedom from "cruel and unusual punishments" as promised in the Eighth Amendment; finally, Mr. Speaker, and perhaps most importantly, the freedom enshrined in the First Amendment, which guarantees "the right of the people peaceably to assemble and to petition the government for a redress of grievances."

It is the job of law enforcement to uphold these freedoms, to uphold our Constitution, to uphold justice even in the most difficult of situations. Beatings and mace and tear gas against our own people exercising their constitutional rights? That is unacceptable. More importantly, it is un-American.

I do sympathize with the tough job our Nation's police officers face now and have faced, and I can understand why they may feel intimidated by the sheer numbers or may mistake the demonstrators' passion for aggression. However, in a humble way, I ask the police officers who are monitoring these protests to act with a rational head, with soberness, with restraint. Violence only breeds violence. Such unwarranted crowd control methods will only serve to create mutual contempt between protesters and the police alike, dividing Americans against Americans and citizens against the police. We don't want that. This is not a nation that supports and encourages that type of activity.

It was only last week, Mr. Speaker, that we—this Nation, the citizens of the greatest country in the history of the world—dedicated a memorial to a man who was the embodiment, the living proof, of the power of civil disobedience and non-violence. It is those who marched peacefully in the face of fire hoses, in the face of dogs attacking them, of police batons striking them all over their bodies, including their heads, who changed America.

Now a new generation follows boldly and audaciously with an American audacity. They follow in the footsteps of those American patriots who dared to disobey the law of the land as a matter of conscience and priority, as a matter of conscience that created this great civil society called the United States of America. They made our Nation better back then, and I believe the Occupy Movement challenges us to make America better now.

Yes, it can be done. America can be better. America must address the issues that those who are now demonstrating peacefully across the land are raising. They are only trying to peacefully redress their grievances. It is their constitutional right. How dare dogs, how dare tear gas, how dare police attack them in the wee hours of the morning?

Mr. Speaker, the mayor of Oakland, California, Mayor Jean Quan, owes the Occupy Movement a sincere, heartfelt apology. Mayor Quan owes the American people a sincere, heartfelt apology. At 3 a.m. yesterday, the Oakland Police invaded the park where the protesters were assembled.

Forty-five years ago in the same city, 45 years ago this very week, an organization that I became a member of, the Black Panther Party, was founded in Oakland, California, as a result of the police brutality of the Oakland Police Department. Forty-five years later, I as a Member of this esteemed body, the House of Representatives, am ashamed to bear witness once again to the same Oakland Police Department violating and attacking and brutalizing innocent citizens who are protesting, bringing their deep-felt grievances to the forefront and engaging in acts of civil disobedience.

Police batons, tear gas, mace, no matter what the weapon is, no matter what the strategy is, they cannot kill this movement. They cannot stop this movement. This occupy movement is going to move forward. It's going to move forward with an accelerated pace because of the actions of the police department in Oakland and in other cities across this Nation.

They have a right to protest. They have a right to make their voices heard. They have a right, as called for in the gospel of Jesus Christ in the Bible, to make their bodies a living sacrifice. These individuals, they are epitomizing the greatness in this hour. It's a thing that we celebrate all across the land.

We celebrated it in Tunisia, we celebrated it in Egypt, we celebrated it in Libya, we celebrated it in Yemen, we celebrated it in China, we celebrated it in other places all across the world. How can we be so hypocritical? How can we be so insensitive? How can we be so arrogant to celebrate civil disobedience in other places across the world and attack the same, the very same actions and attitude here in our Nation when our citizens engage in civil disobedience?

Mr. Speaker, I say that those who are involved in the occupy movement, you are just lighting the first spark in a prairie fire of peaceful demonstrations across this land. Don't give up, don't give out, and please don't give in.

> *It's high time now that the American people stand up for what they believe in and take to the streets to demonstrate to all that we're sick and tired of being sick and tired. We're sick and tired of home foreclosures. We're sick and tired of unemployment. We're sick and tired of being sick and tired, as Fannie Lou Hamer once said.*

Godspeed to you. We need you. You're doing the right thing at the right time for the right reasons. Keep doing what you're doing. Stand up for what you believe in. Stand up for what you believe in.

It's high time now that the American people stand up for what they believe in and take to the streets to demonstrate to all that we're sick and tired of being sick and tired. We're sick and tired of home foreclosures. We're sick and tired of unemployment. We're sick and tired of being sick and tired, as Fannie Lou Hamer once said.

We're just sick and tired. We're sick, yes, of the rising cost of health care. We need to demonstrate and protest the rising cost of health care.

We're sick and tired of the rising gap between those who are sitting high on the hog, the wealthy, the elite, and those who are at the bottom; the rising gap between those who are unemployed and underemployed, who are chronically unemployed and the 1 percent who are reaping all the wealth of this Nation and telling the rest of us that they have a right to the wealth of the Nation, but yet we as American citizens don't have a right to a decent job. We as American citizens don't have a right to decent housing, that we as American citizens don't have a right to a decent education, that we as American citizens don't have a right to decent health care.

How can they look down on us and tell us that we don't have a right to the same opportunities and to the same life-style and to the same benefits? How can they tell the dwindling, disappearing American middle class that they don't have a right to demonstrate?

These are our children, and they want a better future. These are our children, and they are willing to fight for a better future.

These are our children, and they have the courage to stand up against the government, to stand up against the elite, to stand for their rights. And I am proud that our children are standing up and standing for something to try to get some meaning into their lives and try to make this Nation a better Nation.

I'm proud of them and, again, I say to them, don't give up, don't give out, and please don't give in. Godspeed to you.

About Bobby Rush

Born in Albany, Georgia, on November 23, 1946, Bobby Rush is the US Representative for Illinois's First Congressional District, serving since 1993. He grew up in Chicago, and served in the Army from 1963 to 1968. Thereafter, he was active in the civil rights movement as a member of the controversial Black Panther organization. He then earned a bachelor's degree from Roosevelt University in 1973, a master's in political science from the University of Illinois at Chicago in 1974, and another master's at McCormick Theological Seminary in 1978. In 2000, he was challenged for his seat as US Representative by then State Senator Barack Obama. Rush won, and thus holds the distinction of being the only person to beat Obama in an election to date.

6

Privacy and the Internet

Questions and problems surrounding privacy have accompanied the rapid growth of online social networking and ecommerce, prompting individuals and policy makers to consider the proper use of personal information in a variety of contexts, from the classroom to online shopping.

We Will Not Fail Our Children

US Secretary of Education Arne Duncan

In his speech at the second annual Federal Partners in Bullying Prevention Summit, Secretary of Education Arne Duncan outlines the ways in which the Obama administration is working to confront and reduce the problem of bullying. He refers to the deaths of Tyler Clementi and several other young people the previous fall, as well as the true stories of students who were bullied to the point of taking their own lives. Many of their stories are featured in the play The Bullycide Project, *which Duncan discusses. Duncan presents the myriad reasons why students get bullied, adding statistics about how bullying affects academic performance. He also addresses bullying that occurs outside schools, such as cyberbullying, and lists various partnerships and initiatives his office is involved with in the ongoing effort to reduce bullying.*

I want to thank you for being here today. Over the past year, all of us in the Obama administration have been joining forces to address and reduce bullying. I believe we've made real progress—but I know that we have a long way to go.

In *The Bullycide Project*, you saw just how important this work is. These are real-life stories about students who took their own lives after being bullied. They are sobering reminders of exactly how devastating bullying can be. They're also a reminder of how the entire community suffers—parents, classmates and even the child engaged in bullying. It creates a toxic environment and barriers to learning, and in the worst cases, can even lead to the suicides of some of our children.

Last year, when my team at the Department convened this summit, little did we know that soon after, national attention would turn dramatically to this issue. Just weeks later, Tyler Clementi succumbed to the outrageous behavior of people he trusted. Tomorrow marks the anniversary of his suicide—and tragically, Tyler's death isn't the only one. Last fall, several other young people took their lives after being bullied or harassed.

A number of brave parents and relatives are here today because they too lost children, in part, because of bullying. There is no greater heartbreak. But all of them are now working to ensure that other students won't suffer the way their children did.

I want to recognize and thank some of these strong and dedicated people:

- Wendy Walsh and her son Shawn, mother and brother of Seth Walsh, who have worked with schools to protect gay students from bullying;
- Kevin and Tammy Eppling, parents of Matt Eppling, who have led the charge to establish community-based awareness programs and legislation to stop hazing and bullying in schools;

Delivered September 21, 2011. Remarks made at the second annual Federal Partners in Bullying Prevention Summit by Secretary of Education Arne Duncan.

- Eileen Moore, the aunt of Phoebe Prince, who created a guide book called "You Are Not Alone," a suicide prevention resource for dealing with bullying and its victims. Eileen now leads Phoebe's Messengers, a student group with the mission to find solutions for bullying;

- Tammy and Shawn Aaberg, parents of Justin Aaberg, who are working with their local, state, and federal representatives to create stronger and more inclusive anti-bullying policies;

- Masika Bermudez, mother of Jaheem Herrera, who speaks out against harassment and advocates for laws to stop bullying;

- Tricia Behnke, mother of Paige Behnke, who is working to get the message out that suicide is not the answer; and

- Kevin Jacobsen, father of Kameron. He and his wife, Wanda, founded a charitable foundation called Kindness Above Malice (KAM) that is a call for action to all of us to help prevent even one more child and indeed one more family from having to endure the horrific nightmare of teen suicide by bringing awareness and positive solutions to our communities.

I want to thank all of you for your remarkable courage. All of you are leaders who are using your advocacy to prevent bullying. You are working to make schools safe for all children. You are actively working to prevent bullying and to enforce the message that "Enough is enough. It's time to stop the bullying."

Children are bullied for many different reasons—for their race or national origin, for having a disability, actual or perceived sexual orientation, for how they look, or who they date or are friends with, for how they perform in school or on the athletic field, or for how they speak. This bullying is something no child should have to face.

Recent research confirms that bullying affects all students whether in high school or elementary school—even those who only witness it. A recent University of Virginia study linked bullying in high school to lower academic achievement across the school. Schools with high levels of reported bullying had lower passing rates—by an average of 3 to 6 percent across tests—when compared to schools with less reported bullying. Related research tells more of the story: Jaana Junoven and her colleagues at UCLA in a study of middle schools' academic performance found that, over time, bullying can account for a decline of one-and-a-half letter grades in academic subjects. Another study found that students who are chronically rejected and mistreated by peers in elementary school are more likely to perform poorly in academics, and to ultimately avoid school altogether. Ian Rivers' research on students' mental health shows that students who witness bullying are more likely to use tobacco or alcohol, to be depressed, and to miss or skip school.

If you ask kids about bullying, they'll all tell you it's not just at school. Kids can now bully their classmates through e-mail and text messages, on social networking sites, and across the Internet.

But there is some encouraging news. Through our collective efforts we are starting to make a difference, and we are starting to reduce harassment and make

> *We are starting to reduce harassment and make schools and the Internet into better, safer places for students to learn. That is our duty: We cannot fail any more of our children.*

schools and the Internet into better, safer places for students to learn. That is our duty: We cannot fail any more of our children.

Last year, my team at the Department convened this summit to help inform the way forward, shed light on this touchy subject and broaden our impact. We brought together eight federal partners who made a promise to do something to change things for the better. You can read about our work at www.stopbullying.gov, which has received almost half a million visits. I want to commend all of our partners for their efforts in the past year. There has been an unprecedented commitment by both the private and public sectors to understand and address bullying. Campaigns have helped students learn to talk to adults about their problems, encouraged parents to support their children and monitor what they are doing online, and taught kids that bullying is flat out wrong.

At the federal government, we've made progress in developing a uniform definition of bullying and analyzing the effectiveness and comprehensiveness of state anti-bullying laws. Last October, we sent a Dear Colleague letter to school administrators, explaining that they have a legal duty under the federal civil rights laws to prevent discriminatory harassment; and we provided a series of practical examples to help them understand how to address harassment when it does occur. In December, I sent a memo to all Governors and Chief State School Officers outlining the key components of state anti-bullying laws.

This memo serves as a reference to states and districts as they develop or revise anti-bullying legislation and policies. We will continue to work with state and local policymakers and educators to keep children safe, and to provide them with the best learning environment. In June, I issued a Dear Colleague letter reaffirming the rights of students to form Gay-Straight Alliances and other non-curricular clubs under the Equal Access Act. These student groups can and do make schools tolerant and inclusive places, and ensure that all students have the support they need.

We have also focused on vigorously enforcing existing federal laws that speak to this issue. As you heard from our Assistant Secretary Ali, we have greatly stepped up enforcement of civil rights laws through our Office for Civil Rights.

We are also committed to providing technical assistance on a variety of related topics. We partnered with the Office for Juvenile Justice and Delinquency Prevention to host a number of webinars that have reached a nationwide audience, explaining topics like when bullying constitutes discriminatory harassment and how to constructively intervene in bullying situations. Our Safe and Supportive Technical Assistance Center developed training modules specifically for bus drivers after we saw survey results showing that they don't feel prepared to handle bullying on their buses.

Working with the White House, we convened another conference in March. There, the private sector rallied to respond. I want to specifically commend MTV.

After the March 10th White House Conference on Bullying Prevention, MTV partnered with researchers from the MIT Media Lab. They're working on vanguard approaches to detect and deter cyber bullying. The centerpiece of the partnership is "Over the Line?" a Web and iPhone app where young people share and rate personal stories of how technology is complicating social interactions.

More than 9,000 young people have submitted stories about being bullied or harassed and over three hundred thousand have responded to those stories—creating one of the largest bodies of knowledge on youth digital ethics. Today MTV and MIT announced that the wider research community is invited to learn from this data and gain a deeper understanding of the digital behaviors that youth feel cross the line from innocent to inappropriate. We are hopeful this will help fuel innovation in the realm of cyber bullying prevention.

We have absolutely seen a significant commitment from the federal government and leadership from the private sector. I'm happy to report that there's also significant work and progress in states and districts.

In New Jersey, the Anti-Bullying Bill of Rights that took effect September 1 will send a strong message that puts the state, school officials and law enforcement on the side of victims.

Connecticut, for example, recently passed legislation that provides additional guidance on preventing and intervening in bullying and cyber bullying.

In Hawaii, a new state law requires monitoring of schools' compliance with anti-bullying policies.

In Texas, a recent law will expand the definition of bullying to include cyber bullying and to require schools to have policies for reporting and investigating bullying incidents.

And Georgia has recently updated its model bullying policy to make clear that districts are required to report bullying incident data to the state.

There is ongoing work in Florida and North Carolina to update and more clearly define the characteristics of bullying.

In Massachusetts, there are initiatives to provide training for teachers and school personnel to prevent, identify, and respond to bullying.

In North Carolina, a clear and comprehensive list of enumerated characteristics means that all cases of bullying will be addressed.

And finally, today Michigan is announcing a crack down on cyber bullying.

States and our partner agencies are moving forward on a number of fronts, but we all know our work is far from over. As I said a year ago, and as I promise you again today, we remain committed to continuing to provide the guidance and technical assistance to address bullying. It is an educational priority that goes to the heart of student learning and school culture. It is an issue of school safety. We at the Department of Education and our federal partners are not going to fail any more children. We are in this for the long haul.

Truly addressing bullying requires a systematic paradigm shift, so we must find ways to open up lines of communication and change the cultures in our schools so students feel accepted and supported in asserting their own identities.

I want to close by telling you about the hundreds of letters that the President and I have received from parents and students desperately looking for answers. One young girl from Athens, Texas, told me, "I'm being bullied in school and on the bus. I am afraid of telling somebody because they might hear about it and do something bad to me. I don't really like telling on somebody . . . I've told the principals but they didn't do anything about it. I've considered suicide, but that won't help anything . . . that'll only hurt my family. Please give me advice on what to do, steps to make them stop!"

And a mother in Sugarloaf, Pennsylvania, writes "I am going through the problem of bullying with my fifteen year old daughter who is being bullied almost every day. She used to be a straight A student and love school. Now she hates it, and she doesn't want to go and is barely making honors. I have enrolled her in counseling hoping to save her from herself. . . . I cry almost every day knowing this is happening to my child and I am helpless. There is nothing I can do to make the pain go away. We try, the school tries, but these children do not seem to understand. . . . I fear for my daughter, mostly I fear for her from herself." I fear for her from herself.

I have to tell you as a parent and father of two young children—these letters break my heart. But I promise you I will not look the other way when students fear for their safety at school, worry about being bullied, or suffer discrimination and taunts because of their race, sex, religion, sexual orientation, disability, or any other reasons.

And I know President Obama will not allow this on his watch either. As he says, "We must dispel the myth that bullying is just a harmless rite of passage. We have begun to do so, but we cannot become passive and believe we have won this fight until no student feels like they cannot attend school because of the bullying they face."

But none of us can confront this or stop this alone. Nor should we. When we stand together we can address bullying and fight the hatred, bigotry and fear that divide us. Our children deserve no less. And when we do support them, we give them the opportunity to fulfill their true academic and social potential. Thank you for your courage, thank you for your commitment, and most importantly, thank you for the difference you are making in the lives of children. I am proud to be your partner in this effort.

About Anne Duncan

Arne Duncan, the ninth US secretary of education, was nominated by President Barack Obama and confirmed by the US Senate on January 20, 2009. As secretary, he is best known for his Race to the Top initiative, which invites states to compete for federal education funds by submitting proposals for statewide education reforms. Before he began his post as secretary of education, Duncan served as the chief executive officer of the Chicago Public Schools from June 2001 through December 2008, where he was appointed by Mayor Richard M. Daley. In Chicago, Duncan has been praised for raising standardized test scores and criticized for closing neighborhood schools and replacing them with charter schools.

Victim Impact Statement

Jane Clementi

In September 2010, Rutgers University student Tyler Clementi committed suicide after his roommate, Dharun Ravi, watched Clementi and another man, via a webcam, in an intimate encounter in the dorm room Clementi and Ravi shared. Ravi was indicted on counts of invasion of privacy, bias intimidation, tampering with evidence, and other charges. He was convicted on all counts. Speaking on the occasion of Ravi's sentencing, Clementi's mother, Jane, begins by discussing the emotional devastation she felt as a result of losing her son. She imagines what pain and anguish he must have been in when he decided to take his own life. Mrs. Clementi recalls the family's first encounter with Tyler's roommate, Dharun Ravi, who used her son's email address to discover Tyler's online browsing habits and expose him as gay. She explains how Ravi used webcam feeds and social media to ridicule Tyler, and appeals to Judge Berman to deliver a fair and just sentence for the crimes committed against her son.

N.B.: MB refers to the unnamed witness who was captured on video in his meetings with Tyler Clementi.

My world came crumbling apart in September 2010. The devastation of the loss of my son was more than I could bear and the thought of reliving it over again was one of the reasons I had gone along with the more than generous pretrial plea "deal." After having sat through the horrendous and tortuous reenactment of the crimes committed against my son, feeling the pain and anguish that he must have felt during his final days, listening to the lies and deceptions of the defendant, and in light of the jury's unanimous findings for the crimes committed against my son, MB and now our family, by submitting us to the pain and emotional frustration of the trial, I now know I must seek accountability under the laws of our state under the guidance and direction of Judge Berman.

We do not know what Tyler was thinking or why he did what he did since he did not tell us. He obviously hid his feelings and thoughts very well. Even I had no idea of the despair and torment Tyler must have been feeling and I thought I knew him. Tyler and I had been very connected, so much so that I felt like a piece of me died in September 2010. That connection became very real to me again during the trial as most of the time I was listening and watching as if through Tyler's ears, eyes, and mind.

The pain and anguish that I felt during the trial was overwhelming at times. As different pieces of evidence were presented, they would trigger memories, both good and bad, but nonetheless all bittersweet and sad. Even simple things such as Tyler's laptop reminded me how he carefully explored his options and then chose the different features he liked best, including the blue color for the case. And the photos of his dorm room, reminiscing on how carefully we had shopped for all the components of his room, like the lamps and the bedding and all the other accessories. All the dates repeatedly mentioned during the trial, all triggering memories in my head, terrible horrific memories that will forever hold me captive. Some memories seemed good at the time, but have now taken on new meaning for me during and since the trial. As I now have come to a better understanding as to what was really occurring.

One memory I now struggle with most is move-in day. The only day I ever encountered his roommate. Tyler was so excited about the move. I could sense a little nervousness on the morning but still so very excited. We had gotten there early, close to the start time so as to have lots of time to get settled

> *To video chat a live stream of someone's most intimate actions without their consent or knowledge is wrong and it's criminal.*

before the activities of the day would begin. Oddly, his roommate was nowhere to be seen. All of the other rooms were crowded and busting out with people and excitement. But we were alone. We were able to get Tyler completely settled and organized and had left to go to the bookstore to get his books before his roommate even arrived. When we returned with Tyler's books, the roommate and his family were present getting him settled. When we entered the room, we said hello and the only response was from his mother, then his father came over to say hello.

The roommate ignored Tyler, continuing to work on his computer. He didn't even look up. In this tiny 10 by 14 foot room, it is pretty hard to hide or miss 3 people but he never even paused to acknowledge that Tyler was even in the room. He never stopped what he was doing. Nothing, no greeting, no smile, no recognition, no anything, he just continued in silence to work on his computer. Only after his parents called him over did he stop and come the 2 feet towards us to say hello. More to me and my husband than to Tyler and then he went right back to what he was doing. At the time, I thought maybe he was stressed by trying to get his computer set up. But thanks to the defense attorney, I have learned that was wrong, after all, he is such a "computer expert," no stress there. I was also incorrect in thinking that maybe he was shy. Wrong again, according to the defense lawyer he was extremely social and outgoing, making lots of friends in a very short amount of time. So that left me tortured and heartbroken yet again as I sat in the courtroom to think and come to the realization that he came to Rutgers that fall with preconceived ideas about Tyler and he never had any intentions of befriending Tyler or even of being a considerate or trustworthy roommate.

When most people get their roommate's name and email address, they might either go to Facebook, asking "to be friends" or they could send an email and start a conversation. But yet another terribly painful and unbearable realization I had to learn was Tyler's roommate did not follow any of these conventional social graces. No instead he took Tyler's email address put it into different search engines and found out what web sites Tyler frequented. Based on what he found out, he judged Tyler. He decided that he knew all he wanted to know about Tyler. Getting to know Tyler and developing a friendship with Tyler was not what he had in mind. The sad part is what he found out was only one part of who Tyler was. He would never really know Tyler. Not the smart, kind, articulate, humble, funny, talented, caring, thoughtful, generous, trustworthy, and dependable person Tyler was. All he found out was that Tyler was gay.

The fact that Tyler went to the RA shows me just how totally overwhelmed and devastated Tyler must have felt. It was a monumental step that Tyler reached out for assistance. He rarely ever went for help from his teachers or others. He had always been very resourceful. This act of going to the RA shows me just how totally frustrated and out of control Tyler must have thought this situation was. Tyler knew how serious these actions were and he knew the situation needed to be reported to the authorities.

I can't help but still wonder why it was not reported to the police at that time, there may have been a very different outcome.

If setting up the web cam once was not bad enough, doing it a second time, clearly knowing what he would see, and then advertising and promoting it on his public Twitter page is just down right cold and vicious. And to make things even worse, to take credit for disconnecting the web cam, after he knew Tyler had done it and Tyler was not here to speak up for himself, is just malicious and evil. How difficult and torturous it was for me to sit through the lies and deceptions of the defense. I am very grateful to Ms. McClure for allowing the truth on that matter to shine and not get buried. The truth will prevail and it will either set you free or hold you in bondage.

Another devastating part of the trial was learning how many times Tyler went back to his roommate's Twitter page those last few days. The frustration and turmoil must have been just growing faster than the speed of light in Tyler's mind. It appeared from the evidence that this was probably the last thing Tyler looked at on his computer before he left his dorm room for the bridge on Wednesday, September 22, 2010. My question is why didn't his roommate just request a roommate change? Why was he so arrogant, so mean spirited and evil that he would humiliate and embarrass Tyler in front of Tyler's new dorm mates, the very people Tyler was trying to meet and become friends with? How could they all just go along with such meanness? Why didn't any one of them speak up and stop it? How did it spiral so out of control? They knew it was wrong and yet no one stopped it. No one spoke up to the "master mind," the "computer genius." We need to make sure everyone knows that these actions are wrong, they are mean spirited, they are evil and most importantly, they are against the law.

To video chat a live stream of someone's most intimate actions without their consent or knowledge is wrong and it's criminal. Tyler did not know how much was or was not observed. All that was racing through his head was what he was reading on the Twitter and Facebook pages. It is overwhelming and so painful, just thinking about Tyler realizing what had happened and his confusion and distress as he tried to decide what he should do next. What could he do? He went to the RA, really, really big for him, monumental. Tyler must have been beside himself to do that!! The anguish and frustration must have been insurmountable to him. Even now 19 months later, I feel such sadness and grief, which quickly turns to anger and rage coming up from deep within me just thinking about these events and what Tyler must have been feeling. What I want is justice. Many people are watching and I am asking the court to do the right thing. The court needs to show the residents of New Jersey, for that matter the entire country, this was not right, it is not acceptable behavior and it will not be tolerated. I trust The Honorable Judge Berman will interpret the laws and impose the proper sentence that fits the crimes that were committed against my son and MB.

Consequences that are significant enough for the defendant to wake up and realize that what he did was wrong. He broke the law and New Jersey does not tolerate criminal actions without penalties. We are all responsible for our actions and these actions were criminal and require accountability. No one is above the law. Justice must be served.

I would also like to thank the entire Middlesex County Prosecutor's office, specifically Mr. Bruce Kaplan, Ms. Julia McClure, Mr. Chris Shellborn, Lieutenant Randi Colatrella, Investigator Frank Dininno, Agent Nicole Ortiz, Mrs. Jayne Guarino, Mrs. Diane Johnson, Ms. Christi Delgaldo, as well as the court employees, Sergeant Keith Lane and all the officers of the court. Each and every member of this team performed in a professional and courteous manner, with the highest level of character and integrity.

Their knowledge, skill and expertise made the truth shine and the outcome worth all the pain it caused my family. Also their kindness, understanding and compassion helped me to be able to bear a most intolerable situation. Thank you.

About Jane Clementi

Jane Clementi is the mother of Tyler Clementi, a Rutgers student who jumped to his death from the George Washington Bridge after being bullied by his roommate, Dharun Ravi, in September 2010. She and her husband, Joe Clementi, created the Tyler Clementi Foundation in honor of their son. The foundation aims to promote the acceptance of lesbian, gay, bisexual, and transsexual teenagers, to prevent suicide among young people, and to discourage cyberbullying. The Clementis live in Ridgewood, New Jersey.

Online and Overexposed: Consumer Privacy, the FTC, and the Rise of the Cyberazzi

Federal Trade Commission Chair Jon Leibowitz

Commissioner Jon Leibowitz begins by introducing a new study that aims to protect consumer privacy. He compares the paparazzi photos used to invent dubious and sensationalistic stories for the tabloid press to "cyberazzi" data, which creates a picture of our online habits for use by marketing firms. The commissioner points to the potential for this information to be misused, or for it to create an inaccurate portrayal of individuals when taken out of context. He discusses Do Not Track technology, stressing that the Federal Trade Commission (FTC) does not care how it works, as long as it is easy to use and consumers can actively and effectively use it to determine their participation in data tracking. He then explains the latest methods for the FTC to protect children with the Children's Online Privacy Protection Act (COPPA). Liebowitz concludes by stressing that "the FTC is committed to a thriving and innovative Internet through policy recommendations for self-regulatory efforts and strong enforcement."

Thank you Jeff, and let me also extend my thanks to the many other organizers of this event. I'm happy to be here. Jeff will be announcing a new study today, which we haven't yet seen, but I am certain it will move us toward the goal we all share—and it seems to me that goal is shared by many businesses—protecting consumer privacy while ensuring a cyberspace that generates the free content we've all come to expect and enjoy.

Based on reading we have been doing over the last couple of weeks, most of it picked up while waiting in line at the grocery store, we have concluded: Kirstie Alley could have had gastric bypass surgery, and Kim Kardashian almost definitely had a butt lift. Blake Lively and Leo diCaprio's short-lived relationship seems faker than—well, Kim Kardashian's rear end.

And it doesn't look good for Ashton and Demi; she's been nowhere near the set of *Two and a Half Men*.

Thank goodness for the paparazzi. And really, who cares that, of the 1000 words each of their pictures is worth, at best only about 500 are true? Public figures choose to make their livings monetizing their identities; in a free market, it is hardly surprising that photographers and gossip rags want to get in on the action.

It would be a different story, of course, if the paparazzi turned their lenses on those of us who don't have jobs treading the red carpet—if they snapped photos of

Delivered October 11, 2011. Remarks made at the National Press Club, Washington, DC, by Federal Trade Commission Chair Jon Leibowitz. Source: United States Federal Trade Commission. www.ftc.gov.

us in what we thought were our private moments and then sold them without our permission, the resulting montage a detailed and perhaps damaging portrait of our selves.

But you could make the case that this is exactly what happens every time we access the Internet. A host of invisible cyberazzi—cookies and other data catchers— follow us as we browse, reporting our every stop and action to marketing firms that, in turn, collect an astonishingly complete profile of our online behavior. Whenever we click, so do they.

One day you might print out a CDC fact sheet on alcoholism to help your son with a project for health class. Click. Or you order a box of your mother's favorite candy to take her when you go visit. Click. Or you buy the book "The Winner's Guide to Casino Gambling" as a raffle prize for your church's Las Vegas night. Click.

You know you are a dutiful parent, but a potential employer could see a boozy job applicant. You know you are a thoughtful daughter, but a health insurer could see a destined diabetic. You know you are a generous member of the community, but a loan officer could see a risky gambler.

Click. Click. Click.

It is true that paparazzi know who their celebrity subjects are while the cyberazzi may not have linked—at least not publically—our identities to the profiles they are building. But that could happen; disturbingly, it may even become common practice.

Often the buyers of these cyber-snaps are companies that target internet advertising to your particular interests, a beneficial—or at worst innocuous—marketing practice that helps support free web content. But your tracked information doesn't have to stop there; it could be traded throughout an invisible lattice of companies, snowballing into an exhaustive profile of you available to those making critical decisions about your career, finances, health, and reputation.

Of course, most online advertisers are nothing like paparazzi; many companies have strong privacy policies protecting consumers. But we are not presenting a digitally altered picture of the situation. Once you enter cyberspace, software placed on your computer—usually without your consent or even knowledge—turns your private information into a commodity out of your control. And keep in mind: as my former colleague Republican FTC Chairman Debbie Majoras used to say, your computer is your property.

At the FTC, we want you to get that control back. We've been safeguarding privacy since long before the cyberazzi focused their wide angles on the public. Our goal: to stay one step ahead of technology as it races along, finding better hiding places, stronger lenses, and more means to record and store your every move.

The FTC has been working on consumer privacy since the 1970's. In the early days of the Internet, businesses posted privacy policies, which they—and we—expected consumers to read and understand. We soon learned that both were unlikely. Who is going to examine a legal document as long as the Code of Hammurabi, when all that stands between them and free shipping is checking the little box—often conveniently pre-checked for you—that says, "I consent"?

This is not meaningful privacy protection for consumers in cyberspace. With that same space expanding exponentially to allow more and more data collection that is more and more often invisible to consumers, the Commission is looking for another way to allow consumers to cap the lenses of the cyberazzi.

Looking to how celebrities handle paparazzi doesn't provide much guidance: Matt Damon suggested never doing anything in public of any interest. Jude Law counseled tossing root vegetables at the stalkers. The Commission decided to take instead a position that, while organic, was not so in the vegetative sense: In a preliminary report issued by staff in December 2010, we proposed a new framework for safeguarding consumers' personal data flexible enough to allow both businesses and consumers to continue to profit from an innovating, growing, and rich information marketplace. We expect to issue a final report in the coming months.

> **At the FTC, we want you to get that control back. We've been safeguarding privacy since long before the cyberazzi focused their wide angles on the public. Our goal: to stay one step ahead of technology as it races along, finding better hiding places, stronger lenses, and more means to record and store your every move.**

The report puts forth three principles to guide policymakers and industry as they, we hope, work together to protect privacy online.

First, companies in the business of collecting, storing, and manipulating consumer data need to build privacy protections into their everyday business practices—we call this "privacy by design." Companies that collect consumer data should do so only for a specific business purpose, store it securely, keep it only as long as necessary to fulfill its legitimate business need, then dispose of it safely. The more sensitive the data, the stronger the protections should be. To its credit, much of industry is embracing this approach—even before we issued the draft report.

Second, transparency. Any companies gathering information online need to tell consumers what's going on. And by this, I do not mean another three-point font, ten-page document written by corporate lawyers and buried deep within the site. I asked our staff to look at data disclosures on mobile devices; one form took 109 clicks to get through, and the staffer who discovered that is probably the only one who ever made it to click number 109.

Transparency is not an unreasonable request. My daughters can go to any of a number of retail clothing websites, and, with one click, see a clear description of a pair of pants—color, sizes, fit, customer reviews, shipping options. One more click—that's a total of 2, not 109—and they can choose exactly the pants they want, in their sizes and favorite colors, shipped where they want them. Put the guy who designed that page on the job of presenting a meaningful disclosure and consent form.

Third, choice. Consumers should have streamlined and effective choices about the collection and use of their data. That includes choices about when, why, and how cyberazzi follow them into cyberspace. To that end, we proposed a "Do Not Track" mechanism that will allow consumers to decide whether to share information about their browsing behavior. We envision a system consumers can find and use easily and one that all companies employing cyberazzi must respect.

A vision of Do Not Track bears some similarities to the successful Do Not Call program. Now with more than 200 million registered phone numbers, Do Not Call has brought some peace and quiet to Americans' dinner hour; no wonder Dave Barry called it the "most popular federal concept since the Elvis stamp." But unlike Do Not Call, the FTC does not think Do Not Track should be administered by the government. We hope different sectors of industry will work collaboratively to give consumers choices about how and when they are tracked online.

A number of leading online businesses have responded to our call for Do Not Track. Microsoft, Mozilla, and Apple have implemented their own Do Not Track features, and we remain hopeful that Google will join them. A half dozen advertising networks pledged to honor the Mozilla Do Not Track header. And that, I suspect is only the tip of the online advertising iceberg.

The FTC's chief technologist, the wonderful Ed Felten, is participating in the W3C, a key Internet standards-setting body defining technical standards for Do Not Track. In this and other similar endeavors, the FTC supports standards that provide persistent and effective choices but do not interfere with the normal data flows necessary to a thriving Internet. We think this balance can be struck without too much difficulty.

To its credit, the online advertising industry is also focusing on consumer choice architecture. The Digital Advertising Alliance, a coalition of media and marketing associations, is making progress on its "Ad Choices" icon, which consumers can click to opt out of targeted advertising. We are encouraging the industry to partner with browser vendors to ensure that consumer choice is persistent and effective, and that it encompasses not just the advertising the consumer sees, but also the information about the consumer that the advertisers—and others—collect.

Of all the recommendations in the December privacy report, Do Not Track has probably received the most exposure: in fact, it has probably been overexposed, leading to a fuzzy picture of exactly what Do Not Track will do.

To be clear: Do Not Track will not end behavioral advertising, the targeted marketing that funds a wealth of free online content. The FTC has no intention of pulling a Sean Penn on the cyberazzi. Many, if not most, consumers prefer targeted ads: do you really want to scroll through a leggings' montage from Forever 21 when you can instead open your computer right to the announcement of LL Bean's annual chinos' sale?

At the FTC, we are agnostic as to how Do Not Track comes about: it doesn't matter what technology backs the system, so long as it works. But no matter what, it should be easy to use and easy to find.

Industry's interest in developing tracking choices for consumers is heartening; they have the experience and knowledge to draft a flexible, workable approach quickly. If they do not, however, there are signs that Congress might impose a Do Not Track system of its own design on the private sector.

When it comes to the tracking of adults, we believe that, with good faith and full disclosure on all sides, industry will strike a reasonable balance between consumer privacy and the information needs of online advertisers. But the cyberazzi do need to stay away from our kids—at least without parental consent.

The FTC protects children's privacy online through COPPA—the Children's Online Privacy Protection Act—and our Rule implementing the Act. The Rule requires operators of websites and online services directed at children under the age of 13, as well as other online sites and services that knowingly collect information from children under 13, to obtain parental consent before collecting personal information from children.

Last month, we proposed updates to the COPPA Rule to keep pace with both rapid technological change—such as geo-location services, social networks, and tracking cookies—and even more rapid evolution of tech-savvy kids' ability to outwit parental consent. We are seeking public comment on the proposed amendments and will take into account all the comments we expect to receive—from consumer groups, advertisers, children's website operators, and technologists.

While we at the FTC are proud of our work on privacy policy and rules, we are primarily an enforcement agency. Over the last ten years, we've brought more than 100 spam and spyware cases, and 79 Do Not Call cases with over $580 million in civil penalties ordered. We've also brought more than 30 data security cases, most of which ended in companies adopting comprehensive security programs and undergoing independent audits.

You have probably heard about our cases against Google for its Buzz social network, and against Twitter for data security lapses that allowed hackers to gain control of accounts—one sending a tweet purportedly from President Barack Obama offering the chance to win $500 in free gas, and another purportedly from Britney Spears making disturbing comments about her own anatomy. Decorum prevents me from relaying those unauthorized Britney Spears postings.

But you may not have heard about our action against a company called Chitika. Though it's not a household name, Chitika has a sizeable presence behind the scenes delivering targeted online advertising. It offered consumers the chance to opt out of tracking but did not disclose that the opt-out was good for only ten days. To settle FTC charges, Chitika agreed to stop making misrepresentations and only supply real opt-outs that last at least five years.

Here, again, we capped the overly long lens of this cyberazzi. And Chitika has also gone one step further: it has agreed to honor the Do Not Track signal that browser companies like Mozilla have implemented.

Today we are announcing a privacy case against a company called Frostwire, which offers mobile P2P software used by hundreds of thousands of consumers. We charged that Frostwire shared its users' personal cellphone pictures and other data without their consent. Frostwire's default settings, which were extremely difficult to change, had been automatically revealing private photos and videos taken with users' phones to other P2P users around the world—in effect turning all its clients into both unwitting paparazzi and unaware paparazzi victims.

We now have a settlement order against Frostwire prohibiting default settings that automatically share the files users have created. Had Frostwire practiced privacy by design, as our 2010 staff report suggested, it would have built into the software consumers' reasonable expectations that their private photos stay private, and would have avoided a run-in with our agency's team. Had it embraced the transparency principle, it would have provided clearer information to consumers who could make choices about the sharing of personal content like photos and videos.

The bottom line is this: cyberspace need not be a privacy-free zone, a place where, without our consent or knowledge, our every online click is tracked and recorded with the intensity of a "National Enquirer" photographer trying to catch Justin Bieber on a bad hair day. The FTC is committed to a thriving and innovative Internet through policy recommendations for self-regulatory efforts and strong enforcement. By working with all of you in the audience today, I believe we can keep cyberazzi lenses focused on willing subjects and ensure the right of all citizens to choose the public faces we present to the world.

About Jon Leibowitz

A Phi Beta Kappa graduate of the University of Wisconsin with a bachelor's in American history (1980), Jon Leibowitz graduated from the New York University School of Law in 1984 and worked as an attorney in private practice in Washington, DC, from 1984 to 1986. Leibowitz then worked for Senator Paul Simon from 1986 to 1987. He served as chief counsel and staff director for the Senate Subcommittee on Terrorism and Technology from 1995 to 1996 and the Senate Subcommittee on Juvenile Justice from 1991 to 1994. He was chief counsel to Senator Herb Kohl from 1989 to 2000. He was the Democratic chief counsel and staff director for the US Senate Antitrust Subcommittee from 1997 to 2000. Leibowitz served as vice president for congressional affairs for the Motion Picture Association of America from 2000 to 2004. Leibowitz was sworn in as a commissioner on September 3, 2004, and was designated to serve as chair of the Federal Trade Commission on March 2, 2009, by President Barack Obama.

Internet Privacy

The Views of the FTC, the FCC, and NTIA

Edith Ramirez

In testimony given before the House of Representatives, Edith Ramirez, a commissioner of the Federal Trade Commission (FTC), describes the implications for consumer privacy of some routine but little-known uses of consumer data. She summarizes the commission's recent enforcement efforts, including actions against companies as well known as Google and lesser-known companies such as Teletrack and Chitika. Ramirez goes on to enumerate the commission's steps toward the education of children and adults about privacy concerns, citing numerous publications by the commission. On behalf of the FTC, she encourages Congress to enact data security legislation that would standardize the requirements imposed on companies regarding data security, and require companies to notify consumers when the security of their information has been compromised.

Introduction

Chairman Bono-Mack, Chairman Walden, Ranking Member Butterfield, Ranking Member Eshoo, and members of the Subcommittees, I am Edith Ramirez, a Commissioner of the Federal Trade Commission ("FTC" or "Commission").[1]

Privacy has been an important part of the Commission's consumer protection mission for 40 years.[2] During this time, the Commission's goal in the privacy arena has remained constant: to protect consumers' personal information and ensure that they have the confidence to take advantage of the many benefits offered by the dynamic and ever-changing marketplace. To meet this objective, the Commission has undertaken substantial efforts to promote privacy in the private sector through law enforcement, education, and policy initiatives. For example, since 2001, the Commission has brought 34 cases challenging the practices of companies that failed to adequately protect consumers' personal information; more than 100 spam and spyware cases; and 16 cases for violation of the Children's Online Privacy Protection Act ("COPPA").[3] The Commission also has distributed millions of copies of educational materials for consumers and businesses to address ongoing threats to security and privacy. And the FTC examines the implications of new technologies and business practices on consumer privacy through ongoing policy initiatives, such as a recent proposed privacy framework.

Delivered July 14, 2011. Remarks made before the Committee on Energy and Commerce's Subcommittee on Commerce, Manufacturing and Trade and the Subcommittee on Communications and Technology in the US House of Representatives. Source: United States Federal Trade Commission. www.ftc.gov.

This testimony begins by describing some of the uses of consumer data that affect consumers' privacy today. It then offers an overview of the Commission's recent enforcement, education, and policy efforts. While the testimony does not offer views on general privacy legislation, the Commission continues to encourage Congress to enact data security legislation that would (1) impose data security standards on companies, and (2) require companies, in appropriate circumstances, to provide notification to consumers when there is a security breach.[4]

Information Flows in the Current Marketplace

For today's consumer, understanding the complex transfers of personal information that occur offline and online is a daunting task. Indeed, these information flows take place in almost every conceivable consumer interaction. For example, a consumer goes to work and provides sensitive information to her employer, such as her Social Security number, to verify her employment eligibility, and bank account number, so that she can get paid. After work, she uses an application on her smartphone to locate the closest ATM so that she can withdraw cash. She then visits her local grocery store and signs up for a loyalty card to get discounts on future purchases. Upon returning home, the consumer logs onto her computer and begins browsing the web and updates her social networking profile. Later, her twelve-year-old grabs her smartphone and plays games on a mobile app.

All of these activities clearly benefit the consumer—she gets paid, enjoys free and immediate access to information, locates places of interest, obtains discounts on purchases, stays connected with friends, and can entertain herself and her family. Her life is made easier in myriad ways because of information flows.

There are other implications, however, that may be less obvious. Her grocery store purchase history, web activities, and even her location information may be collected and then sold to data brokers and other companies she does not know exist. These companies could use her information to market other products and services to her or to make decisions about her eligibility for credit, employment, or insurance. And the companies with whom she and her family interact may not maintain reasonable safeguards to protect the data they have collected.

Some consumers have no idea that this type of information collection and sharing is taking place. Others may be troubled by the collection and sharing described above. Still others may be aware of this collection and use of their personal information but view it as a worthwhile trade-off for innovative products and services, convenience, and personalization. And some consumers—some teens for example—may be aware of the sharing that takes place, but may not appreciate the risks it poses. Because of these differences in consumer understanding and attitudes, as well as the rapid pace of change in technology, policymaking on privacy issues presents significant challenges.

As the hypothetical described above shows, consumer privacy issues touch many aspects of our lives in both the brick-and-mortar and electronic worlds. In the offline world, data brokers have long gathered information about our retail purchases, and consumer reporting agencies have long made decisions about our eligibility for credit, employment, and insurance based on our past transactions. But new online business models such as online behavioral advertising, social networking, and location-based services have complicated the privacy picture. In addition, the aggregation of data in both the online and offline worlds have in some instances led to increased opportunities for fraud. For instance, entities have used past transaction history gathered from both the online and offline worlds to sell "sucker lists" of consumers who may be susceptible to different types of fraud. In both the online and offline worlds, data security continues to be an issue. The FTC continues to tackle each of these issues through enforcement, education, and policy initiatives.

Enforcement

In the last 15 years, the Commission has brought 34 data security cases; 64 cases against companies for improperly calling consumers on the Do Not Call registry;[5] 586 cases against companies for violating the Fair Credit Reporting Act ("FCRA");[6] 697 spam cases; 15 spyware (or nuisance adware) cases; 16 cases against companies for violating COPPA; and numerous cases against companies for violating the FTC Act by making deceptive claims about the privacy and security protections they afford to consumer data. Where the FTC has authority to seek civil penalties, it has aggressively done so. It has obtained $60 million in civil penalties in Do Not Call cases; $21 million in civil penalties under the FCRA; $5.7 million under the CAN-SPAM Act;[7] and $6.2 million under COPPA. Where the Commission does not have authority to seek civil penalties, as in the data security and spyware areas, it has sought such authority from Congress.

> *For today's consumer, understanding the complex transfers of personal information that occur offline and online is a daunting task. Indeed, these information flows take place in almost every conceivable consumer interaction.*

And these activities do not fully reflect the scope of the Commission's vigorous enforcement agenda, as not all investigations result in enforcement actions. When an enforcement action is not warranted, staff closes the investigation, and in some cases it issues a closing letter.[8] This testimony highlights the Commission's recent, publicly-announced enforcement efforts to address the types of privacy issues raised by the hypothetical scenario described above.

First, the Commission enforces the FTC Act and several other laws that require companies to maintain reasonable safeguards for the consumer data they maintain.[9]

Most recently, the Commission resolved allegations that Ceridian Corporation[10] and Lookout Services, Inc.[11] violated the FTC Act by failing to implement reasonable safeguards to protect the sensitive consumer information they maintained. The companies offered, respectively, payroll processing and immigration compliance services for small business employers. As a result, they both obtained, processed, and stored highly-sensitive information—including Social Security numbers—of employees. The Commission alleged that both companies failed to appropriately safeguard this information, which resulted in intruders being able to access it. The orders require the companies to implement a comprehensive data security program and obtain independent audits for 20 years.

Second, the Commission enforces the FCRA, which, among other things, prescribes that companies only sell sensitive consumer report information for "permissible purposes," and not for general marketing purposes. Last month, the Commission announced an FCRA enforcement action against Teletrack, Inc., which provides consumer reporting services to payday lenders, rental purchase stores, and certain auto lenders so that they can determine consumers' eligibility to receive credit.[12]

The Commission alleged that Teletrack created a marketing database of consumers and sold lists of consumers who had applied for payday loans to entities that did not have a permissible purpose. The Commission asserted that Teletrack's sale of these lists violated the FCRA because the lists were in fact consumer reports, which cannot be sold for marketing purposes. The Commission's agreement with Teletrack requires it to pay $1.8 million in civil penalties for FCRA violations.

Third, the Commission has been active in ensuring that companies engaged in social networking adhere to any promises to keep consumers' information private.[13] The Commission's recent case against Google alleges that the company deceived consumers by using information collected from Gmail users to generate and populate its social network, Google Buzz.[14]

The Commission charged that Google made public its Gmail users' associations with their frequent email contacts without the users' consent and in contravention of Google's privacy policy. As part of the Commission's proposed settlement order, Google must implement a comprehensive privacy program and conduct independent audits every other year for the next 20 years.[15]

Further, Google must obtain affirmative express consent for product or service enhancements that involve new sharing of previously collected data.[16]

Fourth, the Commission has sought to protect consumers from deceptive practices in the behavioral advertising area. Last month, the Commission finalized a settlement with Chitika, Inc., an online network advertiser that acts as an intermediary between website publishers and advertisers.

The Commission's complaint alleged that Chitika violated the FTC Act by offering consumers the ability to opt out of the collection of information to be used for targeted advertising—without telling them that the opt-out lasted only ten days. The Commission's order prohibits Chitika from making future privacy misrepresentations. It also requires Chitika to provide consumers with an effective opt-out mechanism, link to this opt-out mechanism in its advertisements, and provide a notice on its website for consumers who may have opted out when Chitika's opt-out mechanism was ineffective. Finally, the order requires Chitika to destroy any data that can be associated with a consumer that it collected during the time its opt-out mechanism was ineffective.

Finally, the Commission has sought to ensure that data brokers respect consumers' choices. In March, the Commission announced a final order against US Search, a data broker that maintained an online service, which allowed consumers to search for information about others.[17]

The company allowed consumers to opt out of having their information appear in search results for a fee of $10. The Commission charged that, although 4,000 consumers paid the fee and opted out, their personal information still appeared in search results. The Commission's settlement requires US Search to disclose limitations on its opt-out offer and to provide refunds to consumers who had previously opted out.

Education

The FTC conducts outreach to businesses and consumers in the area of consumer privacy. The Commission's well-known OnGuard Online website educates consumers about many online threats to consumer privacy and security, including spam, spyware, phishing, peer- to-peer ("P2P") file sharing, and social networking.[18]

Last month, the FTC issued a new consumer education guide called "Understanding Mobile Apps: Questions and Answers." The guide provides consumers with information about mobile apps, including what apps are, the types of data they can collect and share, and why some apps collect geolocation information.[19] The FTC issued the guide to help consumers better understand the privacy and security implications of using mobile apps before downloading them.

The Commission has also issued numerous education materials to help consumers protect themselves from identity theft and to deal with its consequences when it does occur. The FTC has distributed over 3.8 million copies of a victim recovery guide, *Take Charge: Fighting Back Against Identity Theft*, and has recorded over 3.5 million visits to the Web version.[20]

In addition, the FTC has developed education resources specifically for children, parents, and teachers to help children stay safe online. In response to the Broadband Data Improvement Act of 2008, the FTC produced the brochure *Net Cetera: Chatting with Kids About Being Online* to give adults practical tips to help children navigate the online world.[21] In less than one year, the Commission distributed more than 7 million copies of *Net Cetera* to schools and communities nationwide.

Business education is also an important priority for the FTC. The Commission developed a widely-distributed guide to help small and medium-sized businesses implement appropriate data security for the personal information they collect and maintain.[22]

Another way in which the Commission seeks to educate businesses is by publicizing its complaints and orders and issuing public closing letters. For example, the Commission recently sent a letter closing an investigation of Social Intelligence Corporation, a company that sold reports to employers about potential job applicants.[23] The reports included public information gathered from social networking sites. The investigation sought to determine Social Intelligence's compliance with the FCRA.[24] Although the staff decided to close the particular investigation, the public closing letter served to notify similarly situated businesses that, to the extent they collect information from social networking sites for employment determinations, they must comply with the FCRA. The letter included guidance on the obligations of such businesses under the FCRA. For example, companies must take reasonable steps to ensure the maximum possible accuracy of the information reported from social networking sites. They must also provide employers who use their reports with information about the employers' obligation to notify job applicants if they were denied employment on the basis of these reports, and to provide such applicants with information about their rights under the FCRA.

Policy Initiatives

The Commission reviews its rules periodically to ensure that they keep pace with changes in the marketplace.[25] The Commission is currently reviewing its rule implementing COPPA and anticipates that any proposed changes will be announced in the coming months.[26]

In addition to reviewing rules, the Commission's policy initiatives also include public workshops, reports, and policy reviews to examine the implications of new technologies and business practices on consumer privacy. For example, in December 2009, February 2010, and March 2010, the FTC convened three public roundtables to explore consumer privacy issues, including the issues facing the hypothetical consumer discussed in Section II above.[27]

The roundtables examined the effectiveness of current privacy approaches in addressing the challenges of the rapidly evolving market for consumer information, including consideration of the risks and benefits of consumer information collection and use; consumer expectations surrounding various information management practices; and the adequacy of existing legal and self-regulatory regimes to address privacy interests. At the roundtables, stakeholders across the board emphasized the need to improve the transparency of businesses' data practices, simplify the ability of consumers to exercise choices about how their information is collected and used, and ensure that businesses take privacy-protective measures as they develop and implement systems that involve consumer information.[28]

At the same time, the roundtable commenters and participants urged regulators to be cautious about restricting the exchange and use of consumer data in order to preserve the substantial consumer benefits made possible through the flow of information.

Staff issued a preliminary privacy report in December 2010 ("Staff Report"),[29] which discusses the major themes that emerged from these roundtables, including the ubiquitous collection and use of consumer data; the extent to which consumers are able to understand and to make informed choices about the collection and use of their data; the importance of privacy to many consumers; the significant benefits enabled by the increasing flow of information; and the blurring of the distinction between personally identifiable information and supposedly anonymous or de-identified information.[30] The Staff Report proposed a new framework to guide policymakers and industry as they consider further steps to improve consumer privacy protection.

The Proposed Framework

Second, the FTC staff proposed that companies provide simpler and more streamlined choices to consumers about their data practices. Under this approach, consumer choice would not be necessary for a limited set of "commonly accepted" data practices, thus allowing clearer, more meaningful choice with respect to practices of greater concern. This component of the proposed framework is premised on the notion that consumers reasonably expect companies to engage in certain practices, such as product and service fulfillment, internal operations such as assessing the quality of services offered, fraud prevention, legal compliance, and first-party marketing. Some of these practices, such as a retailer's collection of a consumer's address solely to deliver a product the consumer ordered, are obvious from the context of the transaction, and therefore, consumers' consent to them can be inferred. Others are sufficiently accepted or necessary for public policy reasons that companies need not request consent to engage in them. The Staff Report suggested that by clarifying those practices for which consumer consent is unnecessary, companies will be able to streamline their communications with consumers, which will reduce the burden and confusion on consumers and businesses alike.

The proposed framework included three main concepts. First, FTC staff proposed that companies should adopt a "privacy by design" approach by building privacy protections into their everyday business practices. Such protections include providing reasonable security for consumer data, collecting only the data needed for a specific business purpose, retaining data only as long as necessary to fulfill that purpose, safely disposing of data no longer in use, and implementing reasonable procedures to promote data accuracy. The Staff Report also urges companies to implement and to enforce procedurally sound privacy practices throughout their organizations, including, for example, assigning personnel to oversee privacy issues, training employees on privacy issues, and conducting privacy reviews when developing new products and services. Such concepts are not new, but the Staff Report indicated that the time has come for industry to implement them systematically. Implementation can be scaled, however, to each company's business operations. For example, the Staff Report recommended that companies that collect and use small amounts of nonsensitive consumer data should not have to devote the same level of resources to implementing privacy programs as companies that collect vast amounts of consumer data or data of a sensitive nature.

For data practices that are not "commonly accepted," the Staff Report proposed that consumers should have the ability to make informed and meaningful choices. To be most effective, choices should be clearly and concisely described and offered at a time and in a context in which the consumer is making a decision about his or her data. Depending upon the particular business model, this may entail a "just-in-time" approach, in which the company seeks consent at the point a consumer enters his personal data or before he accepts a product or service. One way to facilitate consumer choice is to provide it in a uniform and comprehensive way. Such an approach has been proposed for behavioral advertising, whereby consumers would be able to choose whether to allow the collection and use of data regarding their online searching and browsing activities. This idea—often referred to as "Do Not Track"—is discussed further below.

Third, the Staff Report proposed a number of measures that companies should take to make their data practices more transparent to consumers. For instance, in addition to providing the contextual disclosures described above, companies should improve their privacy notices so that consumers, advocacy groups, regulators, and others can compare data practices and choices across companies, thus promoting competition among companies. The Staff Report also proposed providing consumers with reasonable access to the data that companies maintain about them, particularly for non-consumer-facing entities such as data brokers. Because of the significant costs associated with access, the Staff Report noted that the extent of access should be proportional to both the sensitivity of the data and its intended use. In addition, the Staff Report stated that companies must provide prominent disclosures and obtain affirmative consent before using data in a materially different manner than claimed when the data was collected.

Finally, the Staff Report proposed that stakeholders undertake a broad effort to educate consumers about commercial data practices and the choices available to them. Increasing consumer understanding of the commercial collection and use of their information is important to both empowering consumers to make informed choices regarding their privacy and facilitating competition on privacy across companies. In addition to proposing these broad principles, the staff sought comment from all interested parties to help guide further development and refinement of the proposed framework. Close to 450 comments were received and the staff expects to issue a final report this year.

Do Not Track

As noted above, the Staff Report included a recommendation to implement Do Not Track—a universal, one-stop choice mechanism for online behavioral tracking, including behavioral advertising.[31] Following the release of the Staff Report, the Commission has testified that any Do Not Track system should include certain attributes.[32]

First, any Do Not Track system should be implemented universally, so that consumers do not have to repeatedly opt out of tracking on different sites. Second, the choice mechanism should be easy to find, easy to understand, and easy to use. Third, any choices offered should be persistent and should not be deleted if, for example, consumers clear their cookies or update their browsers. Fourth, a Do Not Track system should be comprehensive, effective, and enforceable. It should opt consumers out of behavioral tracking through any means and not permit technical loopholes. Finally, an effective Do Not Track system would go beyond simply opting consumers out of receiving targeted advertisements; it would opt them out of collection of behavioral data for all purposes other than product and service fulfillment and other commonly accepted practices.[33]

Of course, any Do Not Track system should not undermine the benefits that online behavioral advertising has to offer, by funding online content and services and providing personalized advertisements that many consumers value. For this reason, any Do Not Track mechanism should be flexible. For example, it should allow companies to explain the benefits of tracking and to take the opportunity to convince consumers not to opt out of tracking. Further, a Do Not Track system could include an option that enables consumers to control the types of advertising they want to receive and the types of data they are willing to have collected about them, in addition to providing the option to opt out completely.[34]

Industry appears to be receptive to the demand for simple choices. Within the last six months, three of the major browsers offered by Mozilla, Microsoft, and Apple announced the development of new choice mechanisms for online behavioral advertising that seek to provide increased transparency, greater consumer control and improved ease of use. Recently, Mozilla introduced a version of its browser that enables Do Not Track for mobile web browsing. In addition, an industry coalition of media and marketing associations, the Digital Advertising Alliance, has continued to make progress on implementation of its improved disclosure and consumer choice mechanism offered through a behavioral advertising icon.

Conclusion

The Commission is committed to protecting consumers' privacy and security—both online and offline. We look forward to continuing to work with Congress on these critical issues.

Notes

1. The views expressed in this statement represent the views of the Commission. My oral presentation and responses to questions are my own and do not necessarily represent the views of the Commission or any other Commissioner. Commissioner William E. Kovacic dissents from this testimony to the extent that it endorses a Do Not Track mechanism. Commissioner J. Thomas Rosch dissents to the portions of the testimony that discuss and describe certain conclusions about the concept of Do Not Track. Commissioner Rosch also has some reservations about the proposals in the preliminary staff privacy report.
2. Information on the FTC's privacy initiatives generally may be found at business.ftc.gov/privacy-and-security.
3. 15 U.S.C. §§ 6501-6508.
4. The Commission has long supported data security and breach notification legislation. *See, e.g.,* Prepared Statement of the Federal Trade Commission, *Data Security,* Before the Subcomm. on Commerce, Manufacturing, and Trade of the H. Comm. on Energy and Commerce, 112th Cong., June 15, 2011, *available at* http://www.ftc.gov/os/testimony/110615datasecurityhouse.pdf (noting the Commission's support for data security and breach notification standards); Prepared Statement of the Federal Trade Commission, *Protecting Social Security Numbers From Identity Theft,* Before the Subcomm. on Social Security of the H. Comm. on Ways and Means, 112th Cong., April 13, 2011, *available at* http://ftc.gov/os/testimony/110411ssn-idtheft.pdf (same); FTC, *Security in Numbers, SSNs and ID Theft* (Dec. 2008), *available at* www.ftc.gov/os/2008/12/P075414ssnreport.pdf; President's Identity Theft Task Force, *Identity Theft Task Force Report* (Sept. 2008), *available at* http://www.idtheft.gov/reports/IDTReport2008.pdf.
5. 16 C.F.R. Part 310.
6. 15 U.S.C. §§ 1681e-i.

7. 15 U.S.C. §§ 7701-7713.

8. *See* http://www.ftc.gov/os/closings/staffclosing.shtm.

9. *See* the Commission's Safeguards Rule, 16 C.F.R. Part 314, implementing provisions of the Gramm-Leach-Bliley Act, 15 U.S.C. § 6801(b), and the Commission's Disposal Rule, 16 C.F.R. Part 682, implementing provisions of the FCRA, 15 U.S.C. §§ 1681e, 1681w.

10. *Ceridian Corp.*, FTC Docket No. C-4325 (June 8, 2011) (consent order), *available at* www.ftc.gov/opa/2011/05/ceridianlookout.shtm.

11. *Lookout Servs., Inc.*, FTC Docket No. C-4326 (June 15, 2011) (consent order), *available at* www.ftc.gov/opa/2011/05/ceridianlookout.shtm.

12. *See U.S. v. Teletrack, Inc.*, No. 1:11-CV-2060 (N.D. Ga. filed June 24, 2011) (proposed consent order), *available at* http://www.ftc.gov/opa/2011/06/teletrack.shtm.

13. *See, e.g., Twitter, Inc.*, FTC Docket No. C-4316 (Mar. 2, 2011) (consent order), *available at* http://www.ftc.gov/opa/2010/06/twitter.shtm (resolving allegations that social networking service Twitter deceived its customers by failing to honor their choices after offering the opportunity to designate certain "tweets" as private).

14. *Google, Inc.*, FTC File No. 102 3136 (Mar. 30, 2011) (consent order accepted for public comment), *available at* www.ftc.gov/opa/2011/03/google.shtm. Commissioner Rosch issued a concurring statement expressing concerns about the terms of the proposed consent agreement, *available at* http://www.ftc.gov/os/caselist/1023136/110330googlebuzzstatement.pdf.

15. This provision would apply to any data collected by Google about users of any Google product or service, including mobile and location-based data.

16. *Chitika, Inc.*, FTC Docket No. C-4324 (June 7, 2011) (consent order), *available at* http://www.ftc.gov/opa/2011/03/chitika.shtm.

17. *US Search, Inc.*, FTC Docket No. C-4317 (Mar. 14, 2011) (consent order), *available at* http://www.ftc.gov/opa/2010/09/ussearch.shtm.

18. *See* www.onguardonline.gov. Since its launch in 2005, OnGuard Online and its Spanish-language counterpart Alerta en Línea have attracted nearly 12 million unique visits.

19. *See* Press Release, FTC, Facts from the FTC: What You Should Know About Mobile Apps (June 28, 2011), *available at* http://www.ftc.gov/opa/2011/06/mobileapps.shtm.

20. See Take Charge: Fighting Back Against Identity Theft, *available at* http://www.ftc.gov/bcp/edu/pubs/consumer/idtheft/idt04.shtm.

21. *See* Press Release, FTC, OnGuardOnline.gov Off to a Fast Start with Online Child Safety Campaign (Mar. 31, 2010), *available at* www.ftc.gov/opa/2010/03/netcetera.shtm.

22. See Protecting Personal Information: A Guide For Business, *available at* www.ftc.gov/infosecurity. Commission, *The FTC's Regulatory Reform Program: Twenty Years of Systematic Retrospective Rule Reviews & New Prospective Initiatives to Increase Public Participation and Reduce Burdens on Business*, Before the Subcomm. on Oversight and Investigations of the H. Comm. on Energy

and Commerce, 112th Cong., July 7, 2011, *available at* http://www.ftc.gov/os/testimony/110707regreview.pdf; Notice Announcing Ten-Year Regulatory Review Schedule and Review of the Federal Trade Commission's Regulatory Review Program (July 7, 2011), *available at* http://www.ftc.gov/os/fedreg/2011/07/110707regulatoryreviewfrn.pdf. More information about the Commission's efforts can be found on the Regulatory Review web page, http://www.ftc.gov/ftc/regreview/index.shtml.

23. Letter from Maneesha Mithal, Associate Director, Division of Privacy & Identity Protection to Renee Jackson, Counsel to Social Intelligence Corporation (May 9, 2011), *available at* www.ftc.gov/os/closings/110509socialintelligenceletter.pdf.

24. FTC staff did not express an opinion on the merits of Social Intelligence's business model.

25. For example, the Commission recently announced plans to enhance the agency's longstanding program to review rules and guides in order to increase transparency and public participation and reduce burden on business. *See, e.g.*, Prepared Statement of the Federal Trade Commission, *The FTC's Regulatory Reform Program: Twenty Years of Systematic Retrospective Rule Reviews & New Prospective Initiatives to Increase Public Participation and Reduce Burdens on Business*, Before the Subcomm. on Oversight and Investigations of the H. Comm. on Energy and Commerce, 112th Cong., July 7, 2011, *available at* http://www.ftc.gov/os/testimony/110707regreview.pdf; Notice Announcing Ten-Year Regulatory Review Schedule and Review of the Federal Trade Commission's Regulatory Review Program (July 7, 2011), *available at* http://www.ftc.gov/os/fedreg/2011/07/110707regulatoryreviewfrn.pdf. More information about the Commission's efforts can be found on the Regulatory Review web page, http://www.ftc.gov/ftc/regreview/index.shtml.

26. *See generally* COPPA Rulemaking and Rule Reviews web page, business.ftc.gov/documents/coppa-rulemaking-and-rule-reviews.

27. *See generally* FTC Exploring Privacy web page, www.ftc.gov/bcp/workshops/privacyroundtables.

28. *See generally* 3rd Roundtable, Panel 4: Lessons Learned and Looking Forward at242, *available at* http://www.ftc.gov/bcp/workshops/privacyroundtables/PrivacyRoundtable_March2010_Transcri pt.pdf (industry and consumer representatives suggesting the need to simplify consumer choice and improve transparency); *Written Comment of Centre for Information Policy & Leadership at Hunton & Williams LLP*, cmt. #544506-00059, *available at* http://www.ftc.gov/os/comments/privacyroundtable/544506-00059.pdf (industry group comment on improving transparency, choice, and accountability on privacy); Leslie Harris, *Written Comment of Center for Democracy & Technology*, cmt. #544506-00067, *available at* http://www.ftc.gov/os/comments/privacyroundtable/544506-00067.pdf (urging companies to adopt privacy by design).

29. *See* A Preliminary FTC Staff Report on *Protecting Consumer Privacy in an Era of Rapid Change: A Proposed Framework for Businesses and Policymakers* (Dec.

1, 2010), *available at* http://www.ftc.gov/os/2010/12/101201privacyreport.pdf. Commissioners Kovacic and Rosch issued concurring statements, *available at* http://www.ftc.gov/os/2010/12/101201privacyreport.pdf at Appendix D and Appendix E, respectively.

30. *Id.* at 22-38.

31. Commissioner Kovacic believes that the endorsement of a Do Not Track mechanism by staff (in the report) and the Commission (in this testimony) is premature. His concerns about the Commission Staff Report are set forth in his statement on the report. *See* FTC Staff Report, *supra* note 29, at App. D. Commissioner Rosch supported a Do Not Track mechanism only if it were "technically feasible" and implemented in a fashion that provides informed consumer choice regarding all the attributes of such a mechanism. *Id.* at App. E. Commissioner Rosch believes that a variety of issues need to be addressed prior to the endorsement of any particular Do Not Track mechanism. *See* Rosch Statement, *supra* note 1.

32. *See, e.g.*, Prepared Statement of the Federal Trade Commission, *The State of Online Consumer Privacy*, Before the S. Comm. on Commerce, Science and Transportation, 112th Cong., Mar. 16, 2011, *available at* http://www.ftc. gov/os/testimony/110316consumerprivacysenate.pdf; Prepared Statement of the Federal Trade Commission, *Do Not Track*, Before the Subcomm. on Commerce, Trade and Consumer Protection of the H. Comm. on Energy and Commerce, 111th Cong., Dec. 2, 2010, *available at* www.ftc.gov/os/ testimony/101202donottrack.pdf (hereinafter "Do Not Track Testimony").

33. As noted in prior Commission testimony, such a mechanism should be different from the Do Not Call program in that it should not require the creation of a "Registry" of unique identifiers, which could itself cause privacy concerns. *See* Do Not Track Testimony, *supra* note 32.

34. For example, use of a Do Not Track browser header would enable consumer customization. The browser could send the header to some sites and not others. Moreover, a particular site could ignore the header to the extent the user has consented to tracking on that site.

About Edith Ramirez

Edith Ramirez has served as a commissioner of the Federal Trade Commission since 2010. A native of Southern California, Ramirez earned a bachelor's in history from Harvard University in 1989 and graduated from Harvard Law School cum laude in 1992, where she served as an editor of the Harvard Law Review. *From 1993 to 1996, Ramirez was an associate at the law firm Gibson, Dunn & Crutcher in Los Angeles. She clerked for the Honorable Alfred T. Goodwin in the United States Court of Appeals for the Ninth Circuit from 1992 to 1993. Prior to joining the FTC, Ramirez was a partner in the Los Angeles law office of Quinn Emanuel Urquhart & Sullivan.*

Index

About the Editor

Writer Brian Boucher has edited the *Representative American Speeches* volume since 2008. He currently serves as associate editor and news editor at *Art in America* magazine, where he has worked for eight years and where he has written articles about artists including Rachel Harrison, Michael Rakowitz, and Gedi Sibony, as well as over a hundred exhibition reviews. In 2006 in *New York* magazine, he published the article "My Roommate the Diamond Thief," the story of an unexpected discovery about a lodger. Boucher lives in New York.